# Revolution & Counter-Revolution in Spain

Felix Morrow

# Revolution & Counter-Revolution in Spain

including "The Civil War in Spain"

**PATHFINDER**

New York    London    Montreal    Sydney

ISBN 0-87348-402-9 paper; ISBN 0-87348-401-0 cloth
Library of Congress Catalog Card Number 74-80372
Manufactured in the United States of America

First edition, 1938
Second (expanded) edition, 1974
Fifth printing, 2002

**Pathfinder**

410 West Street, New York, NY 10014, U.S.A.
Fax: (212) 727-0150
www.pathfinderpress.com
E-mail: pathfinderpress@compuserve.com

PATHFINDER DISTRIBUTORS AROUND THE WORLD:
Australia (and Southeast Asia and the Pacific):
    Pathfinder, Level 1, 3/281-287 Beamish St., Campsie, NSW 2194
    Postal address: P.O. Box K879, Haymarket, NSW 1240
Canada:
    Pathfinder, 2761 Dundas St. West, Toronto, ON, M6P 1Y4
Iceland:
    Pathfinder, Skolavordustig 6B, Reykjavík
    Postal address: P. Box 0233, IS 121 Reykjavík
New Zealand:
    Postal address: P.O. Box 3025, Auckland
Sweden:
    Pathfinder, Domargränd 16, S-129 47, Hägersten
United Kingdom (and Europe, Africa, Middle East and South Asia):
    Pathfinder, 47 The Cut, London, SE1 8LL
United States (and Caribbean, Latin America, and East Asia):
    Pathfinder, 410 West Street, New York, NY 10014

# CONTENTS

# PUBLISHER'S PREFACE

Decades after Franco's army overcame the final defenses of the Republic, interest in the issues of the Spanish Civil War remains high. In reprinting these two contemporary accounts, which have been out of print in the United States for years, the publishers are once again making available what is still the most incisive descriptive analysis available of the Spanish Civil War and the events leading up to it.

Viewed in retrospect, Felix Morrow's work, written as the events themselves unfolded, stands up remarkably well. Its theme throughout is the futility of attempting to defeat Franco through a People's Front coalition with the bourgeoisie. This was the central strategy of both the Stalinists and the Socialists after September 1935. In order to keep the bourgeoisie in the coalition, the workers' organizations had to agree to forswear the most urgent demands of the Spanish peasants and workers: agrarian reform and workers' control of industry. Furthermore, they could not grant Morocco its freedom from Spanish tyranny because this would endanger Spain's relations with the imperialist "democracies" abroad, who would fear for the stability of their own colonial empires.

But the Spanish workers' organizations badly miscalculated. The bourgeoisie declared almost unanimously for Franco, leaving behind only its figureheads in the government; and the imperialist democracies—England, France, and the U.S.—under the guise of "nonintervention" sabotaged the defense of the legally elected, legitimate Spanish Republican government. The Moroccan people, who might have become the allies of a government that granted them their independence, instead proved to be Franco's strongest base of support; and the Spanish workers and peasants, their hopes beaten back by the Republican government, fell prey to demoralization and indifference.

All the major political tendencies in Spain, from the Anarchists to the Stalinists, and from the POUM to the Socialist Party, turned their backs on the independent struggle of the working class in favor of an alliance with the bourgeoisie. So the other major theme in Morrow's narrative is the rôle a revolutionary party could have played had one been created in time to defend the genuinely revolutionary aspirations of the workers and peasants against betrayal by their leaders and government.

Felix Morrow was a leader of the Socialist Workers Party and was on the editorial board of its weekly newspaper, *Socialist Appeal*, which carried his extensive coverage of the Spanish Civil War. He was one of the eighteen American Trotskyists convicted in the notorious Minneapolis Labor Trial in 1941, which was the first use of the Smith Act. After World War II he broke with the SWP.

*The Civil War in Spain: Towards Socialism or Fascism?* was completed just two months after Franco's insurrection and was published that year as a pamphlet by Pioneer Publishers. It was designed to provide a political history of the Spanish Republic, from its beginning in 1931 through the fascist insurrection in July 1936. The insurrection was met by a huge popular upsurge throughout Spain demanding arms to fight the fascists, as well as by a far-reaching social revolution, with factories and lands, and in some cases even shops and cafes, seized by the workers to ensure an efficient organization of the struggle against Franco. A network of popular militias was established under the control of the workers' organizations. By September, when this pamphlet was completed, the People's Front government had effectively regained control of the military struggle and begun to reestablish its authority, with the complicity of the leaders of the workers' organizations.

*Revolution and Counter-Revolution in Spain* was completed in November 1937, after the crushing and outlawing of the left wing of the Spanish Republican movement had been accomplished in

Barcelona in May. With the destruction of the left wing, the hopes for a Republican victory quickly dimmed. By the time of the author's postscript in May 1938, the outcome of the Civil War was clear to all who cared to look.

For this edition, a brief epilogue has been added about the conclusion of the Civil War, as well as a chronology, glossary, and index.

# CHRONOLOGY

## 1930

**January** — Dictator Primo de Rivera resigns; King Alfonso XIII appoints Berenguer to head interim government.

**December** — Liberal officers stage unsuccessful (Jaca) coup

## 1931

**February** — Berenguer resigns.

**April** — Municipal elections bring sweeping victory to Republicans. Alfonso abdicates; Alcalá Zamora is prime minister.

**May** — Clashes between monarchists and workers in Madrid; several churches are burned.

**June** — Elections to Cortes give overwhelming majority to pro-Republican parties. Alcalá Zamora becomes president of Republic; Azaña is prime minister.

**July–Aug.** — Strike wave crushed by Republican government artillery.

## 1932

**January** — Uprisings in Catalonia organized by the FAI.

**August** — Catalan charter of autonomy granted. Unsuccessful coup by monarchist general Sanjurjo.

## 1933

**January** — Anarcho-Syndicalist rising in Barcelona is crushed.

**April** — Municipal elections show big gains for rightists.

**September** — Lerroux replaces Azaña as prime minister.

**October 29** — Falange Española founded in Madrid.

**November** — Elections to Cortes give rightists and monarchists control when CNT abstains; Lerroux confirmed as prime minister, begins to repeal reforms.

## 1934

January — Catalan elections swing to left; Companys becomes Catalan president.

April — Barcelona general strike suppressed.

June — Rural strike movement called by Anarchists.

Oct.–Nov. — Lerroux forms new government, with members of right-wing CEDA of Gil Robles; general strike of Socialists and Anarchists crushed; Lerroux calls in Franco to crush uprising of Asturian miners. Catalan independence is suppressed.

## 1935

August — Seventh Congress of Comintern proclaims People's Front policy.

September — Founding of the POUM.

## 1936

January — Lerroux resigns amid financial scandal; Cortes dissolved.

February — New elections bring People's Front to power; Azaña is prime minister; Anarchists and POUM support People's Front.

April — Socialist and Communist youth groups merge.

May — Azaña becomes president; Casares Quiroga is prime minister.

May–June — Mass strikes in France; French People's Front elected. Leon Blum is prime minister; Daladier is minister of war.

July 13 — Spanish CP declares full support to government.

July 17–21 — Fascist rising begins in Morocco and spreads to Spain. Quiroga replaced by Martínez Barrio and then by Giral.

July 21 — Antifascist Militias Committee formed in Catalonia.

August 15 — France and England sign nonintervention pact.

September — Giral resigns; Largo Caballero becomes prime minister on condition that CP join government. CNT and POUM join Catalan government; Nin becomes minister of justice.

October — Central government ends independence of militias, creates Popular Army; seige of Madrid begins; government approves formation of International Brigades. Franco becomes

Generalissimo in Nationalist Spain.

**November** — Central government, reorganized to include Anarchists, moves to Valencia. International Brigades arrive in Madrid.

**December 16** — POUM expelled from government.

### 1937

**February** — Fall of Málaga.

**April 25** — Bombing of Guernica.

**May** — Government attempt to seize Barcelona telephone exchange from Anarchists leads to new upsurge; Negrin replaces Caballero as prime minister.

**June** — POUM outlawed by central government; leaders arrested; fall of Bilbao.

**October** — Central government moves to Barcelona.

### 1938

**January** — Heavy bombardment of Barcelona begins.

**February** — Fall of Teruel.

**April–June** — Franco reaches coast and cuts Republican Spain in half.

**September** — International Brigades fight final battle in Ebro campaign; Chamberlain and Daladier sign Munich Pact with Hitler.

**November** — International Brigades withdraw from Spain.

### 1939

**January 26** — Barcelona surrenders.

**February 27** — France and Britain recognize Franco while Loyalists still hold a third of Spain. Azaña flees Spain.

**March** — Formation of National Defense Junta to arrange surrender of central government. CP expelled from People's Front. Madrid and Valencia surrender; active hostilities cease.

**April** — United States recognizes Franco.

**August 23** — Stalin-Hitler Pact signed.

# The civil war in Spain

*by Felix Morrow*

# INTRODUCTION

Fascist soldiers and workers' militiamen, entrenched near each other. In a lull in the fighting, they shout arguments back and forth:

"You are sons of peasants and workers," shouts a militiaman. "You should be here with us, fighting for the republic, where there is democracy and freedom."

The retort is prompt; it is the argument with which the peasantry has answered every reformist appeal since the republic came in 1931:

"What did the Republic give you to eat? What has the Republic done for us that we should fight for it?"

In this little incident, reported casually in the press, you have the essence of the problem of the civil war.

The peasantry, which is seventy percent of the population, has yet to be won to the side of the proletariat. It played no rôle in bringing the Republic in 1931. Its passivity and hostility led to the triumph of reaction in November, 1933. It played no part in the proletarian October revolt of 1934. Except in Catalonia and Valencia where the proletariat has declared for confiscation of the land and is already turning it over to the peasantry, and in parts of Andalusia where the landworkers have seized the land themselves, the masses of the peasantry are not yet rising to fight beside the working class.

No civil war as profound as the present one in Spain has ever been won without advancing a revolutionary social program. Yet the sole program of the coalition government headed by Caballero appears to be a military struggle. "Only after victory shall we be allowed to defend the political and social problems of the various groups composing the Left Popular Front," says a government spokesman (*New York Times*, Sept. 20). "There is only one point in our program and that is to win victory." As a matter of actual fact, however, the coalition government's slogan, "Defend the Democratic Republic," *does* contain a social program; but it is the reformist program of defending the "kindest" political instrument of the bourgeois mode of production.

In the great French Revolution, the slogan of "Liberty, Equality and Fraternity" meant, quite concretely, land to the peasants, freedom from serfdom, a new world of labor and enrichment, wiping out the economic power of feudal oppressors, putting France into the hands of the revolutionary bourgeoisie. In the Russian Revolution, the slogan of "Land, Bread and Freedom" successfully rallied the people against Kornilov and Kerensky, because it meant the transformation of Russia. The proletariat of Spain will raise equally revolutionary slogans, or it will not win the civil war.

The Catalonian proletariat has already recognized this great truth. Its revolutionary program will not long remain confined within its own borders. Only today news has come that another party of the People's Front, the Syndicalist party formed after the October revolt by anarcho-syndicalists who recognized the need for participating in political life, has demanded a socialist program for the successful prosecution of the civil war. The Premiership of Caballero, the "extreme" left wing of the Popular Front, is itself a distorted recognition that the masses will not fight for the maintenance of capitalism. But Caballero's former laurels cannot and will not be a substitute for the very concrete content of a program of revolutionary socialism.

In the following pages are told the rich history of revolutionary experience which five short years have brought the Spanish proletariat. Out of the wisdom extracted from that extraordinarily concentrated experience, the Spanish proletariat is learning how to take its own destiny into its own hands. To the lessons of the Russian Revolution are now being added the equally profound lessons of the Spanish Revolution.

*New York, September 22, 1936.*

# The birth of the republic—1931

"Glorious, bloodless, peaceful, harmonious" was the revolution of April 14, 1931. Two days before, the people had voted for the republican-socialist coalition in the countrywide municipal elections; this was enough to finish off Alfonso. The Spanish Republic came so easily. . . . Its advent, however, was almost the only bloodless event connected with the revolution before or since 1931.

For over a century Spain had been attempting to give birth to a new régime. But the paralysis of centuries of senile decay from the days of empire had doomed every attempt. All the more bloody, therefore, was the history of failure and its punishment. Four major revolutions before 1875, followed by four white terrors, were merely crescendoes in an almost continuous tune of peasant revolts and army mutinies, civil wars, regionalist uprisings, army pronunciamentos, conspiracies and counter-plots of court camarillas.

Nor did the modern bourgeoisie, when it belatedly appeared on the scene, proceed to preparing the bourgeois revolution. Modern industry and transportation dates from the Spanish-American War, which brought a new ferment to Spain. The years 1898–1914 are called the "national renascence" (it was also the Indian summer of world capitalism). But the Spanish and Catalonian industrialists who flourished in those two decades vied with the most ancient landowning families in their loyalty to the monarchy. Some—like Count Romanones—were ennobled, purchased great tracts of land and combined in their own persons the old and the new economies; others cemented the bonds between the two by mortgages and intermarriages with the landed aristocracy. The King preserved the trappings of feudalism; but he was scarcely averse to associating with the bourgeoisie in their most dubious economic ventures. Seeking new fields for exploitation, the bourgeoisie secured from Alfonso the conquest of Morocco, begun in 1912. Alfonso's profitable neutrality during the World War endeared him to the bourgeoisie, who for four years found the world market open to their wares.

When that market was taken back by the imperialists after the war, and the Catalonian and Spanish proletariat launched great struggles, and when the workers' and peasants' respect for the régime had been dissolved by the disasters to the army in Morocco, the Catalan industrialists financed Primo de Rivera's *coup*. The dictator's program of public works and insurmountable tariff walls, suppression of the anarcho-syndicalists and compulsory arbitration boards for the socialist unions, gave industry a new impetus and to Rivera and Alfonso the most fervent adulation of the bourgeoisie. The world crisis put an end to Spanish prosperity and Rivera fell with the peseta in January 1930. But the bourgeoisie in the main still clung to Alfonso. Indeed, as late as September 28, 1930, and at a mass meeting protesting the government's course, Alcala Zamora, who was to head the republic, could still end his speech with a paean of praise to the crown.

Meanwhile, in May 1930, the students and workers of Madrid had hoisted red and republican flags, and engaged the police in rifle fire; in September the socialists and the U.G.T. made a pact with the republican groups to finish with the monarchy; revolutionary general strikes followed in Seville, Madrid, Bilbao, Barcelona, Valencia, etc., involving fatal encounters with the armed forces in every instance. A rising of the workers to coincide with a republican mutiny in the army was frustrated when the soldiers' revolt of December 12 was precipitated before the time planned; but the executions of the soldier-leaders inspired a manifesto signed by republican and socialist leaders announcing their object to be the immediate introduction of the republic. The signatories were put in the Model Prison of Madrid—and it became the center of Spanish political life. Premier Berenguer's desperate attempt to provide a Cortes on the old model as a support for Alfonso was defeated by the republican-socialist declaration of a boycott; Berenguer resigned. The municipal elections demonstrated that the masses were for a republic.

It was only at this last moment that the industrialists, frightened by the general strikes, by arming of the workers openly going on, and by the socialist threat of a national general strike, decided the monarchy was a cheap sacrifice to the wolves of the revolution. Then, and only then, when Alfonso himself was agreeing that to fight was futile, did the bourgeoisie also agree to the republic.

The spirit of the new republic is characterized by the fact that the oldest and largest of the republican parties did nothing to bring it into being, and was soon to ally itself with the monarchists. This was the Radical Party of Lerroux. Three decades of Spanish parliamentarism are filled with charges of bribery, blackmailing, cheating and trickery against this party. The Radical demagogues had served the monarchy in the struggle against Catalonian nationalism. The thievery and blackmail for which their French namesakes (now leading the *Front Populaire*) are so notorious, pale by comparison with the bold campaigns which the Spanish Radicals conducted against individual industrialists and bankers and which came to a sudden end in each case when the expected fat envelope had been quietly delivered. Within the Radical Party the normal method of polemic was mutual accusations of corruption and blackmailing. Because of its extremely filthy history, and despite the fact that it was the oldest and largest bourgeois republican party, there was the strongest opposition to its participation in the first republican government. This opposition came even from those Catholics, like

Zamora, who at first seriously wanted the republic and who, having been a Minister under the monarchy, knew best for what class of services Alfonso had used the Radicals.

Despite a great following among the bourgeoisie as the most conservative republican party, Lerroux's Radicals provided no political leadership. They occupied themselves in scrambling for lucrative posts. However, the horror shared by other republicans and socialists, that any touch of scandal should reach the new republic, was a terribly constraining influence on the Radicals. They were happier when they left the government shortly and allied themselves with Gil Robles' clericals—the Radicals, whose chief stock in trade had been anti-clericalism!

The other republican parties, except for the Catalan Left which had peasants in its ranks, were mere makeshifts created for the April elections and had little mass support, for the lower middle class of Spain is tiny and impotent.

The only real support for the republic, therefore, came from the socialist and trade union proletariat. That very fact, however, signified that the republic could be only a transition to a struggle for power between fascist-monarchist reaction and socialism. There was no room, at this late stage, for the democratic republic in Spain.

Unfortunately, however, the socialist leadership did not prepare for the struggle. Instead, it shared the petty-bourgeois outlook of the Azañas.

That outlook was avowedly modeled on the French Revolution of 1789. Spain was presumed to have before it a long course of peaceful development in which the tasks of the bourgeois revolution would be carried out by an alliance between the republicans and the workers. After that—decades after 1931—the republic would be changed into a socialist republic. But that was a long way off! thought the socialist leaders, Prieto, Caballero, de los Rios, Besteiro, del Vayo, Araquistain, who had grown to middle age, at the least, under the almost Asiatic régime of the monarchy. Madrid, chief socialist stronghold, was still much the city of crafts that it had been in the nineties; its socialism was a compound of the provincial reformism of the founder, Pablo Iglesias, and the German Social-Democracy of the worst, the post-war period.

The other major current in the Spanish proletariat, anarcho-syndicalism, commanding in the C.N.T. about half the strength of the socialist U.G.T. unions, dominated the modern industrial city of Barcelona but had changed little since its origin in the Cordoba Congress of 1872. Hopelessly anti-political, it played no rôle in bringing the Republic; then swung in the honeymoon days to a position of passive support, which changed to wild putschism as soon as the rosy haze disappeared. Spain would not find its ideo-logical leadership here. Five years of revolution were needed before anarcho-syndicalism would begin to break with its doctrinaire refusal to enter the political field and fight for a workers' state.

The making of the Soviet Union and its achievements—a peasant country like Spain—were extraordinarily popular in Spain. But the Bolshevik methodology of the Russian Revolution was almost unknown. The theoretical backwardness of Spanish socialism had produced only a small wing for Bolshevism in 1918. What progress it had made by 1930 was cut off by the Comintern's expulsion of practically the whole party for Trotskyist, "Right" and other heresies. Despite the vast backing of the Comintern, the official Communist Party in the ensuing period played no rôle whatever. In March 1932, the Comintern discovered new heresy and wiped out the entire leadership again. Following their "third period" (1929–1934) ideology, the Stalinists denounced united fronts with anarchist or socialist organizations, which they dubbed twins of the fascists; built empty "Red unions" against the C.N.T. and U.G.T.; made empty boasts that they were building peasant Soviets, at a time when they had no following among the proletariat, which must lead such soviets; propagandized for the "intermediary democratic workers and peasants revolution"—a concept repudiated by Lenin in 1917—as distinct from the bourgeois and proletarian revolutions, thereby hopelessly confusing the task of the struggle for the masses with the subsequent struggle for power. The Stalinists dropped this "third period" hodge-podge in 1935—only to pick up the discredited "People's Front" policy of coalitions with the bourgeoisie. First, and last, they played a thoroughly reactionary rôle.

The real Bolshevik tradition was consistently represented in Spain only by the small group, the Communist Left, adhering to the international "Trotskyist" movement. Trotsky himself wrote two great pamphlets, *The Revolution in Spain* several months before the actual arrival of the republic, and *The Spanish Revolution in Danger* shortly afterward, and many articles as events unfolded. No one can understand the dynamics of the Spanish revolution without reading Trotsky's prophetic analyses. On every basic question events have vindicated his writings. To the pseudo-Jacobin doctrines of official socialism he counterposed a Marxist-Leninist proof, rich in concrete grasp of Spanish conditions, of the impossibility of the bourgeois republic undertaking the democratic tasks of the revolution. To the pseudo-leftist nonsense of the Stalinists, he counterposed the specific program by which a revolutionary party could win the Spanish masses and carry them to a victorious revolution.

But the Communist Left was a tiny handful and not a party. Parties are not built overnight, not even in a revolutionary situation. A group is not a party. The Communist Left, unfortunately, failed to understand this, and did not follow Trotsky in his estimation of the profound significance of the leftward development in the socialist ranks after events confirmed Trotsky's predictions. This "leftism" was followed by an opportunist line leading to signing the Popular Front program. It was only after the present civil war broke out that the former Trotskyists (now in the P.O.U.M.) again turned toward a Bolshevik policy.

Thus, the proletariat was without the leadership to prepare it for its great tasks, when the republic arrived. It was to pay dearly for this lack!

# 2

## The tasks of the
## bourgeois-democratic revolution

Five great tasks confronted the bourgeois republic; these must be carried out, or the régime must give way to reaction, monarchical or fascist, or to a new revolution and a workers' state:

### 1. THE AGRARIAN QUESTION

Agriculture was accounting for over half of the national income, almost two-thirds of exports and most of the government's internal revenue; and with seventy per cent of the population on the land, this was the key question for Spain's future.

The division of the land is the worst in Europe. One third owned by great landowners, in some cases in estates covering half a province. Another third owned by a group of "middle owners," more numerous than the great landowners, but also in large estates tilled by sharecroppers and landworkers. Only one third owned by peasants, and most of this in primitively-equipped farms of five hectares or less of dry, poor land—insufficient to support their families. Such good land as peasants own—in the gardening lands of the Mediterranean coast—is divided into dooryard-size patches.

The five million peasant families fall into three categories:

Two million who own the insufficient holdings. Only in the northern provinces are there any number of peasant families who are moderately comfortable. For the most part, these millions of "owners" starve with the landless, hiring themselves out for day-labor whenever they can.

A million and a half sharecroppers renting on a basis of dividing the crop with the landlord, and subject to the threefold oppression of the landlord, the usurer who finances the crop and the merchant who buys it.

A million and a half landworkers hiring themselves out at incredibly low wages and under the best of conditions out of employment from ninety to one hundred fifty days a year. A *good* wage is six pesetas (75 cents) a day.

The direct exploitation on the land is supplemented by tax squeezing. Of the total tax levy collected from the land in the first year of the republic, more than one-half came from the landowning peasants.

The conditions under which millions of peasant families live beggar description. For comparison one must go to the Orient, to the living conditions of the Chinese and Hindu peasantry. Starvation between harvests is a *normal* process. The Spanish press at such times carries numerous reports of whole districts of peasants living on roots and boiled greens. Desperate revolts, seizures of crops, raids on storehouses and periods of guerilla warfare have been part of the history of Spain for a century; but each time it was proven again that the scattered peasantry, without the help of the cities, could not free itself.

The last decades brought the peasant no relief. The halcyon war years, 1914–1918, gave Spanish agriculture an opportunity to enter the world market and secure high prices. The resultant rise in the price of produce and land was capitalized into cash via mortgages by the landowners; the peasants got little of it. The burdens of the collapse of agriculture following the war were, however, quickly shifted onto the peasants. The agricultural crisis, part of the world crisis, aggravated by the tariff barriers raised against Spanish agriculture by England and France, brought the peasant in 1931 to such a plight that whole regions were in danger of extermination by starvation, and with a permanent army of the unemployed on the land.

*The only solution for this dreadful condition was the immediate expropriation of the two-thirds of the land held by landowners, and its division among the peasantry.* Even this would not suffice. With the exception of the gardening regions on the Mediterranean, Spanish agriculture is conducted by primitive methods. Its yield per hectare is the lowest in Europe. Intensive methods of agriculture, requiring training, modern implements, fertilizer, etc., which mean systematic state aid to agriculture, would have to supplement the distribution of the land.

The feudal tenure of the land in France was destroyed by the Jacobins with nothing but benefit to capitalist relations of production. But in Spain of 1931 the land was already exploited under capitalist relations. Land had long been alienable, bought and sold in the market; hence mortgageable and debt-laden. *Hence confiscation of the land would also be confiscation of bank-capital, would be a death-blow to Spanish capitalism, both agricultural and industrial.*

From this perfectly obvious fact, the coalition government drew the conclusion that, therefore, the land could not be confiscated. Instead, elaborate and futile plans were developed, whereby the government, through its Institute for Agrarian Reform, would purchase the landed estates and parcel them out to the peasants on a rental basis. Since Spain is an impoverished land, providing little income to the State, this process would necessarily be a very long one. The government's own figures showed that its method of dividing the land by purchase would take at least a century.

## 2. THE DEVELOPMENT OF SPANISH INDUSTRY

If the republican-socialist coalition could not solve the agrarian question, could it develop the productive forces of industry and transportation?

Compared to the industry of the great imperialist powers, Spain is pitifully backward. Only 8,500 miles of railroad, in a country larger than Germany! With 1.1% of world trade in 1930, she had slightly less than she had had before the war.

The era of development of Spanish industry was short—1898–1918. The very development of Spanish industry in the war years became a source of further difficulties. The end of the war meant that Spain's industry, infantile and backed by no strong power, soon fell behind in the imperialist race for markets. Even Spain's internal market could not long be preserved for her own industry. Primo de Rivera's insurmountable tariff walls brought from France and England retaliation against Spanish agriculture. With agriculture accounting for one-half to two-thirds of exports, this meant a terrific agricultural crisis followed by the collapse of the internal market for industry. That very crisis, in 1931, ushered in the republic.

These facts stared it in the face, but the republican-socialist coalition repeated, as if it were a magic formula, that Spain was only at the beginning of its capitalist development, that somehow they would build industry and commerce, that the world crisis would let up, etc., etc. The republic found nearly a million unemployed workers and peasants and before the end of 1933 the number was a million and a half, who with their dependents accounted for 25% of the population.

With iron logic the Trotskyists showed that weak Spanish industry, under capitalist relations, *can develop only in an expanding world market, and that the world market has been progressively contracting; Spanish industry can be developed only under protection of a monopoly of foreign trade,* but the pressure of foreign capital in Spain and the threat to agricultural exports from France and England means that a bourgeois government cannot create a monopoly of foreign trade.

If the lateness of Spanish industry barred its further development under capitalism, that same lateness (like that of Russia) had resulted in a concentration of its proletariat in large enterprises in a few cities. Barcelona, the largest port and also the largest industrial center, with the industrial towns of Catalonia, alone accounts for fully 45% of the Spanish working class. The Biscay region, Asturias and Madrid account for most of the rest. All in all, Spain has less than two million industrial workers, but their specific gravity, in view of their concentration, is comparable to that of the Russian proletariat.

### 3. THE CHURCH

The separation of Church and State was no mere parliamentary task. To achieve separation, the French Revolution confiscated the Church lands, rallying the peasantry for their seizure; dissolved the religious orders, seized the churches and their wealth, and for many years illegalized and prohibited the functioning of the priesthood. Only then was even the inadequate separation of Church and State achieved in France.

In Spain of 1931 the problem was even more urgent and compelling. By its whole past the Church could not but be the mortal enemy of the Republic. For centuries the Church had prevented any form of progress. Even a most Catholic King, Carlos III, had been compelled to expel the Jesuits in 1767; Joseph Bonaparte had to dissolve the religious orders, and the liberal Mendizabel suppressed them in 1835. The Church had destroyed every revolution of the 19th century; in turn every revolution, every quickening of Spanish life, had been necessarily anti-clerical. Even King Alfonso, after the Barcelona revolt of 1909, had to announce that he would "give expression to the public aspirations for the reduction and regulation of the excessive number of religious orders," and would establish religious freedom. Rome, however, changed Alfonso's mind for him. Every attempt at widening the basis of the régime was frustrated by the Church—the last in 1923, when it vetoed Premier Alhucemas' proposal to call a constituent Cortes and instead backed the dictatorship. No wonder that every period of ferment since 1812 has been followed by burning of churches and killing of clericals.

The economic power wielded by the Church can be gauged from the estimate, given to the Cortes in 1931, that the Jesuit order possessed one-third of the country's wealth. Such lands as had been confiscated after the revolution of 1868 had been so generously indemnified by the reaction, that the Church was launched on a career in industry and finance. Its monopolistic "agricultural credit" banks were the usurers of the countryside and its city banks the partners of industry. The religious orders conducted regular industrial establishments (flour mills, laundries, sewing, clothing, etc.) with unpaid labor (orphans, "students") competing to great advantage against industry. As the established religion it received tens of millions of pesetas each year from the state treasury, was freed of all tax obligations even in industrial production, and received rich fees from baptism, marriage, death, etc.

Its official control of education meant that the student would be safeguarded from radicalism and the peasantry kept illiterate—half the Spanish population could neither read nor write in 1930. The superstition bred by the Church may be realized from the fact that until quite recently papal indulgences sold for a few pesetas each; signed by an archbishop they could be purchased in shops displaying the advertisement: "Bulas are cheap today."

Its robed hordes were a veritable army confronting the republic: eighty to ninety thousand in 4,000 religious houses of the orders, and over 25,000 parish priests—the number in the religious orders alone thus outnumbering the total of high school students and being double the number of college students in the country.

In the first months of the republic the Church moved cautiously in its struggle against the new régime, and advisedly: a pastoral letter advising Catholics to vote for Catholic candidates who were "neither republican nor monarchist" was answered, in May, by mass burning of churches and monasteries. Nevertheless, it was no secret to anyone that the myriad army of monks and nuns and parish priests were vigorously propagandizing from house to house. As in every critical period in Spanish history in which the Church felt itself endangered by a change, it disseminated to the superstitious reports of miraculous incidents—statues seen weeping, crucifixes exuding blood—portents of evil times having come. What would the republican government do about this powerful menace?

The Church question brought the first governmental crisis; Azaña formulated a compromise, which was adopted. The clerical orders were not to be molested unless proven, like any other organization, detrimental to the commonweal, and there was a gentleman's agreement that this would apply only to the Jesuits, who were dissolved in January 1932, having been given plenty of opportunity to transfer most of their wealth to individuals and other orders. Government subventions to the clergy ended formally with the official declaration of disestablishment but were partly retrieved by payments to the Church for education; for the ousting of the Church from the schools was to be a "long term" program. This was the sum total of the government's Church program. Even this pathetically inadequate legislation created a furor among the bourgeoisie; it was opposed, for example, not only by Ministers Zamora and Maura (Catholics), but by the republican Radical, Lerroux, who had made a lifetime career in Spanish politics out of anti-clericalism. Anti-clerical in words and desiring a fairer division of the spoils, the republican bourgeoisie were so intertwined with capitalist-landowner interests which in turn rested on the Church, that they were absolutely incapable of a serious onslaught on its political and economic power.

The Communist Left declared that this was a further proof of the bankruptcy of the coalition government. It could not even fulfill the "bourgeois-democratic" task of curbing the Church. The revolutionists demanded the confiscation of all Church wealth, the dissolution of all orders, the immediate prohibition of religious teachers in schools, the use of Church funds to aid the peasantry in cultivating the land, and called upon the peasantry to seize the Church lands.

## 4. THE ARMY

The history of Spain during the nineteenth and the first third of the twentieth century is a history of military plots and *pronunciamentos*. Called in by the monarchy itself to put a period to opposition, the army's privileged rôle led to pampering of an officer caste. So numerous did the officers become that the whole colonial administration and much of that in the country itself (including the police force, the Civil Guard) was entrusted to them. Alfonso's growing need of army support was used by the officers to entrench themselves. The Law of Jurisdictions of 1905, empowering military tribunals to try and punish civilian libels on the army, made labor and press criticism *lèse majesté*. Even Alfonso's Premier Maura, in 1917, protested that the officers were making civil government impossible. In 1919, disapproving of concessions made to the general strike, the army caste, organized into Officers' Councils for pressure on government and public, demanded the dismissal of the Chief of Police. The War Minister was always one of their men. There was an officer for every six men in the ranks, and the military budget grew accordingly. Indeed, the military budget grew so insupportable that even Rivera tried to cut down the officer caste; the Officers' Councils retaliated by letting him fall without protest, though they had joined him in his original *coup*. Alfonso supported them to the last.

The tradition of an independent and privileged caste was a grave danger for the republic. In a country where the lower middle class is so tiny and undistinguished, the officers have to be drawn from the upper classes, which means that they will be tied by kinship, friendship, social position, etc., to the reactionary landowners and industrialists. Or the officers must be drawn from the ranks, that is from the peasantry and the workers. And haste was needed: control of the army is the life and death question of every régime.

The republican-socialist coalition put this grave problem into the hands of Azaña himself, as Minister of War. He reduced the army by a voluntary system of retirement pay for officers, so reasonable in their eyes that within a few days 7,000 officers agreed to retire with pay. The diminished officer corps remained in spirit what it had been under the monarchy.

The Communist Left denounced this as treachery to the democratic revolution. They demanded dismissal of the whole officer corps and its replacement by officers from the ranks, elected by the soldiers. They appealed to the soldiers to take matters into their own hands, pointing out that the bourgeois republic was treating them just as barbarously as had the monarchy. They sought to draw the soldiers into fraternization and common councils with the revolutionary worker.

The democratization of the army was viewed by the revolutionists as a necessary task, not for the revolutionary overthrow of the bourgeoisie—other organs were needed for that—but as a measure of defense against a return of reaction. The failure of the coalition government to undertake this elementary task of the democratic revolution was simply further proof that only the proletarian revolution would solve the "bourgeois-democratic" tasks of the Spanish revolution.

## 5. THE COLONIAL AND NATIONAL QUESTIONS

The "feudal" monarchy had not only been modern enough to foster the rise, development and decline of bourgeois industry and finance. It was ultra-modern enough to embark on seizure and exploitation of colonies in the most contemporary manner of finance-capitalism. The "national renascence" included the conquest and subjugation of Morocco (1912–1926). In the disaster of Anual (1921) alone, ten thousand workers and peasants, serving under two-year compulsory military service, were destroyed. Seven hundred million pesetas a year was the cost of the Moroccan campaign after the World War. Riots when recruits and reserves were called up and mutinies at embarkation preceded Rivera's *coup*. An alliance with French imperialism (1925) led to a decisive victory over the Moroccan people the next year. A murderously cruel colonial administration proceeded to exploit the Moroccan peasants and tribesmen for the benefit of government and a few capitalists.

The republican-socialist coalition took over the Spanish colonies in Morocco and ruled them, as had the monarchy, through the Foreign Legion and native mercenaries. The socialists argued that when conditions justified they would extend democracy to Morocco and would permit it to participate in the benefits of a progressive régime.

Trotsky and his adherents termed the socialist position an act of treachery against an oppressed people. But for the safety of the Spanish masses, too, Morocco must be set free. The peculiarly vicious legionnaires and mercenaries bred there would be the first force to be used by a reactionary *coup,* and Morocco itself as a military base for the reaction. Withdrawal of all troops and independence for Morocco were immediate demands for which the workers themselves must fight, and incite the Moroccan people to achieve. The liberty of the Spanish masses would be imperiled unless the colonies were freed.

Similar to the colonial question was the issue of *national liberation* of the Catalan and Basque peoples. The strong petty-bourgeois Catalan *Esquerra* (Left) Party derived its chief following from among the militant sharecroppers who should be the allies of the revolutionary workers, but who succumb to the nationalist program of the petty-bourgeoisie, the latter thereby finding a support in the peasantry against the de-nationalizing rôle of big capital and the Spanish state bureaucracy. In the Basque provinces the national question in 1931 led to even more serious consequences; the nationalist movement there was clerical-conservative in control and returned a bloc of the most reactionary deputies in the Constituent Cortes. Since the Basque and Catalonian provinces are also the chief industrial regions, this was a decisive question to the future of the labor movement: how free these workers and peasants from the control of alien classes?

The model for the solution was given by the Russian Bolsheviks, who inscribed in their program the slogan of national liberation, and carried it out after the October revolution. The broadest autonomy for the national regions is perfectly compatible with economic unity; the masses have nothing to fear from such a measure, which in a workers' republic will enable economy and culture to flourish freely.

Any other position than support of national liberation becomes, directly or indirectly, support for the maximum bureaucratic centralisation of Spain demanded by the ruling class, and will be recognized as such by the oppressed nationalities.

Catalonian nationalism had grown under the oppression of the Rivera dictatorship. Hence, a day before the republic was proclaimed in Madrid, the Catalans had already seized the government buildings and declared an independent Catalonian republic. A deputation of republican and socialist leaders rushed to Barcelona, and combined promises of an autonomy statute with dire threats of suppression; the final settlement provided a much-restricted autonomy which left the Catalan politicians with grievances they could display with profitable results in the way of maintaining their following among the workers and peasants. On the pretext that the Basque nationalist movement was reactionary, the republican-socialist coalition delayed a settlement of the question and thereby gave the Basque clericals, threatened by the proletarianization of the region, a new hold on the masses. In the name of getting away from regional prejudices, the socialists identified themselves with the outlook of Spanish bourgeois-imperialism.

Thus, in all fields, the bourgeois republic proved absolutely incapable of undertaking the "bourgeois-democratic" tasks of the Spanish revolution. That meant that the republic could have no stability; it could be only a transition stage, and a short one. Its place would be taken either by military, fascist or monarchical reaction—or by a real social revolution which would give the workers power to build a socialist society. The struggle against reaction and for socialism was a single task, and on the order of the day.

# 3

# The coalition government and the return of reaction, 1931–1933

The revolution of 1931 was not a month old when bloody struggles between soldiers and workers took place.

The cardinal-primate's injunction to Catholics to vote "neither monarchist nor republican" led to mass burning of churches. A monarchist club meeting May 10th was hooted by workers, monarchists fired and wounded workers, and with the spread of the news through Madrid, groups of workers started a round-up of monarchists. The fight against Church and monarchists reached such proportions that the workers involved left the factories for some days to carry on the struggle. The socialists joined the republicans in appealing for calm and return to work; the revolutionists demanded extermination of the monarchist organizations and arrest of their leaders. Worse still, the socialists instructed their militia to help the police maintain law and order. In the ensuing struggles the Civil Guard shot ten workers. A delegation of their comrades demanded of the provisional government the dissolution of the Civil Guard. The government's reply was a declaration of martial law and the troops were called out in all the important cities. Alfonso's police and army, its officer caste still weeping for the banished King, solaced themselves with attacks on those who had caused Alfonso to flee. The workers got their first taste of the republic and of socialist participation in a bourgeois government.

In the work of drafting the new constitution, the socialists viewed the republican-socialist coalition as the permanent government of Spain. It was more important to give the Spanish government strong powers than to provide a free hand for anarchist and communist "irresponsibles" to incite the masses to disorder.

Was there any possible justification for the socialist position? The Spanish socialists argued their support of the government was justified because this was a bourgeois revolution, the completion of which could be achieved by a republican government, and that the "consolidation of the republic" was the most immediate task in warding off the return of reaction. In this argument they echoed the German and Austrian Social-Democracy after the war. But they were flying in the face of the authentic tradition and practice of Marxism.

The revolutions of 1848 had failed, and had been followed by the return of reaction, because of the indecisive course of the petty-bourgeois republicans. Drawing the lessons of 1848, Marx came to the conclusion that the struggle against the return of reaction, as well as the securing of maximum rights for the workers under the new republic, required that in succeeding bourgeois revolutions the proletariat must fight in *organizational and political independence* from the petty-bourgeois republicans.[*]

---

[*] "In the case where a struggle against a common enemy exists, a special kind of alliance is unnecessary. As soon as it becomes necessary to fight such an enemy directly, the interests of both parties fall together for the moment. . . . And then, as soon as victory has been decided, the petty-bourgeoisie will endeavor to annex it for themselves. They will call upon the workers to keep the peace and return to their work in order to avoid (so-called) excesses, and then proceed to cut the workers off from the fruits of victory. . . .

"During the struggle and after the struggle, the workers at every opportunity must put up their own demands in contradistinction to the demands put forward by the bourgeois democrats. . . . They must check as far as possible all manifesta-

Marx's conceptions of strategy were applied in the Russian Revolution of 1905, in which the proletariat created workers' councils (soviets) constituted by delegates elected from factory, shop and street, as the flexible instrument which unified workers of various tendencies in the struggle against Czarism. The Russian workers followed Marx's advice that no special alliance is necessary with even the most progressive sections of the bourgeoisie: both classes strike at the same enemy, but the proletarian organizations pursue their independent aims without the constriction and unnecessary compromise of an alliance—that is, a common program, which could only be the minimum and therefore a bourgeois program— with the bourgeoisie. In February 1917, the soviets were again created at a time when most Marxists thought the question was merely one of bourgeois revolution.

Thus, even for the "bourgeois" revolution, soviets were necessary. And the German and Austrian revolutions taught very different lessons than those which the Spanish socialists chose to draw. For these revolutions, too, had created soviets; but, dominated by reformists, the soviets had been dissolved as soon as capitalism regained stability. The real lessons of the German and Austrian revolutions were that soviets require a revolutionary program; that as organs without political power they cannot continue to exist in-

---

tions of intoxication for the victory and enthusiasm for the new state of affairs, and must explain candidly their lack of confidence in the new government in every way through a cold-blooded analysis of the new state of affairs. They must simultaneously erect their own revolutionary workers' government beside the new official government, whether it be in the form of executive committees, community councils, workers' clubs or workers' committees, so that the bourgeois democratic government will not only lose its immediate restraint over the workers but, on the contrary, must at once feel themselves watched over and threatened by an authority behind which stand the mass of the workers. In a word: from the first moment of the victory, and after it, the distrust of the workers must not be directed any more against the conquered reactionary party, but against the previous ally, the petty-bourgeois democrats, who desire to exploit the common victory only for themselves." (Marx, "Address to the Communist League" *(1850)*, *Appendix 3 to Engels*, "Revolution and Counter-Revolution in Germany", *London, 1933*).

definitely; that one cannot support both the government and the soviets, as the German and Austrian reformists, like the Russian Mensheviks, tried to do; that soviets can begin as powerful strike committees but must end as organs of state power.

Thus have Marx's conclusions of eighty-six years ago been reinforced by every succeeding revolution.

Thus the course taken by the Spanish socialists from 1931 to 1933 was completely alien to Marxism. "Spain is a republic of workers of all classes." This silly phrase was adopted upon socialist initiative as the first article of the constitution

The constitution limited voting to those over the age of 23, and set up a method of Cortes elections which favored coalition tickets and made representation of minority parties almost impossible. When this method later worked against them, the socialist leaders confessed it had been instituted on the assumption that the socialist coalition with the republicans would go on indefinitely!

Compulsory military service was made a constitutional provision, as under the monarchy. The President of the Republic was given power to choose the Premier and to dissolve the Cortes twice in a presidential term of six years, and could be removed during his term only by a three-fifths vote of the Cortes. Provision was also made for a Court of Constitutional Guarantees with powers of nullifying legislation equivalent to those of the United States Supreme Court, and for a difficult system of amending the constitution.

Like the Weimar constitution, the Spanish document contained a great deal of phraseology about social rights but with a "joker" (Article 42) providing for suspension of all constitutional rights; there was immediately adopted the "Law for the Defense of the Republic"—copied almost verbatim from the similar German law. It established as "acts of aggression against the republic": spreading of news likely to disturb the public order or credit; denigration of public institutions; illicit possession of arms; unreasonable refusal to work; lightning strikes. Furthermore, the Minister of the Interior was empowered "in the interests of public order" at any time, to suspend public meetings; to close clubs, associations and unions; to investigate accounts of all associations or unions; to seize illicit arms.

There was also enacted a law continuing Rivera's mixed arbitration boards to settle strikes. "We shall introduce compulsory arbitration. Those workers' organizations which do not submit to it will be declared outside the law," said Minister of Labor Largo Caballero on July 23, 1931. It was made unlawful to strike for political demands, and unlawful to strike unless the workers had presented their demands in writing to the employer ten days before.

Such was the legal structure adopted by the republican-socialist coalition. Not a single deputy voted against it, and it was adopted, December 9, 1931, by 368 ayes and 102 abstentions.

The revolutionists replied by reminding the socialists of the Marxian theory of the state. The Spanish government, regardless of who sits in the cabinet, is a capitalist government. Its powers are powers in the hands of the capitalist class. To give this government the power of suspending constitutional guarantees, or intervening in labor disputes, etc., is an act of treachery against the proletariat. Inevitably these powers will be used against the proletariat.

To limit the voting age to 23 (and this in a southern country where boys of sixteen are active figures in the movement!) is to deprive the working class of a powerful means of drawing into political life the most revolutionary force in the country: the youth. The proletariat least of all need fear the most thorough-going democracy: the electoral scheme means that large sections of the workers and peasantry will not secure representation in the Cortes.

To democratise the bourgeois régime by centering governmental functions in the most representative body, the Cortes, is an elementary tenet of working class policy; to put powers in the hands of a Supreme Court, a president and a cabinet, is a crime against democracy. These smaller bodies are far more susceptible to reactionary influences.

Do we seek to democratise the state so that we shall support it? No! The working class rallies only to its own organizations, its own

class organs. The limited possibilities of democratising the bourgeois state apparatus are important only so far as they enable us to
build, side by side with it, the DUAL POWER of the soviets!

※

The bloody clashes of May were only the beginning. "Spreading
news likely to disturb the public order or credit" was a description
broad enough to cover most anarchist or Marxist criticism. It was
not unusual for Azaña's men to confiscate five out of six successive
issues of a communist paper. The prohibition of lightning strikes
was a deadly blow to syndicalist methods of struggle. Strikes were
driven from the field of battle to the debilitating channels of arbitration boards before the workers had a chance to force favorable
settlements. Socialist organizers advised C.N.T. strikers they would
get better settlements if they joined "the union of the government."
The deepening agricultural crisis led landowners to sharper and
sharper attacks on the living "standards" of sharecroppers and
landworkers; arbitration agreements raising their pay were ignored
and the workers were banned from striking while government agents
went into interminable investigations and discussions with the land
owners.

Unscathed by the meaningless church laws, the clergy raised their
heads, and their demands found spokesmen high in the government. When, in August 1931, the Vicar General of Seville was seized
illegally crossing the border with documents revealing sale and con-
cealment of Jesuit and other church property, the Catholic Ministers in the provisional government, Maura and Zamora, were able
to prevent publication of the documents. Maura retired from the
government with the end of the provisional cabinet in December;
but Zamora, who wished to retire on the principled ground that he
was hostile to the constitutional clauses and the laws dealing with
the Church, was persuaded to accept elevation to the Presidency of
the Republic by socialist votes. From that exalted post Zamora, from
the very first day, aided the clerical forces of reaction.

The socialist, Indalecio Prieto, entered the cabinet as Minister of Finance. At his first move to take control of the Bank of Spain, the government was shaken as by an earthquake. The final "compromise" provided a shifting of cabinet seats, giving the Finance Ministry to a capitalist who named suitable governors for the Bank.

On the last day of the year that ushered in the republic, the peasants of Castilblanco yielded up to the republic the first important group of political prisoners. Meeting with firm resistance an attack by the Civil Guard, the peasant leaders were sent to prison for long terms.

Thereafter, the drama moved to its inexorable ending in reaction. As it became utterly evident that the government's course left reaction not only untouched, but enabled it to grow stronger, the socialist leaders had to speak less of the government's achievements and more of their own organizations. Restive workers were soothed by pointing to the growing numbers in the U.G.T., and to the socialist militia. Revolutionists, however, pointed out that the U.G.T. could not be a bulwark against reaction so long as it supported the government. Struggle against capitalism and support of a bourgeois government are mutually incompatible. The government's prestige is bound up with a record of "maintaining order" so that Minister of Labor Caballero must prevent strikes with the aid of arbitration committees or throttle them if they break out against his will. So, too, the socialist militia: created with the consent of the government and used as an auxiliary to the police, it could be nothing but a display force for parades; a real proletarian militia cannot be pledged to support a bourgeois government nor be limited to the proletarian organizations pledged to loyalty to the régime; it must be a genuinely class weapon which fights for democratic rights without limiting itself to the bounds of bourgeois legality, and which is just as ready to assume the offensive as to fight on the defensive.

In crushing the C.N.T., the troops broadened the repression to the whole working class. Under cover of putting down an anarchist putsch in January 1933, the Civil Guard "mopped up" various groups of troublemakers. An encounter with peasants at Casas Viejas, early in January 1933, became a *cause célèbre* which shook the government to its foundations and opened the road for reaction.

The counter-revolution had taken to arms (August 10, 1932) in Seville, when General Sanjurjo led troops and Civil Guards for restoration of the monarchy (the movement was smashed by the workers of Seville under revolutionary slogans which alarmed Azaña more than did Sanjurjo). Now the counter-revolution discovered that it could out-do the republicans and socialists in demagogic appeals to the masses. The monarchist and Catholic parties sent their own investigating committee to Casas Viejas; they unearthed a terrible story. Under direct orders from Minister of the Interior Quiroga to "take no prisoners," the Civil Guard had descended on the little village where, after two years of patient waiting for the Institute of Agrarian Reform to divide the neighboring Duke's estate, the peasants had moved in and begun to till the soil for themselves. The peasants scarcely could resist the Civil Guard; they were hunted through the fields like animals; twenty were destroyed, others wounded. The survivors were warned by government officials to keep quiet unless they wished the same fate.

Azaña had refused to investigate, and delayed interpellations in the Cortes. Finally, the republican-socialist coalition had to face the music. The monarchist-Catholic deputies wept large tears for massacred peasants and shouted themselves hoarse at such a cruel government. When Azaña finally had to admit the truth about Casas Viejas, he sought to shift the blame to the Civil Guards; but they implicated Quiroga himself. Through it all, the socialist deputies sat silent, and voted a motion of confidence in Azaña-Quiroga. The reactionaries had a real field day: to Casas Viejas they added denunciation of the government for its oppression of the labor press and the large number of political prisoners, mostly workers, in the jails (9,000 was one communist estimate in June 1933). The reactionaries even submitted to the Cortes a bill providing amnesty for all political prisoners, to the enthusiastic vivas of the anarchists.

The workers and, above all, the peasantry were thoroughly bewildered by this bold and successful demagogy. Who were their friends? The republican-socialists had promised land but did not give it. "What did the republic give you to eat?" The republic had killed and jailed the brave peasants of Castilblanco and Casas Viejas. In vain did the socialists argue and plead—the peasants knew their own misery.

The end came quite quickly. In June 1933, Zamora tried to dismiss the coalition but was out-maneuvered, while the socialists announced that any further attempt would be met by a general strike. It proved an empty threat. It is doubtful whether the bewildered and discouraged workers would have responded to a call; they had been held in leash too long! Three months later, Zamora struck again, dismissing the cabinet and simultaneously dissolving the Cortes. Lerroux was appointed Premier.

The elections were held in November; the victory of the coalition of reactionaries and rightists was decisive. The socialists offered many explanations: the embittered anarchists had effectively campaigned for a boycott of the elections; the communists had run separate tickets; the women were under clerical influence and voting the first time; the socialists—running independent tickets in most places, under the pressure of the rank and file—fell victim to their own stupid provisions for electoral machinery; the local bosses and landowners terrorized the villages and bought votes; the elections were fraudulent in many places, etc., etc. But this was a poor alibi and its details, indeed, were proof of the failure of the republican-socialist coalition to win and inspire the masses or to crush the reaction in two and a half years of rule. The cold statistics are that, of 13 million eligibles, 8 million voted and more than half of them voted for the rightist coalition, the "anti-Marxist front," and another million voted for center parties. The petty-bourgeois republicans were wiped out, returning but seven deputies, most of them, like Azaña, owing their election to socialist votes.

As a witness for our analysis of the causes of the victory of reaction, we introduce Indalecio Prieto. In a mood of extreme honesty and frankness, on fleeing to Paris after the October 1934 revolt, Prieto told *Le Petit Journal*, in answer to the question, "How do you explain the discontent in Spain, and the success of Gil Robles in the last elections?":

"Precisely because of the right policy of the left régime," said Prieto. "This government born with the republic and created by the republic became the rampart of forces adverse to the republic. It is true that the left government of Spain carried out the policy of the right before Lerroux and Samper. In this period of perishing capitalism, the Spanish bourgeoisie could not carry through even the bourgeois-democratic revolution."

# 4

## The fight against fascism:
## November 1933 to February 1936

Though governmental crises changed cabinet personnel six times during the next two years, Lerroux's Radicals remained ostensibly at the helm, with either Lerroux or his lieutenants—Samper, Martinez Barrios—as Premier. The Radicals gave a pledge to the left that no Gil Robles man would enter the cabinet. Actually, this arrangement was dictated by Gil Robles. He had studied the methods of Hitler and Mussolini, and felt he dared not openly take power until his fascist movement had acquired a mass base.

It was certainly fitting that this degenerate and reactionary régime should be led by the Radicals, to whose malodorous history we have already referred. A party of such grotesque buffoonery ("Every Nun a Mother!" had been a Lerroux slogan) could exist only so long as capitalist and proletarian camps did not lock in mortal combat; it was soon to dissolve, its finish occasioned, appropriately enough, by a series of scandalous revelations of financial peculations involving the whole party leadership. But for the "bienio negro," the two black years, its cynical satyrs served the austere clericals as Premiers and Ministers.

The legal structure provided by the republican-socialist coalition proved most useful to Lerroux-Gil Robles. Over a hundred issues of *El Socialista* were seized within a year. The Socialist International estimated in September 1934 a total of 12,000 imprisoned workers. The socialist militia was proscribed and its arms confiscated. Workers' meeting halls were closed and their union accounts scanned to discover use of funds for revolutionary purposes. Socialists and other workers elected in the municipal councils were removed. All the laws which the socialists had thought to use against "irresponsibles" were now used against them.

Gil Robles' main problem was to secure a mass base, a difficult task because Spain has an extremely small middle class. Outside of the small group of prosperous peasant-owners in the North—Basque and Navarra—where a force similar to the Austrian clerical-fascist militia was organized, Gil Robles would have much difficulty in recruiting from the lower classes. There were, however, the million and a half unemployed city and land workers: to win them, Gil Robles introduced a bill providing unemployment benefits, seeking to exploit the fact that the unemployed had been neglected by the republican-socialist government. The clericals set up a program of government re-forestation, the work camps being schools for fascism. They set up a youth movement, a "Christian Trade Union Movement" and a "Christian Peasants Movement." Gil Robles even frightened his allies, the landowners of the Agrarian Party, with talk of dividing up the big estates. Even to unfriendly observers it appeared that Gil Robles was rolling up a mass following. But when, after months of patient labor and huge expenditure, the clerical-fascists attempted to show results by marshalling great mass gatherings, they were smashed and disintegrated by the socialist proletariat.

Why? It is true that clerical fascism was often inept. Nevertheless, the lack of a convincing demagogy had not prevented clerical-fascism from smashing the proletariat in Austria. Spanish clerical-fascism did not succeed for the reason that the proletariat, unlike that of Germany, did fight and, unlike the Austrians, fought before it was too late.

For the Spanish proletariat evidenced a real determination not to allow itself to be beaten by fascism. The leftward evolution of the international social-democracy after the defeats of Germany and Austria, came in Spain more rapidly than elsewhere. Caballero joined the left wing, of which the Socialist Youth, deeply critical of both the Second and Third Internationals, was the mainstay. The left wing declared for preparing the proletarian revolution, to be achieved by armed insurrection. The center wing of the party, led by Prieto and Gonzales Pena, publicly pledged, in the Cortes, that any attempt at a fascist régime would be met by armed revolution. Only a small right wing under Besteiro refused to learn from Austria and Germany. In the U.G.T., Caballero introduced a régime of bold struggle and the right-wing socialists who objected were forced to resign from its executive. Precisely because they had been so ideologically dependent on the Kautskys and Bauers, the fall of their teachers enabled the Spanish socialists to make an extraordinarily sharp break with their past. The bourgeoisie, reading proletarian politics by way of bourgeois analogies, thought this was all bluff—until they were scared into conviction by the discovery of large depots of arms in socialist homes and buildings.

With the Socialist Party ready to struggle, the fight against fascism was enormously facilitated, indeed it is not too much to say that only the leftward turn of the Socialist Party made possible, under the existing conditions, the victory over fascism. To have rallied the masses *in spite of* the socialists, would have required a revolutionary party of such calibre and mass proportions as simply did not exist in Spain.

It proved impossible, however, to instill the Socialist Party with the Marxist conception of the insurrection. Even the best of the left socialist leaders held an extremely narrow conception. In pseudo-leftist terms similar to those of the anarchists and the "third-period" Stalinists, the socialists affirmed themselves no longer interested in the course of bourgeois-republican politics—as if the revolution cannot take advantage of, cannot influence, the course of bourgeois politics! For example: the rightists had carried Catalonia in the

November elections, but such was the resurgence of the masses that, only two months later, the left bloc swept the Catalonian municipal elections. The November defeat created a crisis within the C.N.T., part of the leadership demanding an end to boycotting all elections. Hence, a socialist campaign demanding dissolution of the Cortes and new elections could have aided the socialists in rallying the masses, could have torn syndicalists away from the anarchists, could have driven a wedge between Gil Robles and many supporters of Lerroux. Apparently, however, the socialists were afraid of not being left enough.

The broad character of the proletarian insurrection was explained by the Communist Left (Trotskyist). It devoted itself to efforts to build the indispensable instrument of the insurrection: workers' councils constituted by delegates representing all the labor parties and unions, the shops and streets; to be created in every locality and joined together nationally; a veritable mass leadership which as it functioned would succeed in drawing to it all non-party, non-union and anarchist workers seriously desirous of fighting against capitalism. Unfortunately, the socialists failed to understand the profound need of these Workers' Alliances. The bureaucratic traditions were not to be so easily overcome; Caballero, no more than Prieto, could understand that the mass leadership of the revolution must be broader than the party leadership; the socialist leaders thought that the Workers' Alliances meant that they would have merely to share leadership with the Communist Left and other dissident communist groups. Thus, though the Communist Left was persuasive enough to achieve their creation in Asturias and Valencia, and they nominally existed in Madrid and elsewhere, actually in most cases they were merely "top" committees, without elected or lower-rank delegates, that is, little more than liaison committees between the leadership of the organizations involved; and even these were never completed by being joined together through a national committee.

Incredible as it may seem, the fascist scribbler, Curzio Malaparte's *"Technique of the Coup D'état,"* had a great vogue among the socialist leaders. They actually thought Malaparte's preposterous dialogues between Lenin and Trotsky, elaborating a purely putchist conception of seizure of power by small groups of armed men, were genuine transcripts! The socialists seemed to be completely ignorant of the role of the masses in the October revolution of 1917. They failed to tell the masses what the coming revolution would mean to them. Though leading, in June 1934, a general strike of landworkers involving nearly half a million, the socialists did not cement the bond between city and country by rallying the city workers to their aid with pickets and funds; nor was the strike used to systematically propagate the slogan of seizure of the land, although during those same months peasant seizures of land reached their highest peak. As a result, when the bitter strike ended without victory, the class-consciousness of the landworkers, always so much weaker than that of the industrial proletariat, was so shaken that they played no rôle at all in the October insurrection. Nor was the city proletariat prepared to seize the factories and public institutions, and impregnated with the conviction that it was up to them to overthrow capitalism and begin building the new order. Instead, the socialists hinted darkly of their complete preparations to effect the revolution themselves.

In their partial struggles against the fascist menace, however, the socialists acquitted themselves magnificently. Gil Robles put his greatest efforts on three carefully-planned concentrations: that at Escurial, near Madrid, on April 22, 1934; that of the Catalonian landowners in Madrid on September 8th against liberal tenancy laws adopted by the Catalonian government, and that on September 9th at Covadongas, Asturias. Not one of these was successful. The workers declared general strikes covering each area; street car rails were torn up; trains were stopped; food and accommodations were made impossible; roads were blocked by barricades, and with fists and weapons the reactionaries were turned back and dispersed. The small groups of wealthy young bloods and their servants, clergy and landowners, who managed to get through with the aid of the army and Civil Guard, presented such a ludicrous contrast to the forces of their opponents that the clerical fascist claim to represent all Spain received an irreparable blow.

The workers' opposition was re-inforced by the struggle for national liberation. Moves against its semi-autonomous status roused the Catalonian nation; Companys, still in power, had to endorse a series of huge demonstrations against Gil Robles. Finally, the nationalist deputies left the Cortes altogether. Reactionary centralization even drove the conservative Basques into hostility; their municipal councils, in August 1934, met and decided to refuse all collaboration with the government; Lerroux' answer, the arrest of all Basque mayors, only intensified the crisis.

The clerical-fascists dared wait no longer. They had failed to build a mass base; but with every day the opposition grew stronger. The disunity within the workers' ranks was slowly but surely tending to disappear. Despite Lerroux' clever game of gentle treatment for the C.N.T., in order to re-inforce the anti-political elements who were arguing that all governments were equally bad and Lerroux' government no worse than the last, socialist proposals were beginning to meet with acceptances; in a number of strikes the C.N.T. cooperated with the U.G.T., and in several places, notably in Asturias, the anarchists had entered the Workers' Alliances.

Even the Stalinists were compelled to come along. Since November 1933, they had met each socialist step to the left by the foulest kind of invective. Kuusinen, official reporter at the 13th Plenum of the Executive Committee of the Communist International, December 1933, accused the Spanish socialists of taking part "in the preparation for establishing a fascist dictatorship." "There are no disagreements between the fascists and the social-fascists as far as the necessity for the further fascisation of the bourgeois dictatorship is concerned," said the E.C.C.I. "The social-democrats are in favor of fascisation provided the parliamentary form is preserved. . . . What is worrying these people is that in their furious zeal the fascists may hasten the doom of capitalism. The fascisation of social-democracy is proceeding at an accelerated pace." (*Inprecorr,* vol. 14, P. 109.) When in April 1934 the secretary of the Communist Party of Spain, Balbontin, resigned because the Communist International refused to sanction a united front, he was answered: "The social-fascists have to maintain the illusion among the working masses that they are 'enemies' of fascism, and that there is a great struggle between socialism and fascism, as some petty-bourgeois counter-revolutionaries (Balbontin) want to make the workers believe." (*Ibid,* p. 545.) In June 1934, when the socialist Juanita Rico was killed by fascists in Madrid, the Communist Party had to accept the socialist invitation for participation in the mass funeral. But on July 12 it rejected a socialist invitation for joint action and entry into the Workers' Alliances, and declared that "our correct united front tactics enabled us to frustrate the counter-revolutionary plans of the Workers' Alliance." But by September 12 the pressure from its own ranks was irresistible, its delegates taking their seats in the Alliances on September 23—just a few days before the armed struggle began. If the chief exponents of the theory of social-fascism had to join the proletarian united front, the anarchist-led workers of the C.N.T. would soon take the same road. Gil Robles dared wait no longer; he struck.

Zamora named Lerroux to form a new cabinet; three of Gil Robles' nominees entered it. The socialists had declared they would answer such a move with arms. If they now retreated, the initiative would pass to Gil Robles, the masses would be demoralized. The socialists took up the challenge within six hours. At midnight of October 4, the Workers' Alliances and the U.G.T. declared a nationwide general strike.

The stirring events of the next fifteen days are well-enough known not to be repeated here. Despite the absence of real soviets, the lack of clarity concerning the goal of the struggle, the failure to call the peasants to take the land and the workers to seize the factories, the workers heroically threw themselves into the struggle. The backbone of the struggle was broken, however, when the refusal of the C.N.T. railroad workers to strike enabled the government to transport goods and troops. The few hours between the general strike call and the mobilization of the workers' militia was sufficient delay to enable the government to arrest the soldiers who were depended upon to split the army; the failure to arm the workers beforehand could not be made up for within a few hours, while government troops and police were raiding every likely building. There were many outright betrayals of arms depots; many key men fled when victory appeared out of the question. In Catalonia, which should have been the fortress of the uprising, dependence on the petty-bourgeois government of Companys proved fatal; more fearful of arming the workers than of capitulating to Gil Robles, Companys broadcast reassuring statements until, surrounded by Madrid troops, he abjectly surrendered.

And yet, in spite of all this, the workers put up a tremendous struggle. In Madrid, Bilbao and other cities, armed clashes went no further than guerilla sniping by the workers; but the general strikes were carried on for a long period, sustained by the proletariat with exemplary enthusiasm and discipline, and paralyzing industrial and commercial life as no previous struggle had ever done in Spain. The greatest and most glorious struggle took place in Asturias. Here the Workers' Alliances were most nearly like soviets, and had been functioning for a year under socialist and Communist Left leadership. Pena and Manuel Grossi led the miners, who made up for lack of arms by dynamite, tool of their trade, in a victorious insurrection. The "Workers and Peasants Republic" of Asturias gave the land to the peasants, confiscated the factories, tried their enemies in revolutionary tribunals, and for fifteen historic days held off the Foreign Legion and Moorish troops. There is a saying in Spain that had there been three Asturiases, the revolution would have been successful. Only the failure of the rebellion elsewhere enabled the government to concentrate its full force on Asturias.

Nor did there follow a period of pessimism in the workers' ranks. On the contrary, there was widespread recognition that they had not been defeated in a general engagement; the masses had merely gone on strike and confined their fighting to driving off scabs; their ranks were still intact. They would fight again very soon, and this time would know better how to fight. The dread story of how 3,000

Asturian workers had been slaughtered, most of them after surrender, only served to steel the determination of the masses. Gil Robles' attempts to seize workers' headquarters, close down unions, confiscate funds, met with the fiercest resistance. To take the place of the confiscated labor press, illegal organs sprang up and were openly circulated. Executions of October prisoners were met with general strikes. Numerous economic strikes demonstrated the unshaken morale of the proletariat. On May 1, 1935, despite the most frenzied efforts of the government, there was a complete stoppage of work, an absolute paralysis of everything except the public services manned by government troops. The amnesty campaigns, for reprieves of condemned men and release of the prisoners, drew in large sections of the peasantry and the petty-bourgeoisie: the cry of *"Amnistia, amnistia!"* drew hitherto untouched layers into political life. The Radical-clerical régime began to crack.

President Zamora himself dared go no further. Before the struggle was over, he commuted the death sentences of the Catalan chiefs. The Radical Party split, the perspicacious Martinez Barrios—who as Premier in December 1933 ferociously crushed an anarchist putsch—leading an anti-fascist grouping, and joining with Azaña and other republicans, in May, to fight for amnesty. Lerroux himself now retreated, reprieving Pena and 18 other condemned socialists, on March 29; when Gil Robles retaliated by driving his cabinet out of office, Lerroux was named Premier again by Zamora and dissolved the Cortes for a month in which the Radicals ruled alone; on May 4, Lerroux again formed a cabinet with clerical-fascists, this time with Gil Robles himself as Minister of War, but May Day had already made clear the turn of the tide. We now know that Gil Robles then took over the War Ministry for the purpose of preparing the army, arms depots and secret emplacements around Madrid, for the struggle which is now waging, and therefore knew as well as anybody that he would soon be ousted.

Great anti-fascist rallies took place around the demand for dissolution of the Cortes and new elections. Meetings of a hundred thousand, of two hundred thousand, became regular occurrences.

Within the working class, the sentiment for unity was the dominant note. Terribly discredited for their refusal to join the October revolt, the anarchists sought to apologize by pointing to the repressions they were undergoing at the time from Companys and asserted they were ready to join with socialists in the struggle for freedom; Angel Pestana led a split and organized the Syndicalist Party for participation in the coming elections; and even the C.N.T. leadership made it clear they would let their followers vote against the semi-fascist régime. With the tide, most of the bourgeois press turned against Gil Robles. It needed only the final touch of financial scandal involving the Lerroux government. The clerical-fascists had arrived at an impasse; they had to retreat.

They had no idea, however, of the extent of the tidal wave which was to sweep over them. They thought that the February elections would give the balance of power to center groups. So, too, thought Azaña who, eight days before the elections, sought a postponement, fearing the republican-workers' coalition had not had enough time for its propaganda. But the masses of peasants and workers, men and women, had their say. They swept the semi-fascist régime away. And not only at the polls. With the posting of the election returns, the masses came out on the streets. Within four days of the elections Azaña was again at the head of the government and again crying for peace, for the workers to go back to work, banishing any spirit of vengeance. Already he was repeating the phrases, and pursuing the policies of 1931–1933!

# 5

## The People's Front government and its supporters: February 20 to July 17, 1936

*Who are the criminals and traitors responsible for making it possible that, five months after the February days in which the workers drove the clerical-fascists from the government and the streets, the reactionaries can lead the army and police in such a powerful counter-revolution?*

Every serious communist and socialist wants to know the answer to this paramount question, for it has significance not only for Spain, and for France where a similar development is taking place, but for the policies of the proletariat throughout the world.

The answer is: the criminals and traitors are the "left" republican government and its supporters, the Communist Party and the reformist socialists.

When the February elections approached, the left wing socialists were opposed to a joint election ticket with the republicans, because they did not believe the republicans had any real following, and because of the hatred of the masses for these men: Companys' Catalan *Esquerra* had been guilty of treachery in the October revolt; Martinez Barrios' "Republican Union" was merely the remnant of Lerroux' Radicals, singing a new tune for the occasion; Azaña and his left republicans had repudiated the October revolt and admittedly were nothing but a handful of intellectuals. The left socialists were especially outraged when Prieto and the Communist Party agreed to give these republicans a majority in the joint election tickets: the tickets that carried gave the republicans 152 deputies to 116 for the workers' organizations!

But this was not the real crime. Voting blocs for purely electoral purposes are not a matter of principle for revolutionists, although extremely seldom are they warranted by tactical considerations. But such voting agreements must be limited *solely* to the exchange of votes. Before, during and after the election, the proletarian party continues to speak from its *own* platform, with its *own* program, explaining to the workers that it *cannot* arrive at any agreement on *program* with its temporary electoral allies. For a so-called "common program" could be, and was in fact, only the program of the class enemy. This was the real crime, that the Spanish workers' organizations underwrote and guaranteed another charter for the bourgeoisie, necessarily identical with that of 1931–1933.

Prieto forgot that he had said: "In this period of perishing capitalism, the Spanish bourgeoisie could not even carry through the bourgeois-democratic revolution." The Communist Party, slavishly obeying the new international orientation, wiped out its 1931–1933 criticism of the impossibility of the bourgeoisie undertaking the democratic tasks of the revolution, and declared the coalition with the bourgeoisie would carry out these tasks![*]

---

[*] To inveigle the left socialists into the coalition, the Stalinists talked very "left": "The Communist Party knows the danger of Azaña just as well as the Socialists who collaborated with him when he was in power. They know that he is an enemy of the working class. . . . But they also know that the defeat of the CEDA (Gil Robles) would automatically bring with it a certain amount of relief from the repression, for a time at least." (*Inprecorr,* vol. 15, p. 762.) But did the Stalinists propose, then, that once Azaña was in power, the workers should struggle against him? On the contrary. This "enemy of the workers" would fulfill the basic democratic tasks: "land to the peasants, freedom to the oppressed nationalities," "free

The People's Front program was a basically reactionary document:

1. *The agrarian question.* The program states: "The republicans do not accept the principle of the nationalization of the land and its free distribution to the peasants, solicited by the delegates of the Socialist Party." Instead, it promises stimulation of exports, credits, security of tenure for tenants and state purchase of estates for rental to peasants. In other words, the program of 1931, which had already been proven a cruel joke.

2. *Expansion of Spanish economy.* It promises a more efficient system of protective tariffs, institutions to guide industry (a department of commerce, labor, etc.), putting the treasury and the banks at the service of "national reconstruction, without slurring over the fact that such subtle things as credit cannot be forced outside of the sure field of profitable and remunerative effort. The republican parties do not accept the measures of nationalization of the banks proposed by the workers' parties." "Great plans" of public works. "The republicans do not accept the subsidy to unemployment (dole) solicited by the workers' delegation. They believe that the measures of agrarian policy and those which are to be carried out in industry, public works and, in sum, the whole plan of national reconstruction, will fulfill not only its own ends but also the essential task of absorbing unemployment." This, too, like 1931.

3. *The Church.* Only the section on education affects the clergy.

---

Morocco from imperialist oppression." (*Ibid*, p. 639.) In order to justify this open espousal of the Menshevik conception of the bourgeois revolution, the Stalinists had to blacken their own past: Garcia, at the Seventh Congress, denounced the party's leadership of 1931: "Instead of advancing slogans which corresponded to the moment, they expressed themselves against the republic concerning which there were very strong illusions among the masses of the people, and advanced the slogans, 'Down with the bourgeois republic,' 'Long live the Soviets and the dictatorship of the proletariat.' With the expulsion of these renegades (in 1932), our Spanish party began to live and work in a communist manner." (*Ibid*, p. 1310.) But these slogans had been raised not only by the "renegades," but by the party itself, up to the beginning of 1935, by Ercoli, Pieck and the Comintern itself!

The Republic "shall impel with the same rhythm as in the first years of the Republic the creation of primary schools. . . . Private education shall be subject to vigilance in the interest of culture analogous to that of the public schools." We know, from the story of 1931–1933, what rhythm that was!

4. *The army.* The only section that affects the army is that promising investigation and punishment of police abuses under the reaction and dismissal of commanding officers found guilty. Not even the lip-service to democratization of the army which was given in 1931! Thus, the officers' corps is left intact. And in the five months that followed, the People's Front government put off any investigation of the Asturian massacres or other crimes perpetrated by the officers' corps!

5. *The colonial and national questions.* Not a word in the Popular Front program. Morocco remained in the hands of the Foreign Legionnaires until they finally took it over completely on July 18. The semi-autonomous statutes of Catalonia were later restored, but further autonomy not granted. A less liberal arrangement for the Basques.

6. *Democratization of the state apparatus.* Mixed labor boards, Supreme Court, president, censorship, etc.—all were restored as in 1931. The program promised reorganization of the labor boards so that "the interested parties may acquire a consciousness of the impartiality of their decisions"! And, as a final slap in the face, "The republican parties do not accept the workers' control solicited by the socialist delegation."

For this mess of pottage the workers' leaders abdicated the class struggle against the bourgeois republic.

Think of it! The very program for the sake of which the Stalinists and socialists pledged to support the bourgeois republican government, made inevitable the onslaught of reaction. The economic foundations of reaction were left untouched, in land, industry, finance, the Church, the army, the State. The lower courts were hives of reaction; the labor press is filled, from February to July, with accounts of fascists caught red-handed and let free, and workers held on flimsy charges. On the day the counter-revolution broke out, the prisons of Barcelona and Madrid were filled with thousands of political prisoners—workers, especially from the C.N.T., but also many from the U.G.T. The administrative bureaucracy was so rotten with reaction that it fell apart on July 18. The whole diplomatic and consular corps, with a handful of exceptions, went over to the fascists.

The government "impartially" imposed a rigid press censorship, modified martial law, prohibition of demonstrations and meetings unless authorized—and at every critical moment authorization was withdrawn. In the critical days after the assassinations of Captain Castillo and Calvo Sotelo, the working-class headquarters were ordered closed. The day before the fascist outbreak the labor press appeared with gaping white spaces where the government censorship had lifted out editorials and sections of articles warning against the *coup d'état!*

In the last three months before July 18, in desperate attempts to stop the strike movement, hundreds of strikers were arrested in batches, local general strikes declared illegal and socialist, communist, anarchist headquarters in the regions closed for weeks at a time. Three times in June the Madrid headquarters of the C.N.T. was closed and its leadership jailed.

The Stalinist and socialist leaders found it impossible to restrain the hatred of their following for this repetition of 1931–1933. Even that most vociferous supporter of the government, Jose Diaz, secretary of the Communist Party, had to admit:

"The government, which we are loyally supporting in the measure that it completes the pact of the Popular Front, is a government that is commencing to lose the confidence of the workers." And then he adds this most significant admission: "And I say to the left republican government that its road is the wrong road of April 1931." (*Mundo Obrero*, July 6, 1936.)

Thus, in the very moment of pleading with the Asturian miners not to break with the Popular Front, Jose Diaz had to admit that February–July 1936 was a repetition of the disaster of 1931–1933!

When the counter-revolution broke out, the Stalinists asserted that they had not ceased throughout to urge upon the government the necessity of smashing reaction. We have already seen, however, that the Popular Front program protected reaction on every important front.

No urging can change the republican bourgeoisie. Such a coalition government, committed to maintenance of capitalism, must act as Azaña does both in 1931 and in 1936. The government behaves identically in both cases because its program is one of building a Spanish economy under capitalism. That means: *it cannot touch the economic foundations of reaction because it does not want to destroy capitalism.* Azaña's basic program is put succinctly enough in two phrases soon after he came back to power: "No vengeance"; "Gil Robles too will one day be an Azañista." This program is not dictated by psychological weakness but by Azaña's capitalist premises. His government has not been weak, it has made no "mistakes." It has permitted the reactionaries full scope for arming and mobilizing because that is an inevitable consequence of the capitalist nature of the Popular Front program.

Trotsky has laid bare the anatomy of the People's Front government's relation to reaction:

"The officers' corps represents the guard of capital. Without this guard the bourgeoisie could not maintain itself for a single day. The selection of the individuals, their education and training make the officers, as a distinctive group, uncompromising enemies of socialism. That is how things stand in all bourgeois countries. . . . To eliminate four or five hundred reactionary agitators from the army means to leave everything basically as it was before. . . . It is necessary to replace the troops in the barracks commanded by the officers' caste with the people's militia, that is, with the democratic organization of the armed workers and peasants. There is no other solution. But such an army is incompatible with the domination of exploiters big and small. Can the republicans agree to such a measure? Not at all. The People's Front government, that is to say, the government of the coalition of the workers with the bourgeoisie, is in its very essence a government of capitulation to the bureaucracy and the officers. Such is the great lesson of the events in Spain, now being paid for with thousands of human lives."

Just as socialist support of the government in 1933 made impossible the warding off of reaction, so communist-socialist support in 1936 opened the gates for the counter-revolution. But, workers may ask, could they not, while supporting the government, also mobilize the workers and peasants against their enemies? No! Two important examples must suffice:

1. In Albacete province, near Yeste, the peasants seized a big estate. On May 28, 1936, they were attacked by the Civil Guard, 23 peasants killed and 30 wounded. The Minister of Interior greeted this blood-bath by sending a telegram of congratulations to the Civil Guard. The press correctly termed the situation a repetition of that in the Casas Viejas massacre of 1933. The interpellations in the Cortes on June 5 were awaited with bated breath . . . but the communist and socialist deputies proceeded to absolve the government of all responsibility. "We know that the government is not responsible for what has happened, and that it will take measures to prevent its repetition, but these measures must be taken speedily in the interests of the People's Front," said a socialist deputy. "The plot is clear," said the Stalinists:

> The landowners systematically drive the peasants to desperation and when the peasants take means to help themselves the landowners find venal civil guards prepared to shoot them down. The Civil Guard has carried out a blood-bath and the politicians of the right are doing their best to exploit this happening in order to destroy the People's Front. Politically, the Yeste affair was unsuccessful, but it can and will be repeated. . . . The Communist Party was right when it countered the political maneuver of the right by placing the affair on its real basis and demanding that action should be taken against the rich landowners. It pointed out that a struggle must be conducted above all against misery and starvation, which is increased by the caciques and landown-

ers when they sabotage the orders of the government and the republic and refuse the masses bread. *The Communist Party did this by demanding that the agrarian reforms should be accelerated.* (*Inprecorr,* No. 32, July 11, 1936, p. 859.)

In plain words: the struggle against the landowners should be confined to attempts to persuade the government to agrarian reform. Because further struggles of the peasantry, by themselves, in militant action, on the land, which is the only real form of action, lead to events like Yeste, which cause conflict between the masses and the government, and we must avoid breaking the People's Front. "Not breaking the People's Front" can mean only to limit the struggle to friendly persuasion in the arena of parliament!

2. The construction workers of Madrid, over 80,000 strong, went on strike, their main demand being a 36-hour week. The government ordered the workers to arbitrate; and decided on a 40-hour week. The U.G.T. and the communists agreed and instructed their followers to return to work. The C.N.T., however, refused to accept the government settlement and, what is more, the U.G.T. workers followed the anarchists. The Stalinists gave the following "reasons" for calling off the strike:

It is a secret to nobody that after the 16th of February the fascist bosses introduced into their forms of struggle that of pushing the workers to declare conflicts, first, and to prolong their solution afterward, as far as necessary and possible, in order to drive the masses to desperation, which would take the form of sporadic acts without finality or effectiveness . . . but which would confront the workers with the government, because this is one of the conditions . . . for a *coup d'état.* . . . This attitude of the bosses . . . makes it necessary that the construction workers, even though not satisfied with the settlement, put an end to a situation the prolongation of which involves a grave danger for all workers. . . . The moment has arrived to know how to end the strike, without renouncing the possibility created by the settle-

ment of continuing to discuss in the mixed labor board the problem of salaries. (*Mundo Obrero,* July 6.)

In plain words: the bosses insist on fighting you, but this brings
you in conflict with the government—which means that the government has more in common with the bosses than with you!—
and endangers the People's Front. Therefore: end the strike. But
then, why start strikes? However, the logic of reformism does not
always go that far, because then the workers would repudiate it
altogether. The workers, alas, insist on striking. The duty of the
Communist Party is to stop the strike before the government gets
mad. . . .

This policy of confining the struggle against reaction to the parliamentary arena could mean only the eventual defeat of the masses.
For it is a cardinal tenet of Marxism that *the mobilization of the
masses can take place only through militant struggle.* Had the workers followed the Popular Front policy, we would today be mourn-
ing the downfall of the Spanish proletariat.

# 6

# The masses struggle against fascism despite the People's Front: Feb. 16 to July 16, 1936

Fortunately for the future of the Spanish and the international working class, the masses from the first day of the February victory gave no indication of ceasing the struggle. The lessons of 1931–1933 had been burned into their consciousness. If they now, for the moment, were free of the domination of Gil Robles, they had won that freedom, arms in hand, in spite of the treachery of Companys and the "neutrality" of Azaña. The masses did not wait for Azaña to fulfill his promises. In the four days between the elections and Azaña's hasty entry into the government, the masses effectively carried out the amnesty by tearing open the jails; so effectively, in fact, that the Permanent Committee of the old Cortes, including Gil Robles, thereafter unanimously ratified Azaña's amnesty decree, both for fear of the masses in the streets and in order to make it appear that the constituted government remained in control of Spain. Nor did the workers wait for the government decree, and for the decision as to its constitutionality—which came from the Court of Constitutional Guarantees only on September 6!—to get back the jobs of those dismissed after the October revolt; in every shop and factory the workers took along those dismissed and confronted the employers: "Either, or!" Whatever fixing of responsibility for the excesses of October was done, was by the "plebian method" of the aroused workers and peasants. The Stalinist and right wing socialist deputies shouted themselves hoarse, pleading with the workers to leave all this to the People's Front government. The workers knew better!

The hated clergy, rulers of the "black two years," were also dealt with in the time-honored manner of oppressed peasants. Especially after it was clear the government would not touch the clergy, the masses took matters into their own hands. This consisted not only of burning churches, but of ordering the priests to leave the villages under sentence of death if they returned. Out of abject loyalty to the government, the Stalinists vilified the struggle against the clergy: "Remember that the setting fire to churches and monasteries brings support to the counter-revolution!" (*Inprecorr*, August 1, p. 928.) They were listened to no more than was Azaña. In the province of Valencia, where the workers have now smashed the counter-revolution so decisively, there was scarcely a functioning church in June.

In their full force, however, the mass actions began only after a series of events revealing the beginning of a *rapprochement* between the republicans and the reactionaries. Almost all the rightists voted for Barrios as Speaker of the Cortes. In March, Azaña prolonged the press censorship and the state of alarm decreed by the previous reactionary cabinet. On April 4, only eight days before the first municipal elections since 1931 were to be held, Azaña decreed an indefinite postponement, upon the demand of the reactionaries. The day before, Azaña made a speech promising the reactionaries that he would go no further than the limits fixed by the People's Front program, and that he would stop the strikes and seizures of the land. The speech was greeted with delirious joy by the reactionary press. Calvo Sotelo, the monarchist, declared: "It was the expression of a true conservative. His declaration of respect for the law and the Constitution should make a good impression on public opinion." The spokesman of Gil Robles' organization declared: "I support ninety per cent of the speech." On April 15, with many economic strikes going on, the rightists demanded an end to "the state of anarchy." "The troublemakers and fomenters will be exterminated," promised Minister Salvador on behalf of the cabinet. The same day, Azaña delivered a sharp attack on the proletariat: "The government will revise the whole system of defense, in order to put an end to the reign of violence," declared Azaña. "Communism would signify the death of Spain!" The spokesman for the Catalan landowners, Ventosa, hailed him: "Azaña is the only man capable of offering the country security and defense of all legal rights." The same day, emboldened, fascists and Civil Guard officers shot up a workers' street in Madrid.

Such was the governmental atmosphere when, on April 17, the C.N.T. declared a general strike in Madrid in protest against the fascist attack. The U.G.T. had not been asked to join the strike, and at first denounced it, as did the Stalinists. But the workers came out of all the shops and factories and public services, not because they had changed their allegiance, but because they wanted to fight, and only the anarchists were calling them to struggle. As the whole commercial life of Madrid began to be paralyzed, the Stalinists still declared "they may participate later. Their present decision was to support the Azaña government insofar as it takes effective action against the reactionaries." (*Daily Worker*, April 18.) That evening, when in spite of them the strike had proved a huge success, the U.G.T. and the Stalinists belatedly endorsed it before it was called off.

The bourgeoisie realized that the general strike of April 17, and the wave of economic strikes which it inspired, would develop into a proletarian offensive against capitalism and its agency, the government. How to stop this offensive? The army proposed to crush it forcibly. But even among the reactionaries there was serious doubt whether this was possible as yet. Azaña had a much better solution: let the workers' leaders stop the strikes. So, inducted in May as the new president of Spain to the tune of the "International" sung with clenched fists by Stalinist and socialist deputies who had elected him (the reactionaries did not put up an opposing candidate), Azaña asked Prieto to form a coalition cabinet.

Prieto was more than willing to become Premier. But the mere rumor produced such a storm of opposition in the Socialist Party, that he dared not accept. Caballero warned Prieto that he must not enter without the consent of the party; and behind Caballero, and decidedly to the left of him, was most of the party and the U.G.T.

Madrid, strongest of the party organizations, had adopted a new program in April, and was presenting it for adoption by the national convention in June. The program declared the bourgeoisie could not carry out the democratic tasks of the revolution, above all was incapable of settling the agrarian question and that therefore the proletarian revolution was on the order of the day. It was weakened by many grave errors, notably the continued failure to understand the rôle of soviets. But it signified a profound break with reformism.

Logically, that program, accepted by Caballero, should have been accompanied by a decisive break with the Popular Front policy. Logic, however, scarcely guides centrists. Declaring that the government "has not yet entirely exhausted its possibilities," and that trade union unity and merger of the Marxist parties must precede the revolution, Caballero continued to direct the left socialist deputies in alternately abusing the government but supporting it on every crucial question. Nevertheless, in spite of his frequent love feasts of oratory with the Stalinists, the left socialist organ under his control, *Claridad,* continued to be a daily contrast to the organs of the Communist Party and the right wing socialists. *Claridad* effectively exposed the fraudulent character of the agrarian program; showed how Prieto's pet projects of irrigation works were enriching the big landowners while the peasants remained poor, and even carried articles calling upon the peasantry to seize the big estates. Simultaneously, the Stalinists and right wing socialists praised regularly the Quiroga government's agrarian reform! Though Caballero finally had agreed to support Azaña for the presidency, *Claridad* had to carry Javier Bueno's articles denouncing Azaña as the candidate of the rightists. The revolutionary elements among the left socialists were so strong that they had their say despite Caballero.

On the issue of Prieto's entry into the government, Caballero dared not break with his revolutionary following. Equally, however, Prieto dared not submit the question for decision to the national convention. There then took place an extraordinary campaign of pressure to induce the party to let Prieto become Premier. Almost everybody outside the Socialist Party wanted Prieto in the government. The republican press asked for an end of the party conflict—and its solution by Prieto's entry. Barrios' "Republican Union" Party, by this time representing much of the industrial bourgeoisie since Lerroux' Radicals had disappeared, declared it wanted a socialist premier, and that he be Prieto. Miguel Maura, representing the extreme right industrialists and landowners, called for an authoritarian régime, with the Cortes suspended, and carried out by "all republicans and those socialists not contaminated by revolutionary lunacy." The Catalan government and its supporters, including the Stalinists, called for entry of the socialists.

The Stalinists sought to make support of this reactionary demand sound very radical. "If the government continues on this road (the false road of 1931), we will work, not breaking the Popular Front, but strengthening it and pushing it toward the solution of a government of a popular revolutionary type, which will do those things which this government has not understood or has not wished to understand." (*Mundo Obrero,* July 6.) But all that was required to make this government completely identical with that of 1931 was to include in it proletarian hostages!

Even the P.O.U.M., "Workers Party of Marxist Unity," joined the chorus. Formed by a fusion of the so-called Trotskyists with the "Workers and Peasants Bloc," a semi-nationalist Catalan group, it had signed the Popular Front pact, had declared its "independence" of the pact and attacked the concept of the People's Front, only again to support a People's Front for the municipal elections, and again to declare its independence when Azaña decreed the postponement. In order to justify its refusal to enter the Socialist Party, as Trotsky proposed, and thereby throw its forces—numbering only a few thousand even according to its own estimates—on the side of the left wing, it refused to see the profound significance of the development of the left wing. In fact, in *La Batalla* of May 22nd, it denied that there was any real difference between the left and right wings. This false estimate led to deplorable tactics: at a time when the left socialists were engaged in a struggle with the right wing on this question, the P.O.U.M. called for "an authentic Government of the Popular Front, with the direct (ministerial) participation of the Socialist and Communist Parties" as a means to "complete the democratic experience of the masses" and hasten the revolution.

This well-nigh universal pressure failed to weaken the determination of the left socialists. Whereupon Prieto tried desperate measures. Under his control, the National Executive Committee postponed the convention from June to October; outlawed *Claridad* and cut it off from party funds; instructed the district committees to "reorganize" dissident sections, and ran a farcical election to fill vacancies on the executive, not counting the left wing votes. The left wing repudiated these actions, and declared the Prieto leadership had forfeited the confidence of the party.

In spite of all Prieto's moves it was clear that the left wing had the masses. Caballero had been re-elected Secretary of the U.G.T. by overwhelming numbers. And behind Caballero stood much more determined elements. Javier Bueno, a leader of the Asturian rebellion, was speaking at great meetings and demanding not only an end to Prieto's politics, but also to Caballero's. Significant sections of the party had refused to support the Popular Front ticket in the presidential election, and had put up straight socialist tickets. While Caballero's national policy for the U.G.T. was little better than that of the Stalinists, other leaders, on a local or industrial scale, were joining with the C.N.T. in powerful and successful strikes. Permanent committees joined the two unions in the ports, on the ships and on the railroads; port and ship workers thereby won nationwide strikes, and the railroad workers had just voted for a national strike when the revolt broke out. The backward peasant elements in the party were learned enough to know what they wanted. Two days after Vidarte, secretary to the Prieto leadership, had indignantly denied to the United Press the rumor that the socialist peasantry of Badajoz were seizing the land, 25,000 peasant families, socialist-led, took over the big estates. The same thing took place elsewhere; Prieto's attempt to conceal the revolutionary significance of the seizure, by getting the Institute for Agrarian Reform to send in its engineers and legalize the seizure, only encouraged left socialists to repeat the process. The grim miners of Asturias, once the stronghold of the Pricto group, now engaged in political strikes against the government; 30,000 of them struck on June 13, demanding dismissal of the Ministers of Labor and Agriculture (the latter, Funes, a darling of the Stalinists!), and on June 19 fulfilled their threat of having all 90,000 miners cease work. The government managed to get them back to work on June 23, but on July 6 they, and the workers of Oviedo, threatened a general strike against the dismissal by the government of Governor Bosque of Asturias (Calvo Sotelo, chief of the reaction, had received an insulting telegram from the pro-labor governor, and successfully insisted upon his dismissal). The miners repeated their demand, on July 15, and would have gone on strike had not the revolt broken out. In the face of all these unambiguous indications of the revolutionary temper of the socialist proletariat, Prieto dared not risk entry into the cabinet.

Meanwhile, the strike wave reached the proportions of a revolutionary crisis. We can only roughly indicate its magnitude. Every city of any importance had at least one general strike during those five months. Nearly a million were on strike on June 10; a half million on June 20; a million on June 24; over a million during the first days of July. The strikes covered both the cities and the agricultural workers; the latter shattered the traditional village boundaries of struggle, waging, for example, a five weeks' strike covering Malaga province and 125,000 peasant families.

*El Socialista* denounced the tidal wave: "The system is genuinely anarchistic and provokes the irritation of the rightists." *Mundo Obrero* pleaded with the workers that the struggles were bringing them into collision with the Popular Front government. That government, and its provincial governors, threw the Civil Guard against the strikers in desperate attempts to halt the offensive. Particularly desperate measures were taken against the C.N.T. Companys filled the Barcelona jails with anarchists. In Madrid, their headquarters were closed and 180 of them arrested in a raid on May 31; on June 4, Minister Augusto Barcia announced that "if the syndicalists persist in disobeying the orders of the Ministry of Labor, the government proposes to declare syndicalism outside the law." On June 19, the government again closed the C.N.T. headquarters. But this was not 1931, when Caballero himself led the attack on the C.N.T.! The U.G.T. now solidarized itself with its anarcho-syndicalist comrades, and the government had to retreat.

Strikes for political demands against the government also developed. On June 8, a general strike was called in Lerida to force the government to fulfill its promise to feed the unemployed. The Murcia miners went out on June 24 protesting against the government's failure to fulfill electoral promises of bettering conditions. On July 2, the Federation of Agricultural Workers of Andalusia demanded government funds to make up for loss of crops. We have already mentioned the Asturian political strikes. On July 8, students in Barcelona Catholic schools struck, demanding the priests be turned out and lay teachers provided. On July 14, workers demonstrated in Madrid, carrying enlarged photographs of a formal ball held at the Brazilian Embassy, titled, "The republican ministers amuse themselves while the workers die." These are merely examples of political issues raised by the masses. We may be sure that they were not led by supporters of the People's Front!

Neither *El Socialista's* intimations that *Claridad* obtained money from a bank of Catholic reactionaries, nor the filthy slanders of *Mundo Obrero* that the C.N.T. was in league with fascist groups, nor the government's repressive measures, could halt the revolutionary development of the left socialists, the growing unity between C.N.T. and U.G.T. and the tidal wave of strikes.

Nor did the scope for fascist organization and arming provided by the People's Front policy go unresisted by the militant proletariat. They left to *El Socialista* and *Mundo Obrero* pleading with the government to stop the fascists. The revolutionary workers confronted the fascists on the street. From February to the July revolt, these street fights accounted for two deaths and six wounded *per day*. This was, in truth, civil war; and the fascists suffered the greatest casualties. The deadly blows to the morale of the fascist groups also steeled thousands of militants for leadership on July 18.

Finally, the wage and hour improvements won by the strikes, not being followed by an increase in production, of which Spanish industry is deprived by the world crisis, led to price increases; early in July the Madrid press estimated a 20% rise in one month. The workers felt they had been cheated, and prepared for more decisive strikes for more decisive demands. (The identical process is now—mid-September—taking place in France!)

The reaction—which is to say, Spanish capitalism—had pinned its hopes on Azaña for a time; when he proved impotent to stop the workers, its hopes had shifted to Prieto; but the left socialists prevented that solution. There could be no hope, therefore, of a repetition of 1931–1933, and a peaceful return of reaction. The right wing socialists and Stalinists were powerless to prevent the revolutionary development of the Spanish proletariat. Having armed and prepared for the worst, the reactionaries dared not wait until the revolutionary tide overwhelmed them. With ninety-nine per cent of the officer corps, the Foreign Legion and Moorish troops, and most of the fifty provincial garrisons in their hands, Spanish capitalism revolted against impending doom.

# 7

# Counter-revolution and dual power

## 1. THE TREACHERY OF THE PEOPLE'S FRONT GOVERNMENT

Azaña and the People's Front government answered the counter-revolution by attempting to come to terms with it.

Hopelessly compromised by their People's Front policy, the Stalinists have attempted to explain away this treachery by inventing a distinction between "weak" republicans like Barrios and "strong" ones like Azaña. The truth is that Azaña *led* the attempt to compromise with the fascist generals and that all the republican groups were implicated in his move.

Here, collected from *El Socialista* and *Claridad*, are the indisputable facts:

On the morning of July 17, General Franco, having seized Morocco, radioed his manifesto to the garrisons. It was received at the naval station near Madrid by a loyal operator and promptly revealed to the Minister of the Navy. But the government did not divulge the news until 9 o'clock of the 18th; and then it issued only a reassuring note that Spain was completely under government control. Two other notes were issued by the government later in the day, the last

at 3:15 P.M., when the government had full and positive information of the scope of the rising, including the seizure of Seville. Yet
that final note said:

> The Government speaks again in order to confirm the abso-
> lute tranquility of the whole Peninsula.
>
> The Government acknowledges the offers of support which it
> has received [from the workers' organizations] and, while being
> grateful for them, declares that the best aid that can be given to
> the Government is to guarantee the normality of daily life, in
> order to set a high example of serenity and of confidence in the
> means of the military strength of the State.
>
> Thanks to the foresighted means adopted by the authorities,
> a broad movement of aggression against the republic may be
> deemed to have been broken up; it has found no assistance in the
> Peninsula and has only succeeded in securing followers in a frac-
> tion of the army in Morocco. . . .
>
> These measures, together with the customary orders to the
> forces in Morocco who are laboring to overcome the rising, per-
> mit us to affirm that the action of the Government will be suffi-
> cient to reëstablish normality. (*Claridad*, July 18.)

Having thus refused to arm the workers, and justified its treacherous refusal by this incredibly dishonest note, the cabinet of Azaña
went into an all-night conference. There, Azaña had Quiroga's cabinet of Azaña's Left Republicans resign; and appointed as Premier
the former lieutenant of Lerroux, Martinez Barrios, head of the
Republican Union Party. Barrios and Azaña picked a "respectable"
cabinet of Barrios men and Right Wing Republicans outside the
People's Front. This cabinet, too, was committed to refusing to arm
the workers.

*Rather than arm the workers*—their allies in the People's Front,
who had put them into power!—*Azaña and the republicans were preparing to make peace with the fascists, at the expense of the workers.
Had Azaña carried out his plan, the fascists would have conquered Spain.*

But in the very hours that the ministers huddled together in the presidential palace, the proletariat was already mobilizing. In Madrid itself the Socialist Youth militia was distributing its scant store of arms; was throwing up barricades on key streets and around the Montaña barracks; was organizing its patrols for house to house seizures of reactionaries; at midnight had launched the first attack on the barracks. In Barcelona, remembering the treachery in October 1934 of this same President of Catalonia, Companys, the C.N.T. and P.O.U.M. ("Workers Party") militants had stormed several government arms depots on the afternoon of the 18th. By the time the garrison revolted, at one the next morning, the armed workers had surrounded the troops in an iron ring, arming eager recruits with equipment seized from the fascists, and with whatever could be confiscated from the department stores; later the militia seized the regular arsenals. The Asturian miners had outfitted a column of six thousand for a march on Madrid, before the ministerial crisis was well over. In Malaga, the strategic port opposite Morocco, the ingenious workers, unarmed, had surrounded the reactionary garrison with a wall of gasoline-fired houses and barricades. In Valencia, refused arms by the Madrid governor, the workers prepared to face the troops with barricades, cobble-stones and kitchen-knives—until their comrades within the garrison shot the officers and gave arms to the workers. In a word: without so much as a by your leave to the government, the proletariat had begun a war to the death against the fascists. Companys and Azaña found themselves confronted by the first regiments of the Red Army of the Spanish proletariat.

The Azaña-Barrios scheme for a deal with the fascist generals collapsed because the workers had prevented it. And for no other reason! Thanks only to their utter distrust of the government, the masses were able to prevent their betrayal. Independent mobilization, under their *own* leadership, with their *own* banners—only this prevented the victory of fascism.

Thus it was that, side by side with the formal power still held by the government, there arose the "unofficial" but far more substantial power of the armed proletariat—the "dual power," Lenin called it. One power, that of Azaña and Companys, was already too weak to challenge the existence of the other; the other, that of the armed proletariat, was not yet strong enough, not yet conscious enough of the necessity, to dispense with the existence of the other. The phenomenon of "dual power" has accompanied all proletarian revolutions; it signifies that the class struggle is about to reach the point where either one or the other must become undisputed master; it is a critical balancing of alternatives on a razor edge; a long period of equilibrium is out of the question, either one or the other must soon prevail!

The crushing of the counter-revolution will make infinitely more likely the establishment of a workers' and peasants' government. The interests of the bourgeoisie are not, therefore, served by a victory over the fascist generals: the true interests of Spanish capitalism lie in a victory of the counter-revolution or, what is the same thing, a compromise with it. That is why the People's Front government behaved so treacherously in the first days of the counter-revolution. That is why the People's Front government continued to behave treacherously thereafter. Surrounded by armed workers, the republicans dared not openly go over to the enemy; but their policy, at the front and in the rear, permitted the counter-revolution success after success. This was the plain meaning of the change of government after the fall of Irun. It was clear enough in the statement to the press by a spokesman for the Caballero cabinet, who

> dwelt at length on the improvement of the morale of the militia by Largo Caballero's assumption of the premiership last week.
>
> "They know now that they are being directed intelligently . . . They know that if they die, it will not be the fault of the haphazard and weak-kneed command which characterized the last administration.
>
> "We shall now take the offensive and attack the Rebels where they are weak, where we want to attack them instead of, as before, attacking where they are strong and able to repel us." (*N.Y. Times,* Sept. 7.)

If so damning an indictment of the Azaña-Giral government is made by those who will yet have to explain to the proletariat why they permitted such a government to direct the struggle for the first seven weeks, the whole truth must be much, much worse.

The ostensible justification for the People's Front was that it secured the aid of the republicans against counter-revolutionary fascism. The People's Front, however, served the opposite function: it prevented the proletariat from tearing away from the republican politicians the petty-bourgeoisie who, in all victorious revolutions, throw in their lot with the proletariat when they see it determinedly striking out for a new and rich life under a new social order. The People's Front subordinated both the petty-bourgeoisie and the proletarian masses to the treacherous leadership of the bourgeois politicians. Only the dual power of the proletariat has so far prevented the victory of reaction.

## 2. THE DUAL POWER IN CATALONIA

Precisely in Catalonia, where the People's Front was weakest, the dual power has developed most decisively, and made the four Catalonian provinces the most impregnable fortress of the civil war.

The C.N.T. and the F.A.I. (Iberian Anarchist Federation), leading most of the Catalonian proletariat and much of the peasantry, was never part of the People's Front. The P.O.U.M., after much vacillation, finally broke with the People's Front, made a sharp turn to the left, and with extraordinary rapidity grew into a mass party in Catalonia in the two months of civil war. Thus, the only proletarian adherents to the People's Front in Catalonia are the U.G.T., incomparably weaker here than the C.N.T., and the Stalinist organization, the so-called "United Socialist Party." Far from weakening its capacities for struggle, as the People's Front apologists had been declaring, it was this relative freedom from bourgeois ties that enabled the Catalonian masses to conquer the counter-revolution at home and to come to the aid of the rest of Spain. Herein lies a profound lesson for those who still believe in the People's Front!

The Catalonian proletariat understands that civil war must be fought by *revolutionary methods,* and not under the slogans of bourgeois democracy. It understands that civil war cannot be fought by military methods alone, but that the *political methods,* arousing the great masses to action, can even take the army away from its reactionary officers. It directs the struggle, at the front and in the rear, not through agencies of the government but through organs controlled by the proletarian organizations.

The "Central Committee of Anti-Fascist Militias of Catalonia" directs the struggle. The anarchists have three representatives for the C.N.T. and two for the F.A.I. The U.G.T. was given three, though it is small, to encourage similar organization elsewhere. The P.O.U.M. has one, the peasant organization one, and the Stalinists one. The left bourgeois parties have four, making a total of fifteen. In actuality, the Central Committee is dominated by the C.N.T., the F.A.I. and the P.O.U.M.

For these have a program so fundamentally different from that of Madrid, that the U.G.T. and the Stalinists are dragged along only because they fear to be cast aside, and the left bourgeoisie because they are at the mercy of the armed proletariat. That program is identical with that raised by the Bolsheviks in August 1917 in the struggle against Kornilov's counter-revolution:

*Workers' control of production, arousing the highest pitch of initiative and enthusiasm of the proletariat. Mobilization of the armed masses, independent of government control. Vigilance against betrayal by the government and no renunciation, not for a moment, of the sharpest criticism of it. And the drawing into the struggle of the peasantry by the only slogan which can vitalize the starving and backward countryside: LAND TO THOSE WHO TILL IT!*

As soon as the counter-revolution began, the C.N.T. took over all transportation, public utilities and big industrial plants. Democratic control is ensured by election of factory committees based on proportional representation. Such committees have also been set up to control production in those shops and factories still privately owned.

Direction of economic life is now in the hands of the "Council of Economy," which, while still linked to the old order, finds itself compelled at least to talk about socialistic measures. It has five members from the anarcho-syndicalists, one from the P.O.U.M., one from the U.G.T. and one from the Catalonian government. On August 19, it issued its program, which includes: collectivization of landed estates, to be run by landworkers' unions; collectivization of public utilities, transportation and big industry; collectivization of establishments abandoned by their owners; workers' control of banks until they are nationalized; workers' control of all establishments continuing under private ownership; absorption of unemployed in collectivized agriculture and industry; electrification of Catalonia; monopoly of foreign trade to protect the new economic order.

In the midst of civil war the factory committees are demonstrating the superiority of proletarian methods of production. The C.N.T.-U.G.T. committee running the railways and subways reports that by eliminating high salaries of directors, sinecures and waste, tens of thousands of pesetas have been saved, wages of most workers raised to create equalization of pay, extension of the lines is planned, fares will be reduced, trains run on time, and the six-hour day will soon be introduced!

The metal plants have been transformed into munitions works, the automobile factories are producing armored cars and airplanes. The latest dispatches show that the Madrid government depends greatly on Catalonia for these all-important war supplies. A considerable part of the forces protecting the Madrid front were dispatched there by the Catalonian militia.

Few realize the significance of the successful campaign being fought by the Catalonian militia on the Zaragoza-Huesca front. In the plans of the fascist generals Zaragoza, seat of the War College and one of the biggest army garrisons, was to have been for eastern Spain what Burgos has been in the west. But the rapidity with which the Catalonian proletariat crushed the Catalonian garrisons and marched westward into Aragon defeated the fascist plans.

The Catalonian militia marched into Aragon as an army of social liberation. They have been able to paralyze the mobility of the reactionary army by rousing the peasantry as the Madrid forces have been unable to. Arriving in a village, the militia committees sponsor the election of a village anti-fascist committee, to which are turned over all the large estates, and the crops, supplies, cattle, tools, tractors, etc. belonging to big landowners and reactionaries. The village committee organizes production on the new basis and creates a village militia to carry out socialization and fight reaction. Captured reactionaries are placed before the general assembly of the village for trial. All property titles, mortgages and debt documents in the official records go into a bonfire. Having thus transformed the world of the village, the Catalonian columns can go forward, secure in the knowledge that every village so dealt with is a fortress of the revolution!

The Catalonian government continues to exist, passes decrees approving the steps taken by the proletariat, pretends that it is leading the struggle. The Madrid government abets this pretense, by consulting with Companys, but then it must go on to transact all business with the militia and factory committees. At the end of July Companys made a "clever" attempt to recoup power, by reorganizing the Catalonian cabinet, three members of the Stalinist "United Socialist Party" entering it. But this maneuver fell through in a few days. The anarcho-syndicalists served notice on the Stalinists that they considered their entry into the cabinet as disruption of the proletarian bloc, and the Stalinists were compelled to resign from the cabinet. Such little influence as the government still has, by virtue of its representation in the Council of Economy and the Central Committee of Anti-Fascist Militias, will undoubtedly tend to disappear as these organs, in accordance with the proposal of the P.O.U.M., are broadened into elective bodies of delegates from the militia and factories.

The revolutionary course of the Catalonian proletariat and its consequent successes in production and at the front constitute the most damning indictment of the Popular Front policy which is still being pursued in Madrid. Only on the road taken by the Catalonian proletariat can the Spanish masses defeat the counter-revolution!

## 3. THE MADRID RÉGIME

While the Catalonian workers were ensuring for themselves the power which had fallen from the hands of the government, the right wing socialists and the Stalinists were busily putting the power back into the hands of the Madrid government. As a result, the relation of the government and the proletarian organizations is almost the opposite to that prevailing in Catalonia.

We have already seen how treacherous was the policy of the Azaña-Giral government. Yet it was to this government that the right wing socialists and Stalinists ceded all power!

There is not the slightest difference between the outlook of the bourgeoisie and these "leaders" of workers. The workers' militia must limit its struggle to the defense of the republic, that is, to the maintenance of capitalism, to support the bourgeois government loyally, not to dream of socialism. The Stalinists issued a manifesto on August 18, wildly praised by the bourgeois press for good and sufficient reason: it does not include a *single* social demand! Not a word about seizure of the land, freedom for Morocco, workers' control of production—nothing but abject loyalty to the bourgeoisie! Nor is this all. The Stalinists want no workers' state even after the crushing of the counter-revolution: "It is absolutely false that the present workers' movement has for its object the establishment of a proletarian dictatorship after the revolution has terminated," declares the Stalinist chief, Hernandez, on August 10. "It cannot be said we have a social motive for our participation in the war. We Communists are the first to repudiate this supposition. We are motivated exclusively by a desire to defend the democratic republic." Any property seized is purely as a temporary defense measure, declare the Spanish Stalinists. (*Daily Worker*, September 18). To realize how alien to Leninism is such craven nonsense, one has only to recall Lenin's injunctions, in the midst of the Kornilov struggle, against any political support to the government, and his program of fighting the counter-revolution by seizing the land and establishing workers' control of production. Having recruited most of its following under People's Front slogans since February, the Stalinist party can use them for the most shameless devotion to a bourgeois régime of which any proletarian party has ever been guilty.

The left socialists distinguished themselves from the Stalinist position, by an editorial entitled, "Dialectic of War and Revolution":

> Some people are saying: "Let us smash fascism first, let us finish the war victoriously, and then there will be time to speak of revolution and to make it if necessary." Those who are saying this have not contemplated maturely upon the formidable dialectical process which is carrying us all along. The war and the revolution are one and the same thing. They not only do not exclude or hinder each other, but supplement and support each other. The war needs the revolution for its triumph, in the same way that the revolution has required the war. . . . It is the revolution in the rear that will make more assured and more inspired the victory on the fields of battle. (*Claridad*, August 22.)

This correct conception, impressed upon the left socialists by the example of the Catalonian proletariat is then, however, given a typical centrist distortion by the editors of *Claridad,* by the simple process of crediting to the Catalonian government the achievements actually carried through by the workers. The editorial ends:

> The clear historic vision exemplified by the Catalonian Generalidad deserves only praise. It has decreed governmental measures that reflect the inextricable relation between the war and the revolution. To expropriate rebellious capital and to collectivize it is the best way of collaborating for triumph and to extract from the war the maximum social conquests, as well as to destroy the enemy's economic power. . . . On this point and on the organization of the parties and unions around the government

to make the war and the revolution simultaneously, Catalonia is a beacon for Castile and the rest of Spain.

On no question has the anti-proletarian character of the Stalinist program been revealed so much as when the Azaña-Giral government attempted to create a new army. The bourgeoisie recognized that, despite the subordination of the workers' militia to the military commands of the general staff, the internal structure of the militia, organized in separate columns adhering to the various proletarian parties and unions and led by elected workers, rendered hopeless any attempt to secure actual bourgeois control over them. Whereupon the government called for enlistment of ten thousand reserve soldiers as a separate force under direct government control. The Stalinist manifesto of August 18 supported this counter-revolutionary proposal, in accordance with the conception of the militia which *Mundo Obrero* had declared on August 11:

> No. Nothing of militias ruled by parties and organizations. But neither of militias of parties or of unions. They are militias that have their fundamental base in the People's Front, faithful to the politics of the People's Front.

"Some comrades have wished to see in the creation of the new voluntary army something like a menace to the rôle of the militias," said *Mundo Obrero,* August 21. The Stalinists denied such a possibility: "What is involved is to complement and reinforce the militia to give it greater efficacy and speedily end the war." And it ended its defense of the governmental proposal: "Our slogan, today as yesterday, is the same for this. Everything for the People's Front and everything through the People's Front."

This thoroughly reactionary position was exposed by *Claridad.* The left socialist organ examined the reasons offered for the creation of the new army. It showed that the claim that it would provide additional forces is false, since "the number of men now incorporated in the militias or who desire to join it can be considered virtually unlimited." The claim that the reserve soldiers would provide the military experience lacking by the militias is negated by the fact that those reserves "that have not wished to join the armed forces until now would not be animated by the same political and combative ardor that induced the militiamen to enlist." Having disposed of the excuses for the new army, the left socialists bluntly concluded:

> To think of another type of army to be substituted for those who are actually fighting and who in certain ways control their own revolutionary action, is to think in counter-revolutionary terms. That is what Lenin said *(State and Revolution):* "Every revolution, after the destruction of the state apparatus, shows us how the governing class tries to reestablish special bodies of armed men at 'its' service, and how the oppressed class attempts to create a new organization of a type capable of serving not the exploiters but the exploited."
>
> We are sure that this counter-revolutionary thought, which would be as impotent as it is inept, has not passed through the government's mind; but the working class and the petty bourgeoisie, who are saving the republic with their lives, must not forget these accurate words of Lenin, and must take care that the masses and the leadership of the armed forces, which should be above all the people in arms, should not escape from our hands. (*Claridad,* August 20.)

Not those who usurp the prestige of the Russian revolution only to betray its principles in service to the bourgeoisie, not the Stalinists, but the vanguard of the left socialists teach the Spanish proletariat the Leninist conception of the class nature of the army!

The different conceptions of the nature of the present struggle also come into conflict on other questions. The anarcho-syndicalists, the P.O.U.M. and the Socialist Youth, recognizing to varying degrees the treacherous rôle of the bourgeoisie, demand the cleansing from all institutions of all doubtful elements, and insist on retaining arms in the rear to guard against bourgeois betrayal. The Stalinists, on the other hand, have the same "broad" definition of "anti-fascists" as the republicans, and raise the slogan, "Not One Rifle Idling in the Rear!" So broad, indeed, is their conception of anti-fascists that *Claridad* protested, August 19 and 20, that the Stalinist-controlled "Alliance of Anti-Fascist Writers" was harboring counter-revolutionaries. The contemptible campaign of the bourgeoisie and the Stalinists for disarming the rear was well answered by the C.N.T. leader, Garcia Oliver in *Solidaridad Obrera,* deftly turning the point against them: "We desire that our comrades, taking account of the situation, make an inventory of the war material they control and proceed to make a study of *what is indispensable to them to assure the necessary safeguarding of the revolutionary order in the rear,* sending on what they do not need."

We may summarize the character of the régime of Azaña-Giral by stating one deadly fact: *it continued to censor the press of the workers' organizations whose members were dying at the front.* Even the abject *Mundo Obrero* learned what a Popular Front government is: its issue of August 20, having published a photograph deemed objectionable, was confiscated! *Claridad,* daily bearing the stigmata of the censor, reports this fact. The Stalinists of course, suppressed outside of Spain the existence of this intolerable and shameful condition.

### 4. THE CABALLERO CABINET

We have no doubt at all that Caballero's entry into the government was greeted with the utmost joy by large sections of the proletariat. He had stood far to the left of the Stalinists and Prieto, and the militia especially must have felt that Caballero was delivering them out of the hands of the treacherous republicans.

We have no means of knowing at this moment how much of this joy was quickly dissipated a few days ago when, after driving out the anarcho-syndicalists, the republican "defenders" of San Sebastian turned it over intact to the enemy; and when these same republicans, upon retreating to the stronghold of Bilbao, put the 40,000 militiamen to such use-that most of the opposing army of General Mola has been sent to the Madrid and Zaragoza front. The northern front has been betrayed, and that has happened since Caballero took over the government.

What is Caballero's program? No word has come from him. Is his program a "minimum," that is a bourgeois one, satisfactory to the five bourgeois members of his cabinet? Is it the program of Prieto and the Stalinists, which is the bourgeois program? What is the basic difference between the cabinet of Caballero and that of his predecessor? That Caballero is more sincere? But, as Lenin said once for all, no one has yet invented a sincerometer. What is basic is the program. If Caballero's program does not differ from his predecessor's, his conduct of the struggle will be no different.

The Spanish proletariat will have to take the road on which the Catalonian proletariat has begun to march. There is no other road to victory!

Who are the rank and file soldiers of Franco's armies, and why are there so few desertions from his ranks? They are mainly sons of peasants, serving their two-year period in the army. They can be won over, induced to desert, to shoot their officers, by winning their families to the side of the workers. How? By aiding them to seize the land. That slogan should have been raised after the February 16 victory; the failure to do so is the explanation of the fact that the southern provinces, including a stronghold of the Stalinists, Seville, can be in the hands of the fascists. "What did the Republic give you to eat?" The result is much passivity among the peasants. Within the territories held by them, the workers must aid the peasants in seizing and distributing the large estates. By ten thousand channels that fact, transforming the peasants' world, will be carried into the provinces held by the fascists . . . and anti-fascist peasants will spring out of the ground, and Franco's armies will melt away.

Thousands of workers have paid with their lives because their organizations did not fight to give land to the peasants. Thousands more are dying because their organizations did not raise the slogan of freedom for the Spanish colonies. Yet, even now, that slogan and a bold campaign of propaganda in Morocco would disintegrate far more easily than by bullets the Moorish legions of Franco.

Catalonia has shown what prodigious tasks of production the proletariat will undertake once it is in control of the factories. Yet the workers' committees in Madrid which at first took over the public utilities and many big plants were thereafter subordinated to the government's bureaucratic administration. This constriction is not bettered because the government now includes a socialist delegation. Until the workers are masters in the factories, those factories will not become fortresses of the revolution.

Above all, it is intolerable that the workers shall do the drudgery and the dying, without a voice in the direction of the struggle. Caballero has announced the re-opening of the Cortes on October 1. That is a cruel joke! That Cortes no more reflects the sentiment of the people than the nineteenth resembles the twentieth century! Ages have gone by, measured politically, since the republican bourgeoisie was guaranteed a majority on February 16 by workers' votes. The only authentic voice of the people today would be a National Congress of the elected delegates of the militia who are fighting, the workers who are producing and transporting, and the peasants who are providing the food. Only such a soviet, issuing from factory, militia and village committees, is competent to speak for Spain today.

Every one of these basic needs of the revolution can be carried out only against the will of the republican bourgeoisie. That means going far beyond the People's Front. But such "disruption" will mean a "loss" only to the treacherous republican politicians and the substantial capitalists; the main sections of the petty-bourgeoisie will cast their lot with the new social order, as they did in the Russian Revolution.

Caballero's partners in the cabinet, the Stalinists, have made clear their deadly opposition to the revolutionary program: "The slogan today is all power and authority to the People's Front Government." (*Daily Worker,* Sept. 11.) That slogan means just what it says! Lenin's slogan, "All power to the soviets," meant *no* power to the coalition government. The Stalinist slogan means *no* power to the embryo soviets, the factory, militia and village committees. As Stalinism sacrificed the German revolution to the maintenance of the European *status quo,* so it is now seeking to sacrifice the Spanish revolution to the maintenance of the Franco-Soviet Alliance. Stalinism will not raise the slogan of freedom for Morocco because that would embarrass French colonial policy. Stalinism will not go over the People's Front to the Spanish revolution because that would bring the revolution immediately on the order of the day in France and Stalinism, pervaded like all bureaucracy with a cynical lack of faith in the masses, prefers a strong bourgeois French ally to the possibility of a Soviet France. The essence of Stalinist policy is: "Socialism in one country—and in no other country." The Stalinists have become open, shameless enemies of the proletarian revolution. Fortunately for the world proletariat, Stalinism in Spain does not command the forces it held in leash in Germany—and precisely because the lessons of Germany have entered the consciousness of the Spanish proletariat.

Great forces are available for the proletarian victory. In the crucible of civil war they will be welded into a single revolutionary party. The contradiction between the traditional anti political theory of anarcho-syndicalism and its present political-revolutionary practice will inevitably burst asunder its trade union form of organization. Already, thousands upon thousands of C.N.T. adherents have joined the P.O.U.M. That organization, counting in its cadres the most experienced revolutionary elements in the country, has swerved considerably away from its centrist course,[*] but its main forces are limited to Catalonia and Valencia. We may be sure that the most important cadres in the rest of Spain, the revolution-

---

[*] How sharply, indeed, one may measure by contrasting its policy with that of its "international organization", the International Committee of Revolutionary Socialist Unity (S.A.P. of Germany, I.L.P. of England) whose manifesto to the Spanish proletariat does not contain a single word of criticism of the Popular Front! And this, first, "cautious" word from this claimant to the title of revolutionary center is dated August 17!

aries among the left socialists, who have long been chafing at Caballero's vacillation, will enter the revolutionary stream. Even the inexperienced cadres of the Stalinist organization will provide their best elements for the new revolutionary party. The revolution, as always, will have a broader leadership than that of any party; but the gigantic tasks it will pose will be the final goal to the unification of the revolutionary currents of all the parties.

## 5. SPAIN AND EUROPE

*Claridad* has been publishing a box, "Prophetic Texts," of a few lines, different each day, from Trotsky's *History of the Russian Revolution*. The choice of Trotsky is not accidental. It reflects a major preoccupation of Spanish revolutionists; the problem of the European revolution. Technologically backward and fearing military intervention by Hitler and Mussolini, the Spanish revolutionists have been keenly aware of the inextricable relation between their revolution and that of Europe, especially France. For this reason they turn to Trotsky, the authoritative spokesman of revolutionary internationalism.

On July 30, only a few days after the struggle began, Trotsky dealt with this problem, and with the meaning of the Spanish events for France. His closing words are keener than any I could choose to close:

"Certainly, the Spanish proletariat, like the French proletariat, does not want to remain disarmed before Mussolini and Hitler. But to defend themselves against these enemies it is first necessary to crush the enemy in one's own country. It is impossible to overthrow the bourgeoisie without crushing the officers' corps. It is impossible to crush the officers' corps without overthrowing the bourgeoisie. In every victorious counter-revolution, the officers have played the decisive rôle. Every victorious revolution that had a profound social character destroyed the old officers' corps. This was the case in the Great French Revolution at the end of the eighteenth century, and this was the case in the October Revolution in 1917. To decide on such a measure one must stop crawling on one's knees before the Radical bourgeoisie. A genuine alliance of workers and peasants must be created against the bourgeoisie, including the Radicals. One must have confidence in the strength, initiative and courage of the proletariat and the proletariat will know how to bring the soldier over to its side. This will be a genuine and not a fake alliance of workers, peasants and soldiers. This very alliance is being created and tempered right now in the fire of civil war in Spain. The victory of the people means the end of the People's Front and the beginning of Soviet Spain. The victorious social revolution in Spain will inevitably spread out over the rest of Europe. For the Fascist hangmen of Italy and Germany it will be incomparably more terrible than all the diplomatic pacts and all the military alliances."

# Revolution and counter-revolution in Spain

*by Felix Morrow*

|

# Why the fascists revolted

At dawn, July 17, 1936, General Franco assumed command of the Moors and Legionnaires of Spanish Morocco, and issued a manifesto to the army and the nation to join him in establishing an authoritarian state in Spain. In the next three days, one by one, almost all of the fifty garrisons in Spain declared for fascism. The basic sections of the capitalists and landlords, having already participated in Franco's conspiracy, fled into fascist-held territory or out of Spain either before or after the rising. It was clear immediately that this rising had nothing in common with the *pronunciamento* movements whereby the Spanish army had so often supported one bourgeois faction against another. It was not a "handful of generals," but the ruling class as a whole, which was directing its armed minions in an assault, above all, against the economic, political and cultural organizations of the working class.

Franco's program is identical in fundamentals with that of Mussolini and Hitler. Fascism is a special form of reaction, the product of the period of capitalist decline. To see this fully one has only to compare Franco's régime with that of the monarchy. The last Alfonso's record is a bloody account of massacres of peasants and workers, of terrorism and assassination of proletarian leaders. Yet side by side with the systematic measures of repression, the monarchy permitted a restricted existence to economic and political organizations of the working class and to municipal and national organs of parliamentary democracy. Even under the Primo de Rivera dictatorship (1923–1930), the Socialist party and the UGT led a legal existence; indeed, Largo Caballero, head of the UGT, was a Councillor of State under Rivera. In other words, even the reactionary monarchy sought part of its mass support in the organized proletariat, through the mediation of reformist leaders like Prieto and Caballero. Similarly, a system of legal unions and social-democratic parties existed in the empires of Wilhelm and Franz Joseph. Even under Tsar Nicholas there was a measure of legality for unions, cooperatives and the labor press, in which the Bolsheviks were able to work though themselves illegal: *Pravda* had a circulation of 60,000 in 1912–1914.

As contrasted to these reactionary régimes, the special character of fascism consists in its extirpation of any and all independent organizations of the working class. Capitalism in decline finds impossible even the most elementary concessions to the masses. One by one, those capitalist countries which arrive at a complete impasse, take the road of fascism.

Italy, a "victor" in the World War, weakly developed in basic industries, could not compete with more advanced countries in the imperialist race for markets. Strangling in its economic contradictions, the capitalist class of Italy could find a way out only over the broken bones of the workers' organizations. The hordes of the "petty bourgeoisie gone mad," organized and uniformed by Mussolini, trained as hoodlums, were finally unleashed for the special task of crushing the workers' organizations.

The bourgeoisie does not light-mindedly take to fascism. The Nazi movement of Germany had almost no bourgeois support in its *putsch* of 1923. In the ensuing decade, it secured financial support only from a few individual capitalists until 1932. The bourgeoisie of Germany hesitated for a long time before it accepted the instrumentality of Hitler; for fifteen years it preferred to lean on the social-democratic leaders. But at the height of the world economic crisis, technically advanced Germany, handicapped by the Versailles Treaty in its imperialist conflicts with England, France and America, could "solve" its crisis temporarily, in capitalist terms, only by destroying the workers' organization which had existed for three-fourths of a century.

*Fascism is that special form of capitalist domination which the bourgeoisie finally resorts to when the continued existence of capitalism is incompatible with the existence of organized workers.* Fascism is resorted to when the concessions, which are a product of the activities of trade unions and political parties of labor, become an intolerable burden on the capitalist rulers, hence intolerable to the further existence of capitalism. For the working class, at this point, the issue is inexorably posed for immediate solution: either fascism or socialism.

Spanish capitalism had arrived at this point when Franco revolted. His movement, though incorporating the remnants of Spain's feudal aristocracy, is no more "feudal" in basic social character than was that of Mussolini or Hitler.

The chief industry of Spain, agriculture, accounting for over half the national income, almost two-thirds of exports and most of the government's internal revenue, with seventy per cent of the population living on the land, was in desperate straits. The division of the land was the worst in Europe: one third owned by great landowners, in some cases in estates covering half a province; another third held by more numerous owners but also in large estates; only one third owned by peasants, and most of this in primitively equipped farms of five hectares[*] or less of extraordinarily dry, poor land, insufficient to support their families, and necessitating day labor on the big estates to eke out an existence. Thus, most of the five million peasant families were dependent on sharecropping or employment on the big estates.

---

[*] One hectare equals 2.4 acres.

Spanish agriculture was conducted by primitive methods. Its yield per hectare was the lowest in Europe. Increased productivity required capital investment in machinery and fertilizers, employment of technicians, re-training of the peasants. From the landowners' standpoint it was cheaper to continue primitive methods at the expense of the peasantry. The one recent period of good prices for produce, the war years, 1914–1918, which gave Spanish agriculture a temporary opportunity to profiteer in the world market, instead of being used to improve the land, was capitalized into cash via mortgages obtained by the landowners. Driven out of the world market after the war, Spanish agriculture collapsed. The general agricultural crisis, first preceding and then part of the world crisis, aggravated by the tariff barriers raised against Spanish agriculture by England and France, led to widespread unemployment and starvation.

Precisely at the depth of the crisis, in 1931, the rise of the republic gave a new impetus to the organization of agricultural workers' unions. The resultant wage raises seem pitiful enough. A good wage was six pesetas (seventy-five cents) a day. But even this was a deadly menace to the profits of the Spanish landowners, in the epoch of the decline of European agriculture. The great plains of South America and Australia were providing wheat and beef to Europe at prices which were dealing European agriculture a blow incomparably more serious than that dealt by the produce of North America during the epoch of capitalist expansion. *Thus, the existence of agricultural workers' unions and peasants' organizations was incompatible with the further existence of landed capitalism in Spain.*

The landowners got a breathing space during the *bienio negro,* the "two black years," of September 1933 to January 1936, when the reactionary governments of Lerroux-Gil Robles terrorized the masses and put down the revolt of October, 1934. During that period, day wages on the land fell to two or three pesetas. But the masses soon rallied. Gil Robles' attempt to build a mass fascist organization failed, both through his own ineptitude and under the blows of the workers. The Asturian Commune of October, 1934, though crushed by Moors and Legionnaires, became the inspiration of the masses, and Lerroux-Gil Robles gave way to the Popular Front in February, 1936, rather than wait for a more decisive onslaught by the proletariat. The agrarian workers and peasants built even more formidable unions from February to July, 1936, and the precarious condition of agricultural profits drove the landowners and their allies, the Catholic hierarchy and the banks, to a speedy resort to arms to destroy the workers' organizations.

The capitalists in industry and transportation were likewise at an impasse

The era of expansion of Spanish industry had been short: 1898–1918. The very development of Spanish industry in the war years became a source of further difficulties. The end of the war meant that Spain's industry, infantile and backed by no strong state power, soon fell behind in the imperialist race for markets. Even Spain's internal market could not long be preserved for her own industry. Primo de Rivera's attempt to preserve it by insurmountable tariff walls brought from France and England retaliation against Spanish agriculture. The resultant agricultural crisis caused the internal market for industry to collapse. In 1931, this country of twenty-four millions had nearly a million unemployed workers and peasants, heads of families; before the end of 1933 the number was a million and a half.

With the end of the *bienio negro,* the workers' economic struggles took on extraordinary scope. Conscious of having freed themselves from the domination of Gil Robles by their own efforts, the masses did not wait for Azaña to fulfill his promises. In the four days between the elections of February, 1936, and Azaña's hasty assumption of the premiership, the masses effectively carried out the amnesty by tearing open the jails. Nor did the workers wait for the government decree, and for the decision as to its constitutionality—which came from the Court of Constitutional Guarantees only on September 6, nearly two months after Franco's revolt!—to get back the jobs of those dismissed after the October, 1934 revolt. In the shops and factories the workers took along those dismissed, and put them back to work. Then, beginning with a general strike on April 17, 1936, in Madrid, there began a great movement of the masses, often including political demands, but primarily for better wages and conditions.

We can only roughly indicate the magnitude of the great strike wave. The strikes covered both the cities and the rural districts. Every city and province of any importance had at least one general strike during February–July, 1936. Nearly a million were on strike on June 10, a half million on June 20, a million on June 24, over a million during the first days of July.

Spanish capitalism could scarcely hope to solve its problems by expanding its markets for manufactured goods. That road was closed to it externally by the great imperialist powers. Internally, the only way to expand was to create a prosperous landed peasantry, but that meant dividing the land. The city capitalist and landed proprietor were often one and the same person, or bound together by family ties. In any event, the summit of Spanish capitalism, the banks, were inextricably bound up with the interests of the landowners, whose mortgages they held. No real road of development was open to Spanish capitalism. But it could temporarily solve its problems in one way: by destroying the trade unions which were endangering its profits.

Bourgeois democracy is that form of capitalist state which leans on the support of the workers, secured through the reformist leaders. The capitalists of Spain concluded that democracy was intolerable, and that meant that bourgeois democracy and reformism were finished in Spain.

Mussolini declared he had saved Italy from Bolshevism. Unfortunately, the truth is that the workers' post-war upsurge had already receded, thereby facilitating Mussolini's assumption of power. Hitler said the same, at a time when the workers were hopelessly divided and disoriented. Franco had need of the same myth for justifying his resort to arms. What *was* true, in Italy, Germany and now in Spain, is that democracy could no longer exist. Precisely the fact that fascism had to seize power, even though there was no immediate danger of a proletarian revolution, is the most conclusive evidence that democracy was finished.

Franco's rebellion left only two alternatives: either fascism would conquer, or the working class, rallying the peasantry by giving it the land, would destroy fascism and with it the capitalism in which it is rooted.

The Stalinists and social-democrats, seeking theoretical justification for their collaboration with the liberal bourgeoisie, declare that the roots of fascism in Spain are feudal. For the Stalinists, this is an entirely new theory, concocted *ad hoc*. Spanish fascism is no more feudal than is Italian. The backwardness of industry in both countries cannot be overcome within the capitalist framework, since neither can compete with the advanced industrial countries in the epoch of declining world markets. They could only secure temporary stabilization by cutting their labor costs below the European level, and to do this required crushing every form of labor organization. Spanish agriculture is backward and "feudal" in its operating methods. But land has been bought, sold and mortgaged, like any other commodity, for two centuries. Hence, the land question is a *capitalist* question.

The Stalinists blandly resort to "feudalism" as an explanation of the Spanish civil war and denounce as fascist agents anyone who dares to differ. Stalinist journalists writing outside the party press, however, are less fortunate. They have to deal with certain obvious phenomena. If the struggle is one against feudalism, why is the industrial bourgeoisie on the side of Franco?

The Stalinist journalist, Louis Fischer, writes:

> Strangely enough, Spain's small industrialist class supported the reactionary position taken by the landlords. The industrialists should have welcomed a land reform which would create a home market for their goods. But they believed that more than economics was involved. They feared that the granting of land to the peasantry would rob the owning classes of political power. The manufacturers, therefore, who should have encouraged the

republic in its attempts to stage a peaceful revolution which would have enriched the country, actually leagued themselves with the backward looking landlords to prevent all amelioration and reform. ("The War in Spain," published by *The Nation.*)

It does not occur to Fischer to wonder whether landlord and capitalist are not often one and the same, or of the same family, or whether the manufacturer, dependent on the banks, is not fearful for the banks' mortgages on the land. But even as Fischer poses the problem, the answer is clear. The manufacturer fears the diminution of the political power of the owning classes. Why? Because the weakening of the police power permits the workers in his factory to organize and make inroads into his profits. Fischer's own labored explanation gives the show away. Spanish fascism is the weapon not of "feudalism" but of capitalism. It can be fought successfully by the working class and the peasantry, and by them alone.

# 2

## The bourgeois 'allies' in the People's Front

The stake of the workers' parties and unions in the struggle against fascism was clear: their very existence was at stake. As Hitler and Mussolini before him, Franco would physically destroy the leadership and active cadres of their organizations and leave the workers in forced disunity, each an atom at the mercy of concentrated capital. The struggle against fascism was, therefore, a life and death question not only to the masses of the workers but also even to the reformist leaders of the workers. But this is not the same as to say that these leaders knew how to fight against fascism. Their most fatal error was their assumption that their bourgeois allies in the People's Front were equally vitally concerned to fight against fascism.

Azaña's Republican Left, Martinez Barrio's Republican Union, Companys' Catalan Left, had compacted with the Socialist and Communist parties and the UGT—with the tacit consent of the anarchists, whose masses voted for the joint tickets—in the elections of February 16, 1936. The Basque Nationalists had also joined. These four bourgeois groups, therefore, found themselves on the other side of the barricades from the big bourgeoisie on July 17.

Could they be depended on to cooperate loyally in the struggle against fascism?

We said no, because no vital interest of the liberal bourgeoisie was menaced by the fascists. The workers were in danger of losing their trade unions, without which they would starve. What comparable loss was faced by the liberal bourgeoisie? Undoubtedly, in a totalitarian state, the professional politicians would have to find other professions; the liberal bourgeois press would go under (if we grant that the bourgeois politicians and journalists would not go over to Franco entirely). Both Italy and Germany have demonstrated that fascism refuses to become reconciled to individual democratic politicians; some are jailed, others must emigrate. But all these constitute minor inconveniences. The *basic strata* of the liberal bourgeoisie go on as before the advent of fascism. If they do not share the special favors extended by the fascist state to those capitalists who had joined the fascists before victory, they do share the advantages of low wages and curtailed social services. Only to the same extent as all other capitalists are they subject to the fascist exactions, via party or government, which are the stiff price which capitalism pays for the services of fascism. The liberal bourgeoisie of Spain had only to look at Germany and Italy to be reassured for the future. While the trade union officials have been extirpated, the liberal bourgeoisie has found elbow room in which to be assimilated. What is at work here is a *class criterion:* fascism is the enemy primarily of the working class. *Hence, it is absolutely false and fatal to assume that the bourgeois elements in the Popular Front have a crucial stake in prosecuting seriously the struggle against fascism.*

Second, our proof that Azaña, Barrios, Companys and their ilk cannot be loyal allies of the working class, rested not merely on deductive analysis, but upon concrete experience—the record of these worthies. Since the socialists and Stalinists in the People's Front have suppressed the facts about their allies, we must give some space to this question.

From 1931 to 1934, the Comintern called Azaña a fascist, which was certainly incorrect, although it accurately pointed to his systematic oppression of the masses. As late as January, 1936, the Comintern said of him:

> The Communist Party knows the danger of Azaña just as well as the socialists who collaborated with him when he was in power. They know that he is an enemy of the working class. . . . But they also know that the defeat of the CEDA (Gil Robles) would automatically bring with it a certain amount of relief from the repression, for a time at least. (*Inprecorr,* vol. 15, p. 762.)

The last phrase is an admission that repression will come from the direction of Azaña himself. And it did come, as José Diaz, Secretary of the Communist party, was compelled to admit just before the civil war broke out:

> The government, which we are loyally supporting in the measure that it completes the pact of the Popular Front, is a government that is commencing to lose the confidence of the workers, and I say to the left republican government that its road is the wrong road of April 1931. (*Mundo Obrero,* July 6, 1936.)

One must recall the "wrong road of April 1931" to realize what an admission the Stalinists were making, after all their attempts to differentiate the coalition government of 1931 from the Popular Front government of 1936. The coalition of 1931 had promised land to the peasants and gave them none because the land could not be divided without undermining capitalism. The coalition of 1931 had refused the workers unemployment relief. Azaña, as Minister of War, had not touched the reactionary officer caste of the army, and had enforced the infamous law, under which all criticism of the army by civilians was an offense against the state. As Premier, Azaña had left the swollen wealth and power of the church hierarchy intact. Azaña had left Morocco in the hands of the Legionnaires and Moorish mercenaries. Only against the workers and peasants had Azaña been stern. The annals of 1931–1933 are the annals of his government's repressions of the workers and peasants. Elsewhere* I have told this story at length.

Azaña, as *Mundo Obrero* admitted, proved no better as head of the Popular Front government of February–July 1936. Again his régime rejected the idea of distribution of the land, and put down the peasantry when it attempted to seize it. Again the church remained in full control of its great wealth and power. Again Morocco remained in the hands of the Foreign Legionnaires until they finally took it over completely on July 17. Again strikes were declared illegal, modified martial law imposed, workers' demonstrations and meetings broken up. Suffice it to say that in the critical last days, after the assassination of the fascist leader, Calvo Sotelo, the working class headquarters were ordered closed. *The day before the fascist outbreak the labor press appeared with gaping white spaces where the government censorship had lifted out editorials and sections of articles warning against the coup d'état!*

In the last three months before July 17, in desperate attempts to stop the strike movement, hundreds of strikers were arrested *en masse,* local general strikes declared illegal and regional headquarters of the UGT and CNT closed for weeks at a time.

The most damning insight into Azaña was provided by his attitude toward the army. Its officer caste was disloyal to the core toward the republic. These pampered pets of the monarchy had seized every opportunity since 1931 to wreak bloody vengeance against the workers and peasants upon whom the republic rested. The atrocities they committed in crushing the revolt of October, 1934, were so horrible that criminal punishment of those responsible was one of Azaña's campaign promises. But he brought not a single officer to trial in the ensuing months. Mola, director of Public Safety of Madrid under the dictatorship of Berenguer—Mola who had fled on the heels of Alfonso while the streets echoed with the masses' cries of "Abajo Mola"—this Mola was restored to his generalship in the army by Azaña, and despite his close association with Gil Rob-

---

* *The Civil War in Spain,* September, 1936, Pioneer Publishers.

les in the *bienio negro,* was military commander of Navarre at the moment of the fascist revolt, and became chief strategist of the Franco armies. Franco, Goded, Queipo de Llano—all had similarly malodorous records of disloyalty to the republic and yet Azaña left the army in their hands. More, he demanded that the masses submit to them.

Colonel Julio Mangada, now fighting in the anti-fascist forces, who had been court-martialed and driven out of the army by these generals because of his republicanism, is authority for the fact that he had repeatedly informed Azaña, Martinez Barrio, and other republican leaders, of the plans of the generals. In April, 1936, Mangada published a thoroughly documented pamphlet which not only exposed the fascist plot, but proved conclusively that President Azaña was fully informed of the plot when, on March 18, 1936, upon the demand of the general staff, his government gave the army a clean bill of health. Referring to "rumors insistently circulating concerning the state of mind of the officers and subalterns of the army," "the Government of the Republic has learned with sorrow and indignation, of the unjust attacks to which the officers of the army have been subjected." Azaña's cabinet not only repudiated these rumors, describing the military conspirators as "remote from all political struggle, faithful servitors of the constituted power and guarantee of obedience to the popular will," but declared that "only a criminal and torturous desire to undermine it [the army] can explain the insults and verbal and written attacks which have been directed against it." And finally, "the Government of the Republic applies and will apply the law against anyone who persists in such an unpatriotic attitude."

No wonder that the reactionary leaders praised Azaña. On April 3, 1938, Azaña made a speech promising the reactionaries that he would stop the strikes and seizures of the land. Calvo Sotelo praised it: "It was the expression of a true conservative. His declaration of respect for the law and the constitution should make a good impression on public opinion." "I support ninety per cent of the speech," declared the spokesman of Gil Robles' organization. "Azaña is the only man capable of offering the country security and defense of all legal rights," declared Ventosa, spokesman of the Catalan land-owners. They praised Azaña, for he was preparing the way for them.

Though the army was ready to rebel in May, 1936, many reactionaries doubted whether this was possible as yet. Azaña pressed upon them his solution: let the reformist leaders stop the strikes. His offer was accepted. Miguel Maura, representing the extreme right industrialists and landowners, called for a strong régime of "all republicans and those socialists not contaminated by revolutionary lunacy." So, having been elevated to the presidency, Azaña offered the premiership to the right-wing socialist, Prieto. The Stalinists, the Catalan Esquerra, the Republican Union of Barrio, as well as the reactionary bourgeoisie, supported Azaña's candidate.

The left socialists, however, prevented Prieto from accepting. For the reactionary bourgeoisie, the Prieto premiership would have been, at most, a breathing space to prepare further. Having failed to secure it, they plunged into civil war.

Such was the record of Azaña's Republican Left. That of the other liberal-bourgeois parties was, if anything, worse. Companys' Catalan Esquerra had ruled Catalonia since 1931. Its Catalonian nationalism served to hold in leash the more backward strata of peasants while Companys used armed force against the CNT. On the eve of the October, 1934, revolt he had reduced the CNT to semi-legal status, with hundreds of its leaders jailed. It was this situation which had moved the CNT so unwisely to refuse to join the revolt against Lerroux-Gil Robles, declaring that Companys was just as much a tyrant; while Companys, faced with the choice between arming the workers and knuckling under to Gil Robles, had chosen the latter.[*]

As for the Republican Union of Martinez Barrio, it was nothing more than the reconstituted remnants of Gil Robles' allies, Lerroux's

---

[*] The *Estat Catala*, a split-off from the Esquerra, combining extreme separatism with anti-labor hooliganism, had provided its khaki-shirt members for strike-breaking; had disarmed workers during the October, 1934 revolt. This organization, too, after July 19, turned up in the "anti-fascist" camp!

Radicals. Barrio himself had been Lerroux's chief lieutenant, and had served as one of the premiers in the *bienio negro,* putting down with great cruelty an anarchist rising in December, 1933. He had perspicaciously left the sinking ship of the Radicals when it became clear that the crushing of the October, 1934, revolt had failed to stem the masses, and made his début as an "anti-fascist" in 1935 by signing a petition for amnesty for political prisoners. When Lerroux fell after a financial scandal his following turned to Barrio.

The fourth of the bourgeois parties, the Basque Nationalists, had collaborated closely with the extreme reactionaries of the rest of Spain until Lerroux had sought to curb ancient provincial privileges. Catholic, led by the big landowners and capitalists of the four Basque provinces, the Basque Nationalists had supported Gil Robles in crushing the Asturian Commune of October, 1934. They were from the first uncomfortable in their alliance with the workers' organizations. That they did not go over to the other side of the barricades immediately, is to be explained by the fact that the Biscayan region was a traditional sphere of influence of Anglo-French imperialism and as such hesitated to enter the alliance with Hitler and Mussolini.

These, then, were the "loyal," "reliable," "honorable" allies of the Stalinist-reformist leaders in the struggle against fascism. If in peace time the liberal bourgeoisie had refused to touch the land, the church or the army, because they did not want to undermine the foundations of private property, was it conceivable that now, with arms in hand, the liberal bourgeoisie would loyally support a war to the finish against reaction? If Franco's army was crushed, what would happen to the liberal bourgeoisie which, in the last analysis, had maintained its privileges only because of the army? Precisely because of these considerations, the Franco forces moved boldly, taking it for granted that Azaña and Companys would come to heel. Precisely because of these considerations, Azaña and the liberal bourgeoisie *did attempt to come to terms with Franco.*

The Stalinists and reformists, compromised by their People's Front policy, have connived with the liberal bourgeoisie in suppressing almost completely from the outside world the cold facts which reveal the treachery of which Azaña and his associates were guilty in the first days of the revolt. But here are the indisputable facts:

On the morning of July 17, 1936, General Franco, having seized Morocco, radioed his manifesto to the Spanish garrisons, instructing them to seize the cities. Franco's communications were received at the naval station near Madrid by a loyal operator and promptly revealed to the Minister of the Navy, Giral. But the government did not divulge the news in any form until the morning of the 18th and then it issued only a reassuring note:

> The Government declares that the movement is exclusively limited to certain cities of the protectorate Zone [Morocco] and that nobody, absolutely nobody on the Peninsula [Spain], has added to such an absurd undertaking.

Later that day, at 3 P. M., when the government had full and positive information of the scope of the rising, including the seizure of Seville, Navarre and Saragossa, it issued a note which said:

> The Government speaks again in order to confirm the absolute tranquillity of the whole Peninsula.
>
> The Government acknowledges the offers of support which it has received [from the workers' organizations] and, while being grateful for them, declares that the best aid that can be given to the Government is to guarantee the normality of daily life, in order to set a high example of serenity and of confidence in the means of the military strength of the State.
>
> Thanks to the foresighted means adopted by the authorities, a broad movement of aggression against the republic may be deemed to have been broken up; it has found no assistance in the Peninsula and has only succeeded in securing followers in a fraction of the army in Morocco. . . .
>
> These measures, together with the customary orders to the forces in Morocco who are laboring to overcome the rising, per-

mit us to affirm that the action of the Government will be sufficient to re-establish normality. (*Claridad,* July 18, 1936.)

This incredibly dishonest note was issued to justify the government's refusal to arm the workers, as the trade unions had requested.
But this was not all. At 5:20 and again at 7:20 P.M., the government
issued similar notes, the last declaring that "in Seville . . . there were
acts of rebellion by the military elements that were repelled by the
forces in the service of the government." Seville had then been in
the hands of Queipo de Llano for most of the day.

Having deceived the workers about the true state of affairs, the
cabinet went into an all-night conference. Azaña had Premier Casares Quiroga, a member of his own party, resign, and replaced him
with the more "respectable" Barrio, and the night was spent hunt-
ing up bourgeois leaders outside the Popular Front who could be
induced to enter the cabinet. With this rightist combination, Azaña
made frantic attempts to contact the military leaders and come to
an understanding with them. The fascist leaders, however, took the
overtures as a sure sign of their victory, and refused Azaña any form
of face-saving compromise. They demanded that the republicans
step aside for an open military dictatorship. Even when this became known to Azaña and the cabinet ministers, they took no steps
to organize resistance. Meanwhile, garrison after garrison, apprised
of the government's paralysis, took heart and unfurled the banner
of rebellion.

Thus, for two decisive days, the rebels marched on while the government besought them to save its face. It made no move to declare
the dissolution of rebellious regiments, to declare the soldiers absolved from obeying their officers. The workers, remembering the
*bienio negro,* remembering the fate of the proletariat of Italy and
Germany, were clamoring for arms. Even the reformist leaders were
knocking at the doors of the presidential palace, beseeching Azaña
and Giral to arm the workers. In the vicinity of the garrisons, the
unions had declared a general strike to paralyze the rebellion. But
folded arms would not be sufficient to face the army. Grim silence

enveloped the Montaña barracks in Madrid. The officers there, in accordance with the plan of the rising, were waiting for the garrisons surrounding Madrid to reach the city, when they would join forces. Azaña and Giral and their associates waited helplessly for the blow to fall.

And, indeed, could it be otherwise? The camp of Franco was saying: We, the serious masters of capital, the real spokesmen of bourgeois society, tell you that democracy must be finished, if capitalism is to live. Choose, Azaña, between democracy and capitalism. What was deeper in Azaña and the liberal bourgeoisie? Their "democracy" or their capitalism? They gave their answer by bowing their heads before the onward marching ranks of fascism.

On the afternoon of July 18, the chief worker-allies of the bourgeoisie, the National Committees of the Socialist and Communist parties, issued a joint declaration:

> The moment is a difficult one, but by no means desperate. The Government is certain that it has sufficient resources to overcome the criminal attempt. . . . In the eventuality that the resources of the Government be not sufficient, the republic has the solemn promise of the Popular Front, which gathers under its discipline the whole Spanish proletariat, resolved serenely and dispassionately to intervene in the struggle as quickly as its intervention is to be called for. . . . The Government commands and the Popular Front obeys.

But the government never gave the signal!
Fortunately, the workers did not wait for it.

# 3

# The revolution of July 19

The Barcelona proletariat prevented the capitulation of the republic to the fascists. On July 19, almost barehanded, they stormed the first barracks successfully. By 2 P.M. the next day they were masters of Barcelona.

It was not accidental that the honor of initiating the armed struggle against fascism belongs to the Barcelona proletariat. Chief seaport and industrial center of Spain, concentrating in it and the surrounding industrial towns of Catalonia nearly half the industrial proletariat of Spain, Barcelona has always been the revolutionary vanguard. The parliamentary reformism of the socialist-led UGT had never found a foothold there. The united socialist and Stalinist parties (the PSUC) had fewer members on July 19 than the POUM. The workers were almost wholly organized in the CNT, whose suffering and persecution under both the monarchy and republic had imbued its masses with a militant anti-capitalist tradition, although its anarchist philosophy gave it no systematic direction. But, before this philosophy was to reveal its tragic inadequacy, the CNT reached historic heights in its successful struggle against the forces of General Goded.

As in Madrid, the Catalan government refused to arm the workers. CNT and POUM emissaries, demanding arms, were smilingly informed they could pick up those dropped by wounded Assault Guards.

But CNT and POUM workers during the afternoon of the 18th were raiding sporting goods stores for rifles, construction jobs for sticks of dynamite, fascist homes for concealed weapons. With the aid of a few friendly Assault Guards, they had seized a few racks of government rifles. (The revolutionary workers had painstakingly gathered a few guns and pistols since 1934.) That—and as many autos as they could find—was all the workers had when, at five o'clock on the morning of the 19th, the fascist officers began to lead detachments from the barracks.

Isolated engagements before paving-stone barricades led to a general engagement in the afternoon. And here political weapons more than made up for the superior armament of the fascists. Heroic workers stepped forward from the lines to call upon the soldiers to learn why they were shooting down their fellow toilers. They fell under rifle and machine-gun fire, but others took their place. Here and there a soldier began shooting wide. Soon bolder ones turned on their officers. Some nameless military genius—perhaps he died then—seized the moment and the mass of workers abandoned their prone positions and surged forward. The first barracks were taken. General Goded was captured that afternoon. With arms from the arsenals the workers cleaned up Barcelona. Within a few days, all Catalonia was in their hands.

Simultaneously the Madrid proletariat was mobilizing. The left socialists distributed their scant store of arms, saved from October, 1934. Barricades went up on key streets and around the Montaña barracks. Workers' groups were looking for reactionary leaders. At dawn of the 19th the first militia patrols took their places. At midnight the first shots were exchanged with the barracks. But it was not until the next day, when the great news came from Barcelona, that the barracks were stormed.

Valencia, too, was soon saved from the fascists. Refused arms by the governor appointed by Azaña, the workers prepared to face the troops with barricades, cobblestones and kitchen knives—until their comrades within the garrison shot the officers and gave arms to the workers.

The Asturian miners, fighters of the Commune of October, 1934, outfitted a column of five thousand dynamiters for a march on Madrid. It arrived there on the 20th, just after the barracks had been taken, and took up guard duty in the streets.

In Málaga, strategic port opposite Morocco, the ingenious workers, unarmed at first, had surrounded the reactionary garrison with a wall of gasoline-fired houses and barricades.

In a word, without so much as by-your-leave to the government, the proletariat had begun a war to the death against the fascists. The initiative had passed out of the hands of the republican bourgeoisie.

Most of the army was with the fascists. It must be confronted by a new army. Every workers' organization proceeded to organize militia regiments, equip them, and send them to the front. The government had no direct contact with the workers' militia. The organizations presented their requisitions and payrolls to the government, which handed over supplies and funds which the organizations distributed to the militias. Such officers as remained in the Loyalist camp were assigned as "technicians" to the militias. Their military proposals were transmitted to the militiamen through the worker-officers. Those Civil and Assault Guards still adhering to the government soon disappeared from the streets. In the prevailing atmosphere the government was compelled to send them to the front. Their police duties were taken over by worker-police and militiamen.

The sailors, traditionally more radical than soldiers, saved a good part of the fleet by shooting their officers. Elected sailors' committees took over control of the Loyalist fleet, and established contact with the workers' committees on shore.

Armed workers' committees displaced the customs officers at the frontiers. A union book or red party card was better than a passport for entering the country. Few reactionaries managed to get out through the workers' cordon.

The revolutionary-military measures were accompanied by revolutionary-economic measures against fascism. Why this happened, if the world-historical scheme called merely for "defense of the republic," the Stalinist-democrats have yet to explain.

Especially was this true in Catalonia where, within a week from July 19, transport and industry was almost entirely in the hands of CNT workers' committees, or where workers belonged to both, CNT-UGT joint committees. The union committees systematically took over, re-established order and speeded up production for wartime needs. Through national industries stemming from Barcelona, the same process spread to Madrid, Valencia, Alicante, Almeria and Málaga although never becoming as universal as in Catalonia. In the Basque provinces, however, where the big bourgeoisie had declared for the democratic republic, they remained masters in the factories. A UGT-CNT committee took charge of all transportation in Spain. Soon factory delegations were going abroad to arrange for exports and imports.

The peasants needed no urging to take the land. They had been trying to take it since 1931; but Casas Viejas, Castilblanco, Yeste, were honored names of villages where the peasants had been massacred by Azaña's troops because they had taken land. Now Azaña could not stop them. As the news came from the cities, the peasants spread over the land. Their scythes and axes took care of any government official or republican landowner injudicious enough to bar their way. In many places, permeated by anarchist and left-socialist teachings, the peasants organized directly into collectives. Peasant committees took charge of feeding the militias and the cities, giving or selling directly to the provisioning committees, militia columns and the trade unions.

Everywhere the existing governmental forms and workers' organizations proved inadequate as methods of organizing the war and revolution. Every district, town and village created its militia committees, to arm the masses and drill them. The CNT-UGT factory committees, directing all the workers, including those never before organized, developed a broader scope than the existing trade union organizations. The old municipal administrations disappeared, to be replaced, generally, by agreed-upon committees giving representation to all the anti-fascist parties and unions. But in these the Esquerra and Republican Left politicians seldom appeared. They were replaced by workers and peasants who, though still adhering to the republican parties, followed the lead of the more advanced workers who sat with them.

The most important of these new organs of power was the "Central Committee of Anti-fascist Militias of Catalonia," organized July 21. Of its fifteen members, five were anarchists from the CNT and FAI, and these dominated the Central Committee. The UGT had three members, despite its numerical weakness in Catalonia, but the anarchists hoped thereby to encourage similar committees elsewhere. The POUM had one, the Peasant Union (Rabassaires) one, and the Stalinists (PSUC) one. The bourgeois parties had four.

Unlike a coalition government which in actuality rests on the old state machine, the Central Committee, dominated by the anarchists, rested on the workers organizations and militias. The Esquerra and those closest to it—the Stalinists and the UGT  merely tagged along for the time being. The decrees of the Central Committee were the only law in Catalonia. Companys unquestioningly obeyed its requisitions and financial orders. Beginning presumably as the center for organizing the militias, it inevitably had to take on more and more governmental functions. Soon it organized a department of worker-police; then a department of supplies, whose word was law in the factories and seaport.

In those months in which the Central Committee existed, its military campaigns were inextricably bound up with revolutionary acts. This is evident from its campaign in Aragon, on which the Catalan militias marched within five days. They conquered Aragon as an army of social liberation. Village anti-fascist committees were set up, to which were turned over all the large estates, crops, supplies, cattle, tools, etc., belonging to big landowners and reactionaries. Thereupon the village committee organized production on the new basis, usually collectives, and created a village militia to carry out socialization and fight reaction. Captured reactionaries were placed before the general assembly of the village for trial. All property titles, mortgages, debt documents in the official records, were consigned to the bonfire. Having thus transformed the world of the village, the Catalonian columns could go forward, secure in the knowledge that every village so dealt with was a fortress of the revolution!

Much malicious propaganda has been spread by the Stalinists concerning the alleged weakness of the military activity of the anarchists. The hasty creation of militias, the organization of war industry, were inevitably haphazard in all unaccustomed hands. But in those first months, the anarchists, seconded by the POUM, made up for much of their military inexperience by their bold social policies. In civil war, *politics* is the determining weapon. By taking the initiative, by seizing the factories, by encouraging the peasantry to take the land, the CNT masses crushed the Catalonian garrisons. By marching into Aragon as social liberators, they roused the peasantry to paralyze the mobility of the fascist forces. In the plans of the generals, Saragossa, seat of the War College and perhaps the biggest of the army garrisons, was to have been for Eastern Spain what Burgos became in the west. Instead, Saragossa was immobilized from the first days.

Around the Central Committee of the militias rallied the multitudinous committees of the factories, villages, supplies, food, police, etc., in form joint committees of the various anti-fascist organizations, in actuality wielding an authority greater than that of its constituents. After the first tidal wave of revolution, of course, the committees revealed their basic weakness: they were based on mutual agreement of the organizations from which they drew their members, and after the first weeks, the Esquerra, backed by the Stalinists, recovered their courage and voiced their own program. The CNT leaders began to make concessions detrimental to the revolution. From that point on, the committees could have only functioned progressively by abandoning the method of mutual agreement and adopting the method of majority decisions by democratically elected delegates from the militias and factories.

The Valencia and Madrid regions also developed a network of anti-fascist joint militia committees, worker-patrols, factory committees, and district committees to wipe out the reactionaries in the cities and send the militia to the front.

Thus, side by side with the official governments of Madrid and Catalonia there had arisen organs predominantly worker-controlled, through which the masses organized the struggle against fascism. In the main, the military, economic and political struggle was proceeding independently of the government and, indeed, in spite of it.

How are we to characterize such a régime? In essence, it was identical with the régime which existed in Russia from February to November, 1917—a régime of *dual power*. One power, that of Azaña and Companys, without an army, police or other armed force of its own, was already too weak to challenge the existence of the other. The other, that of the armed proletariat, was not yet conscious enough of the necessity to dispense with the existence of the power of Azaña and Companys. This phenomenon of dual power has accompanied all proletarian revolutions. It signifies that the class struggle is about to reach the point where either one or the other must become undisputed master. It is a critical balancing of alternatives on a razor edge. A long period of equilibrium is out of the question; either one or the other must soon prevail! The "revolution of July 19" was incomplete, but that it was a revolution is attested to by its having created a régime of dual power.

# 4

# Toward a coalition
# with the bourgeoisie

In every other period of dual power—Russia of February–November, 1917, Germany of 1918–19 are the most important—the bourgeois government continued to exist, thanks only to the entry into it of representatives of the reformist workers' organizations, who thereby became the main prop for the bourgeoisie. The Mensheviks and Social Revolutionaries not only defended the Provisional Government within the Soviets but also sat with the bourgeois ministers in the government. Ebert and Scheidemann wielded a majority in the Soldiers' and Workers' Councils but simultaneously sat in the government. In Spain, however, for seven critical weeks, no workers' representative entered the cabinet.

Not that the bourgeoisie did not want them there, nor that workers' leaders were not available and willing! On the evening of July 19, when full confirmation of the workers' conquest of Barcelona arrived, Azaña finally abandoned the attempt to form a "peace cabinet" under Barrio. Giral became premier. Azaña and Giral asked Prieto and Caballero to enter the cabinet. Prieto was more than willing. Caballero refused Giral's proposal, and Prieto dared not enter without him.

In Catalonia, during the last days of July, Companys took three Stalinist leaders into his cabinet. But in three days they were forced to resign, at the demand of the anarchists, who denounced their entry as disruption of the leading rôle of the Central Committee of Militias.

Thus, for seven weeks, the bourgeois governments remained isolated from the masses, unprotected by reformist ministers. Nor did the conduct of the republicans enhance their prestige. The more cowardly functionaries fled to Paris. The CNT *Solidaridad Obrera* published day after day a "Gallery of Illustrious Men," of republicans who had fled. The government had in its possession one of the largest gold reserves outside those of the big imperialist powers—over six hundred millions in dollars—yet made no effort during those first two months to purchase arms abroad. It praised France's attempts to organize "non-intervention." It cried out against the workers' seizure of the factories and organization of war production. It denounced the district committees and worker-patrols which were cleansing the rearguard of reactionaries.

The Catalan-bourgeois régime, led by the astute Companys (he had once been a lawyer for the CNT and had a keen knowledge of the workers' movement), riding a revolutionary upsurge far more intense than that in Madrid, behaved much more cleverly than Azaña-Giral. In the first red weeks it sanctioned without question all steps taken by the workers. But it was even more isolated in Barcelona than was the Madrid cabinet.

The Madrid and Barcelona governments lacked the indispensable instrument of sovereignty: armed force. The regular army was with Franco. The regular police no longer had any real independent existence, having been swallowed up in the flood of armed workers. Though itself denuded of its police, most of whom had either volunteered or been sent, under workers' pressure, to the front, the Madrid bourgeoisie had looked askance at the official status conceded to the worker-leadership of the militias by the Catalan government. The discreet explanation offered by the Esquerra leader, Jaime Miravittles, tells volumes:

The Central Committee of Militias was born two or three days after the [subversive] movement, in the absence of any regular public force and when there was no army in Barcelona. For another thing, there were no longer any Civil or Assault Guards. For all of them had fought so arduously, united with the forces of the people, that now they formed part of the same mass and had remained mixed up with that. In these circumstances, weeks went by without it being possible to reunite and regroup the dispersed forces of the Assault and Civil Guards. (*Heraldo de Madrid*, September 4, 1936.)

Yet, the fact is, despite the rise of dual power, despite the scope of the power of the proletariat in the militias and their control of economic life, the workers' state remained embryonic, atomized, scattered in the various militias and factory committees and local antifascist defense committees jointly constituted by the various organizations. It never became centralized in nationwide Soldiers' and Workers' Councils, as it had been in Russia in 1917, in Germany in 1918–19. Only when dual power assumes such organizational proportions is there put on the order of the day the choice between the prevailing régime and a new revolutionary order of which the Councils become the state form. The Spanish revolution never rose to this point despite the fact that the real power of the proletariat was far greater than the power wielded by the workers in the German revolution or, indeed, than that wielded by the Russian workers before November. *Locally* and in each militia column, the workers ruled; but at the top there was only the government! This paradox has a simple explanation: there was no revolutionary party in Spain, ready to drive through the organization of soviets boldly and single-mindedly.

But isn't it a far cry from the failure to create the organs to overthrow the bourgeoisie, to the acceptance of the rôle of class collaboration with the bourgeoisie? Not at all. In a revolutionary period the alternatives are poised on a razor-edge: either one or the other. Every day is as a decade in peacetime. Today's "realism" becomes tomorrow's avenue to collaboration with the bourgeoisie. Civil war is raging. The liberal bourgeoisie offers to co-operate in fighting the fascists. It is obvious that the workers should accept their aid. What are the limits of such co-operation? The "sectarian" Bolsheviks, in the struggle against Kornilov, set exceedingly sharp limits. Above all, they gathered power in the hands of the soviets.

In the very heat of the struggle against the Kornilov counter-revolution in September, 1917, when Kerensky and the other bourgeois ministers in the coalition government were certainly shouting for smashing Kornilov, as much as Azaña and Companys were declaiming against Franco, the Bolsheviks warned the workers that the Provisional Government was impotent and that only the soviets could defeat Kornilov. In a special letter to the Central Committee of the Bolsheviks, Lenin castigated those who uttered "phrases about the defense of the country, about supporting the Provisional Government." "We will fight, we are fighting against Kornilov, even as Kerensky's troops do, but we do not support Kerensky," said Lenin. "On the contrary, we expose his weakness. There is the difference. It is rather a subtle difference, but it is highly essential and one must not forget it." And there was not the slightest thought of waiting until the struggle against Kornilov was over before taking state power. On the contrary, declared Lenin, "even tomorrow events may put power into our hands, and then we shall not relinquish it." (Works, Vol. XXI, Book I., p. 137) Lenin was ready to collaborate with Kerensky himself in a military-technical union. But with this pre-condition, already existing: the masses organized in *class* organs, democratically elected, where the Bolsheviks could contend for a majority.

Without developing soviets—workers' councils—it was inevitable that even the anarchists and the POUM would drift into governmental collaboration with the bourgeoisie. For what does it mean, in practice, to refuse to build soviets in the midst of civil war? It means to recognize the right of the liberal bourgeoisie to *govern* the struggle, i.e., to dictate its social and political limits.

Thus it was that all the workers' organizations, without exception, drifted closer and closer to the liberal bourgeoisie. In the intervening weeks, Azaña and Companys recovered their nerve, as they saw that the inroads of the workers were not to be consummated by the overturn of the state power. Azaña gathered together every officer who, caught behind the lines, proclaimed himself for the republic. At first the officers could deal with the militias only through the militia committees. But the Bolshevik method of using the technical knowledge of the officers without giving them power over the soldiers, can be employed only during the height of the transition from dual power to a workers' state, or by a soviet régime. Little by little the officers pushed their way to direct command.

The government's control of the treasury and of the banks—for the workers, including the anarchists, had stopped short at the banks, merely instituting a form of workers' control which was little more than guarding against disbursements to fascists and encouraging capital loans to collectivized factories—gave it a powerful lever in encouraging the considerable number of foreign-owned enterprises (which had not been seized), in placing governmental representatives in the factories, in intervening in foreign trade, in providing room for quick growth to small factories and shops and traders that had been spared from collectivization. Madrid, controlling the gold reserves, used them as an unanswerable argument in Catalonia in instances where Companys proved powerless. Under contemporary capitalism, finance capital dominates manufacturing and transportation. This law of economics was not abrogated because the workers had seized the factories and railroads. All that the workers had done in seizing these enterprises was to transform them into *producers' co-operatives,* still subject to the laws of capitalist economics. Before they could be freed from these laws, all industry and land, *together with* bank capital and gold and silver reserves, would have to become the property of a workers' state. But this required overthrowing the bourgeois state. The manipulation of finance capital to curb the workers' movement is a phase of the Spanish struggle which will deserve the most careful and detailed study, and undoubtedly will provide new insights into the nature of the bourgeois state. This weapon was openly unleashed in its full force much later, but even in the first seven weeks its guarded use enabled the régime to recover much lost ground.

In the very first weeks the government, feeling its way, returned to the use of one of the instruments of state power most hated by the workers, the press censorship. It was hated particularly because of the government's use of it during the last days before the fascist rebellion, when socialist and anarchist warnings against the imminent civil war were deleted. Azaña hastened to assure the press that the censorship would be limited to military news; but this was merely a bridge to general censorship. The unreserved supporters of the Popular Front, the Stalinists and Prieto Socialists agreed without a murmur. An objectionable feature in the Stalinist *Mundo Obrero* of August 20 led to suppression of the issue. Caballero's *Claridad* grumblingly acceded. The anarchists and the POUM followed. Only the Madrid organ of the Anarchist Youth refused entry to the censor. But censorship was not a separate problem: it would inevitably be the prerogative of the state power.

In August, the CNT entered the Basque "Defense Junta" which was not a military organization at all, but a regional government in which the Basque big bourgeois party held the posts of finance and industry. This, the first time in history that anarchists participated in a government, was reported by the anarchist press without explanation. A great opportunity was presented to the POUM to win the CNT workers to struggle for a workers' state, but the POUM made no issue of the Basque government—for the POUM acted identically in Valencia.

The "Popular Executive," with bourgeois participation, was constituted in Valencia as a regional government, and here the POUM entered too. In those days the POUM's central organ, *La Batalla*, was calling for an all-workers' government in Madrid and Barcelona: the contradiction between this slogan and the Valencia step was passed by without comment.

Formed within two days of the uprising as a military center, the

Central Committee of the Catalan Militias began to undertake collaboration with the bourgeoisie in economic activities as well. Transformation of the Central Committee into a body of democratically elected delegates from the factories and militia columns would have given it more power and authority and, at the same time, would have reduced the rôle of the bourgeoisie to its actual strength in the militias and factories. This was the only way out of the dilemma. But the CNT was blind to the problem, and the POUM kept silent.

Finally, on August 11, the Council of Economy was formed on the initiative of Companys to centralize economic activity. Here it was, despite the bait of a radical economic program, an undisguised question of socio-economic collaboration under the hegemony of the bourgeoisie. But the CNT and POUM entered it.

Thus, in every sphere, the bourgeoisie edged its way back. Thus, the workers were carried, step by step, toward governmental coalition with the bourgeoisie.

To understand this process clearly, we must now examine more closely the political conceptions of the workers' organizations.

# 5

# The politics of the
# Spanish working class

### The right-wing socialists

Prieto, Negrin, Besteiro, clung consistently to the theory that
Spain had before it a considerable period of capitalist development.
Besteiro and others had disgraced themselves by denouncing the
workers' resort to arms in October, 1934. But Prieto, Negrin and
their main associates had comported themselves at least as well as
Caballero in the Asturian fighting and the general strike without,
however, changing their political perspective. They had carried the
party, in spite of left-wing opposition, into the electoral coalition
of February, 1936. The left socialists had, however, prevented Prieto's
entry into the cabinet. Prieto had clearly indicated that, were the
left wing successful in gaining control of the party, he was prepared to fuse with Azaña's Republican Left. He had gone so far, in
the months before the civil war, as to join with Azaña in denouncing the strike epidemic. In their political conceptions the right-
wing socialists were, indeed, simply petty-bourgeois republicans
who, in the struggle against the monarchy, had correctly estimated
that mass support could be had only by socialist coloration. In the
republican arena opened in 1931, the first test had revealed them

to be blood-brothers of Azaña.

Himself a Basque industrialist of considerable wealth, Prieto's *El Liberal* of Bilbao was one of the most influential organs among the bourgeoisie. Decades of class collaboration had given him the full confidence of the Basque bourgeoisie. More than any other figure, Prieto provided the link which united the Catholic, narrow-minded Basque capitalists, Azaña's cosmopolitan and cynical intellectuals, and the Stalinist forces. Callous, ruthless, able, Prieto had none of the subjective fears of the Scandinavian and British Labor party leaders. He recognized the full significance of the policy embarked on by Stalin when the civil war began, and thereafter greeted the Stalinist spokesmen as ideological brothers.

### The Stalinists

The political program of Stalinism in 1936 appeared very different from its ultra-left denunciations of Azaña, Prieto, Caballero, the anarchists, as "fascists" and "social fascists" in 1931. Yet the basic policy remained the same. In 1936, as in 1931, the Stalinists wanted no proletarian revolution in Spain.

Walter Duranty, unofficial apologist for the Kremlin, in 1931 described its attitude:

> The first Soviet comment on the events in Spain appears in the leading editorial in *Pravda* today, but the organ of the Russian Communist Party seems none too jubilant over the prospects of the revolutionary struggle which it clearly expects will follow Alfonso's downfall. . . .
>
> The unexpectedly pessimistic tone of *Pravda* . . . perhaps is to be explained by Soviet anxiety lest the events in Spain disturb European peace during the present critical period of the five-year plan. Rightly or wrongly, it is believed here that the peace of Europe hangs literally on a thread, that the accumulation of armaments and national hatreds are much greater than before the war and make the present situation no less dangerous than the Spring of 1914, and that Spanish fireworks

might easily provoke a general conflagration. (*New York Times,* May 17, 1931.) Paradoxically enough, it appears that Moscow is not overdelighted by this circumstance—in fact it may almost be said that if the Spanish revolution "swings left" as Moscow now expects, Moscow will be more embarrassed than pleased . . .

. . . For, first, the Soviet Union is excessively and perhaps unduly nervous about a war danger and "views with alarm" any event anywhere that may upset the European status quo. . . . Secondly, the Kremlin's policy today stands much more on the success of socialist construction in Russia than upon world revolution. . . . (*New York Times,* May 18, 1931.)

In 1931, the Kremlin had secured its goal by a policy of non-collaboration with the rest of the proletarian parties. The communists were thus isolated from the mass movement by union-splitting, no united front of organizations, attacks on other working-class meetings, etc. In 1931, the Kremlin had wanted nothing but maintenance of the status quo in Europe. In 1936, however, the Comintern adopted a new perspective, embodied in the Seventh Congress. The new course was to maintain the status quo as long as possible, this time not merely by preventing revolutions, but by active class collaboration with the bourgeoisie in the "democratic countries." This collaboration was designed, in the event of war breaking out, to provide Russia with England and France as its allies. The price Russia was offering to pay for an alliance with Anglo-French imperialism was the subordination of the proletariat to the bourgeoisie. "Socialism in a single country" had revealed its full meaning as "no socialism anywhere else."

Lenin and the Bolsheviks were realists enough to allow the Soviet state to utilize conflicts between various capitalist powers even to the extent of using one against another in the event of war. Even more fundamental to their revolutionary politics, however, was the doctrine that, whatever the Soviet's military alliances, the proletariat in every country has the unalterable duty to oppose its "own" bourgeoisie in war, to overthrow it in the course of the war, and to replace it with a workers' revolutionary government which is the only possible real ally of the Soviet Union.

This fundamental tenet of Marxism was repudiated by the Seventh Congress of the Comintern. The French Communist party was already openly proclaiming its readiness to support its bourgeoisie in the coming war. Despite this, England's coolness had largely negated the Franco-Soviet pact. Even under Blum the pact had not yet led to conferences between the two general staffs. The Spanish civil war provided the Kremlin with an opportunity to prove once for all to both French and English imperialists that, not only did the Kremlin intend to encourage no revolution, it was prepared to take the lead in crushing one that had nevertheless started.

Apparently not even all of the foreign Stalinist correspondents in Barcelona realized, in the first days of the civil war, that the Comintern had actually set itself the task of unraveling this all but completed revolution. On July 22, the London *Daily Worker* carried a leading article: "In Spain, Socialists and Communists fought shoulder to shoulder in armed battle to defend their trade unions and political organizations, to guard the Spanish Republic and to defend democratic liberties so that they could advance *towards a Spanish Soviet Republic.*" And the same day, its Barcelona representative, Frank Pitcairn, wired: "Red Militia Crushes Fascists, Triumph in Barcelona." "The united working-class forces have already gained the upper hand. Streets here are being patrolled by cars filled with armed workers who are preserving order and discipline. Preparations are going forward for the organization of a *permanent* workers' militia."

The Spanish Stalinists, however, joined Prieto and Azaña in appeals to the workers not to seize property. The Stalinists were the first to submit their press to the censorship. They were the first to demand liquidation of the workers' militias, and the first to hand their militiamen over to Azaña's officers. The civil war was not two months old when they began—what the government did not dare until nearly a year later—a murderous campaign against the POUM and the Anarchist Youth. The Stalinists demanded subordination to the bourgeoisie, not merely for the period of the civil war, but afterward as well. "It is absolutely false," declared Jesus Hernandez, editor of *Mundo Obrero* (August 6, 1936), "that the present workers' movement has for its object the establishment of a proletarian dictatorship after the war has terminated. It cannot be said we have a social motive for our participation in the war. We communists are the first to repudiate this supposition. We are motivated exclusively by a desire to defend the democratic republic."

*L'Humanité,* organ of the French Communist Party, early in August published the following statement:

> The Central Committee of the Communist Party of Spain requests us to inform the public, in reply to the fantastic and tendentious reports published by certain newspapers, that the Spanish people are not striving for the establishment of the dictatorship of the proletariat, but know only one aim: the defense of the republican order, while respecting property.

As the months passed, the Stalinists adopted an even firmer stand against anything but a capitalist system. José Diaz, "beloved leader" of the Spanish party, at a plenary session of the Central Committee, March 5, 1937, declared:

> If in the beginning the various premature attempts at "socialization" and "collectivization," which were the result of an unclear understanding of the character of the present struggle, might have been justified by the fact that the big landlords and manufacturers had deserted their estates and factories and that it was necessary at all costs to continue production, now on the contrary they cannot be justified at all. At the present time, when there is a government of the Popular Front, in which all the forces engaged in the fight against fascism are represented, such things

are not only not desirable, but absolutely impermissible. (*Communist International,* May, 1937.)

Recognizing that the danger of a proletarian revolution came first of all from Catalonia, the Stalinists concentrated enormous resources in Barcelona. Having practically no organization of their own there, they recruited into their service the conservative labor leaders and petty-bourgeois politicians, by way of a fusion of the Communist Party of Catalonia with the Catalan section of the Socialist party, the "Socialist Union" (a nationalist organization limited to Catalonia), and "Catala Proletari," a split-off from the bourgeois Esquerra. The fusion, the "Unified Socialist Party of Catalonia" (PSUC), affiliated to the Comintern. It had only a few thousand members at the beginning of the civil war but unlimited funds and hordes of Comintern functionaries. It took over the moribund Catalan section of the UGT and, when the Generalidad decreed compulsory syndicalization of all employees, recruited the most backward workers and clerks, who preferred this respectable institution to the radical CNT. But the biggest mass base of the Stalinists in Catalonia was a federation of traders, small businessmen, and manufacturers, the "Federaciones de Gremios y Entidades de Pequenos Comerciantes e Industriales," (GEPCI) which in July was dubbed a union and affiliated to the Catalan UGT. The so-called Catalan section operated in complete independence from the Caballero-controlled National Executive of the UGT. Thereupon, as the chief and most vigorous defenders of the bourgeoisie, the PSUC recruited heavily from the Catalan Esquerra.

The Stalinists followed a similar course in the rest of Spain. From the first, the CNT Agricultural Union and the UGT Peasant and Land Workers Federation—both supporting collectivization of the land accused the Stalinists of organizing separate "unions" of the richer peasants who were opposed to the collectives. The Stalinist party grew more rapidly than any other organization, for it opened its doors wide. Dubious bourgeois elements flocked to it for protection. As early as August 19 and 20, 1936, Caballero's organ, *Claridad,* accused the

Stalinist "Alliance of Anti-Fascist Writers" of harboring reactionaries.[*]

When, after three long months of boycott, in the third week of October the first Soviet planes and guns finally arrived, the Communist party—which up to then had been on the defensive, unable to counter the sharp criticism of the POUM on Stalin's refusal to send arms—received a terrific impetus. Thenceforward its proposals were inextricably linked with the threat that Stalin would send no more planes and arms. Ambassador Rosenberg, in Madrid and Valencia, and Consul-General Antonov-Ovseyenko in Barcelona, made political speeches plainly indicating their preferences. When, at the November celebration of the anniversary of the Russian Revolution in Barcelona (at a parade participated in by all the bourgeois parties!), Ovseyenko ended his speech with "long live the Catalan people and its hero, President Companys," the workers were left in no doubt on which class the Kremlin was placing its approval.[†]

We have only sketched the Stalinist policy sufficiently to place it in the picture. We shall see it grow more openly, ruthlessly counterrevolutionary in the ensuing year.

## Caballero: The left socialists and the UGT

Largo Caballero belonged to the same generation as Prieto. Both had reached middle age under the monarchy and modelled them-

---

[*] H.N. Brailsford, the British Socialist and People's Frontist, says: The Communist party "is no longer primarily a party of the industrial workers or even a Marxist party" and "this development must be permanent. This prediction I base on the social composition of the C.P. both in Catalonia and in Spain." (*New Republic,* June 9, 1937.)

[†] One extraordinary incident deserves reporting. On November 27, 1936, *La Batalla* was able to demonstrate that the CNT, UGT, Socialist party, Republican Left—all favored POUM representation in the Madrid Defense *Junta;* yet the POUM was not represented. How was it possible for Stalinist opposition alone to prevent the POUM, with its militia columns on all fronts, from being represented? Could the Stalinists alone wield a veto? The answer was that the Soviet Embassy had intervened. "It is intolerable that, on account of the aid they furnish us, they should attempt to impose upon us definite political norms, definite vetoes, to intervene

selves upon the German Social Democrats of the right wing. As head of the UGT, Caballero had silently accepted the suppression of the Anarchist-led CNT by Primo de Rivera. More, he had sanctioned it by accepting a state councillorship from the dictator. He had joined the 1931–1933 coalition cabinet as Minister of Labor and had sponsored a law continuing Rivera's mixed arbitration boards to settle strikes. "We shall introduce compulsory arbitration. Those workers' organizations which do not submit to it will be declared outside the law," he declared on July 23, 1931. Under his ministry, it was unlawful to strike for political demands or without ten days' written notice to the employer. No trade union or any other labor meeting could be held without police witnesses present. Side by side with Prieto, Caballero had defended the repressions of the land-hungry peasants, the thousands of political arrests.

After the collapse of the 1931–1933 coalition, a strong left wing developed, first in the Socialist Youth, demanding a re-orientation of the party. In 1934, Caballero unexpectedly declared for it. He had, said his friends, read Marx and Lenin for the first time after being ousted from the government. Nevertheless, Caballero's group made no serious preparations for the October, 1934, uprising. In Madrid, their chief stronghold, the rising never went beyond a general strike. On trial for inciting the insurrection—he was acquit-

---

and even to direct our politics," complained *La Batalla*. The Madrid Defense Council incident, Ovseyenko's November speech, Rosenberg's addresses, were the public incidents which aroused the POUM; through their cabinet post in the Generalidad they knew of even more serious incidents to which they could not refer while in the government.

Consul-General Ovseyenko's note to the press, answering the POUM, probably has no parallel in all previous diplomatic history. It read like an editorial in *Mundo Obrero*, denouncing the "fascist manoeuvres" of the POUM, as an "enemy of the Soviet Union." But before the year was up, Ovseyenko went further. On December 7, the POUM called upon the Generalidad to offer a place of asylum to Leon Trotsky. Before the Generalidad could answer, the Soviet Consul-General declared to the press (*La Prensa* reported it here) that if Trotsky were permitted to enter Catalonia, the Soviet government would cut off all aid to Spain. Truly, bureaucratic despotism could go no further!

ted—Caballero denied the charge.

On record against coalitions, and for proletarian revolution, Caballero nevertheless agreed to the electoral coalition of February, 1936, and supported Azaña's cabinet in the Cortes on all basic questions. Caballero's position, in effect, was that he would not repeat his rôle as Minister of Labor in the 1931–1933 coalition but that he would support Azaña from outside the cabinet, thereby being free to criticize. This was scarcely revolutionary irreconcilability. It was merely a form of critical loyalty, offering no threat to the bourgeois régime. During the February–July (1936) strike wave, Caballero incurred sharp criticism, both from the CNT and his own ranks, for discouraging strikes. An ardent advocate of fusion of the socialist and communist parties, he was mainly responsible for the fusion of the socialist and Stalinist youth. He had recouped his standing with the left wing of the party, however, by leading the fight to prevent Prieto from accepting the premiership. In the ensuing struggle, Prieto's Executive had outlawed *Claridad* (Caballero's paper), reorganized pro-Caballero party districts, and indefinitely postponed the party convention. A split would have come, but the civil war intervened and, for the sake of presenting a picture of harmony, the Caballero forces had conceded to Prieto the national center of the party.

At the height of the workers' movement during the first weeks of the civil war, Caballero came into sharp collision with the Azaña-Prieto-Stalinist bloc. So long as discipline in barracks, management of feeding, lodging and payrolls, were in the hands of the workers' organizations, and the militias freely organized discussions on political questions, the bourgeois-military caste could have no hope of securing real supremacy. Accordingly, the government, as a first feeler, called for enlistment of ten thousand reserve soldiers as a separate force under direct government control. The Stalinists defended the proposal. "Some comrades have wished to see in the creation of the new voluntary army something like a menace to the rôle of the militias," said *Mundo Obrero*, August 21. The Stalinists denied the very possibility and ended: "Our slogan, today as yesterday, is the same for this. Everything for the People's Front and everything through the People's Front."

This thoroughly reactionary position was effectively exposed by the UGT organ, *Claridad:*

> To think of another type of army to be substituted for those who are actually fighting and who in certain ways control their own revolutionary action, is to think in counter-revolutionary terms. That is what Lenin said (*State and Revolution*): "Every revolution, after the destruction of the state apparatus, shows us how the governing class tries to re-establish special bodies of armed men at 'its' service, and how the oppressed class attempts to create a new organization of a type capable of serving not the exploiters but the exploited."
>
> We . . . must take care that the masses and the leadership of the armed forces, which should be above all the people in arms, should not escape from our hands. (*Claridad,* August 20, 1936.)

Nevertheless, Caballero and the rest of the left-socialist leadership, in those critical early weeks, drew closer to Azaña, Prieto and the Stalinists. The dual power was proving a cumbersome and inadequate method of organizing the struggle against the fascist forces. Only two alternatives presented themselves inexorably: either join a coalition government, or replace the bourgeois power entirely by a workers' régime.

Here, however, programmatic errors showed their terrible practical results. In April, 1936, the leading group of the left socialists, the Madrid organization, had adopted a new program, declaring for the dictatorship of the proletariat. What organizational form would it take? Luis Araquistain, Caballero's theoretician, argued that Spain needed no soviets. The April program had consequently embodied in it the conception that "the organ of the proletarian dictatorship will be the Socialist party." But the left socialists had been prevented by Prieto's postponement of the congress from assuming formal control of the party, and had desisted from further struggle for control, when the civil war broke out. Furthermore, according to their program, they would have to wait until the party included a majority of the proletariat. This programmatic failure to provide for united action through workers' councils (soviets) in which socialists, communists, anarchists, Poumists, etc., would be gathered together with the deepest layers of the masses, this distorted notion of the lessons of the Russian Revolution, was a fatal error for the left socialists to make, and especially in Spain, with its anarchist traditions. They were saying precisely what the anarchist leaders had been accusing both communists and revolutionary socialists of meaning by the proletarian dictatorship.

The road to the proletarian dictatorship lay clearly before the proletariat. What was needed was to give the factory committees, militia committees, peasant committees, a democratic character, by having them elected by all of the workers in each unit; to bring together these elected delegates in village, city, regional councils, which in turn would send elected delegates to a national congress. True, the soviet form would not of itself solve the whole problem. A reformist majority in the executive committee would decline the assumption of state power. But the workers could still find in the soviets their natural organs of struggle until the genuinely revolutionary elements in the various parties banded together to win a revolutionary majority in the congress, and establish a workers' state.

The road lay clearly before the proletariat but, not accidentally, the program for that road was not the heritage of the left socialists. Caballero would criticize, grumble, excoriate, but he offered no alternative to the coalition with the bourgeoisie. Finally, he became its head.

## CNT-FAI: The National Confederation of Labor and the Anarchist Iberian Federation

The followers of Bakunin had older roots in Spain than the Marxists. The CNT had been traditionally anarchist in leadership. The tide of the October Revolution had, for a short time, overtaken the CNT. It had sent a delegate to the Comintern Congress in 1921. The anarchists had then resorted to organized fraction work and

recaptured it. Thenceforward, while continuing its traditional epi-
thets against political parties, Spanish anarchism had in the FAI a
highly centralized party apparatus through which it maintained
control of the CNT.

Ferociously persecuted by Alfonso and Primo de Rivera to the
point where it actually dissolved for a time, the CNT from 1931 on
commanded an undisputed majority in the industrial centers of
Catalonia and strong movements elsewhere. After the civil war began, it undoubtedly was larger than the UGT (some of whose biggest sections lay in fascist territory).

Hitherto, in the history of the working class, anarchism had never
been tested on a grand scale. Now, leading great masses, it was to
have a definitive test.

Anarchism has consistently refused to recognize the distinction
between a bourgeois and workers' state. Even in the days of Lenin
and Trotsky, anarchism denounced the Soviet Union as an exploiters' régime. Precisely the failure to distinguish between a bourgeois
and proletarian state had already led the CNT, in the honeymoon
days of the revolution of 1931, to the same kind of opportunist
errors as are always made by reformists—who also, in their way,
make no distinction between bourgeois and workers' states. Overcome by the "fumes of the revolution," the CNT had benevolently
greeted the bourgeois republic: "Under a régime of liberty, the bloodless revolution is still more possible, still easier than under the monarchy." (*Solidaridad Obrera,* April 23, 1931.) By October, 1934, it
swung to the equally false extreme of refusing to join with the republicans and socialists in the armed struggle against Gil Robles
(with the honorable exception of the CNT regional organization in
Asturias).

Now, in the far more powerful fumes of "the revolution of July
19," when the accustomed boundary lines between bourgeoisie and
proletariat were smeared over for the time being, the anarchists'
traditional refusal to distinguish between a bourgeois and workers'
state led them slowly, but decisively, into the ministry of a bourgeois state.

The false anarchist teachings on the nature of the state, it might seem, should logically have led them to refuse governmental participation in any event. Already running Catalan industry and the militias, however, the anarchists were in the intolerable position of objecting to the necessary administrative co-ordination and centralization of the work they had already begun. Their anti-statism "as such" had to be thrown off. What *did* remain, to wreak disaster in the end, was their failure to recognize the distinction between a workers' and a bourgeois state.

Class collaboration, indeed, lies concealed in the heart of anarchist philosophy. It is hidden, during periods of reaction, by anarchist hatred of capitalist oppression. But, in a revolutionary period of dual power, it must come to the surface. For then the capitalist smilingly offers to share in building the new world. And the anarchist, being opposed to "all dictatorships," including dictatorship of the proletariat, will require of the capitalist merely that he throw off the capitalist outlook, to which he agrees, naturally, the better to prepare the crushing of the workers.

There is a second fundamental tenet in anarchist teaching which led in the same direction. Since Bakunin, the anarchists had accused the Marxists of over-estimating the importance of state power, and had characterized this as merely the reflection of the petty-bourgeois intellectual's pre-occupation with lucrative administrative posts. Anarchism calls upon the workers to turn their backs on the state and seek control of the factories as the real source of power. The ultimate sources of power (property relations) being secured, the state power will collapse, never to be replaced. The Spanish anarchists thus failed to understand that it was only the collapse of the state power, with the defection of the army to Franco, which had enabled them to seize the factories and that, if Companys and his allies were allowed the opportunity to reconstruct the bourgeois state, they would soon enough take the factories away from the workers. Intoxicated with their control of the factories and the militias, the anarchists assumed that capitalism had *already* disappeared in Catalonia. They talked of the "new, social economy," and

Companys was only too willing to talk as they did, for it blinded them and not him.

## The POUM

Here was a rare opportunity for even a small revolutionary party. Soviets cannot be built at will. They can be organized only in a period of dual power, of revolutionary upheaval. But in the period which calls for them, a revolutionary party can further their creation, in spite of the opposition of the most powerful reformist parties. In Russia, the Mensheviks and Social Revolutionaries, particularly after July, sought to siphon off the strength of the soviets into the government, sought to discourage their functioning or the creation of new ones, without success despite the fact that these reformists still wielded a majority in the soviets. In Germany, the social democratic leadership sought, even more determinedly since they had the Russian lessons fresh before them, to prevent the creation of the workers' and soldiers' councils. In Spain, the direct hostility of the Stalinists and Prieto, the "theoretical" opposition of Caballero and the anarchists, would have been of no avail, for the basic units of the soviets were already there, in the factory, militia and peasant committees, and needed only democratization and bringing together in the localities. A single example, in POUM-controlled industrial towns like Lerida or Gerona, of delegates elected in every factory and shop, joining with delegates from the workers' patrols and the militias to create a workers' parliament which would function as the ruling body of the area, would have electrified Catalonia and initiated an identical process everywhere.

The POUM was the one organization which seemed suited to undertake the task of creating the soviets. Its leaders had been the founders of the communist movement in Spain. It had, however, basic weaknesses. Its majority came from the Workers and Peasants Bloc of Maurin, whose cadre had collaborated with Stalin in the 1924–1928 period in sending the Communist Party of China into the bourgeois Kuomintang "bloc of four classes"; in creating farmer-labor and "two-class" parties "of workers and farmers" (a fancy name for a bloc with reformists and the liberal bourgeoisie)—and, in a word, in the whole opportunist course of those disastrous years. Maurin and his followers had broken with the Comintern not on these basic questions but on other issues—the Catalonian national question, etc.—when the Comintern had turned to dual unionism, "social fascism," etc., in 1929. Moreover, the fusion of the Maurinists with the former Communist Left (Trotskyists), led by Andres Nin and Juan Andrade—whose previous failure to sharply differentiate themselves from the Maurinist ideology had been the subject of years of controversy with the International Left Opposition—was an unprincipled amalgamation, in which the Communist Left elements had adopted a "joint" program which was simply Maurin's old conceptions, of which Trotsky had said as early as June, 1931:

> All that I have written in my latest work, *The Spanish Revolution in Danger,* against the official policy of the Comintern in the Spanish question, applies entirely to the Catalonian Federation (Workers and Peasants bloc) . . . it represents a pure "Kuomintangism" transported to Spanish soil. The ideas and the methods against which the Opposition fought implacably when it was a question of the Chinese policy of the Kuomintang, find their most disastrous expression in the Maurin program. . . . A false point of departure during a revolution is inevitably translated in the course of events into the language of defeat. (*The Militant*, August 1, 1931.)

The first fruits of the fusion had scarcely been reassuring. After months of campaigning against a coalition with the bourgeoisie, the POUM had overnight entered the electoral coalition of February, 1936, It renounced the coalition after the elections, but on the very eve of the civil war (*La Batalla,* July 17) called for "an authentic Government of the Popular Front, with the direct [ministerial] participation of the Socialist and Communist Parties" as a means to "complete the democratic experience of the masses" and hasten the revolution—an absolutely false slogan, having nothing in common with the Bolshevik method of demonstrating the necessity of the workers' state and the impossibility of reforming the bourgeois state by forcing the reformists to assume governmental power *without* the bourgeois ministers.

Nevertheless, many had the hope that the POUM would take the lead in organizing the soviets. Nin now stood at the head of the party. He had been in Russia during the early years of the Russian Revolution, a leader of the Red International of Labor Unions. Would he not resist the provincialism of the Maurinist cadres? The POUM workers, better trained politically than the anarchists, played a great rôle, entirely out of proportion to their numbers in the first revolutionary weeks, in seizing the land and factories. From a party of about 8,000 on the eve of civil war, the POUM grew quickly, though remaining primarily a Catalonian organization. In the first months it quadrupled its numbers. Even more quickly its influence grew, as evidenced by the fact that it recruited over ten thousand militiamen under its banner.

The rising tide of coalitionism, however, engulfed the POUM. The theoretical premises for it were already there, in the Maurinist ideology, to which Nin had signed his name in the fusion. The POUM leadership clung to the CNT. Instead of boldly contending with the anarcho-reformists for the leadership of the masses. Nin sought illusory strength by identifying himself with them. The POUM sent its militants into the smaller and heterogeneous Catalan UGT instead of contending for leadership of the millions in the CNT. It organized POUM militia columns, circumscribing its influence, instead of sending its forces into the enormous CNT columns where the decisive sections of the proletariat were already gathered. *La Batalla* recorded the tendency of CNT unions to treat collectivized property as their own. It never attacked the anarcho-syndicalist theories which created the tendency. In the ensuing year, it never once made a principled attack on the anarcho-reformist leadership, not even when the anarchists acquiesced in the expulsion of the POUM from the Generalidad. Far from leading to united action with the CNT, this false course permitted the CNT-FAI leadership, with perfect impunity, to turn its back on the POUM.

More than once, in the days of Marx and Engels, and in the first revolutionary years of the Comintern, a weak national leadership had been corrected by its international collaborators. But the POUM's international connections stood to the right of the Spanish party. The "International Committee of Revolutionary Socialist Unity"—chiefly the I.L.P. of England and the S.A.P. of Germany—issued a manifesto to the Spanish proletariat on August 17, 1936, which did not contain a single word of criticism of the Popular Front! The S A P was shortly to go over to Popular Frontism itself, while the I.L.P. embraced the Communist party in a "Unity Campaign." Such were the ideological brethren for whom Nin and Andrade had renounced "Trotskyism," the movement for the Fourth International. True enough, the Fourth Internationalists were small organizations compared to the reformist parties of Europe. But they offered the POUM the rarest and most precious form of aid: a consistent Marxist analysis of the Spanish events and a revolutionary program to defeat fascism. Nin was more "practical," and abdicated the opportunity to lead the Spanish revolution.

# 6

## The program of the Caballero coalition government

Is it necessary, at this late date, to explain that the cabinet of three Caballero men, three Prieto men, two Stalinists, and five bourgeois ministers, which was established on September 4, 1936, was a bourgeois government, a typical cabinet of class collaboration?

Apparently it is still necessary, for as late as May 9, 1937, a resolution of the National Executive Committee of the Socialist Party, U.S.A., characterized this régime as "a provisional revolutionary government."

In turning over the premiership, Giral said: "I remain as a cabinet minister in order to demonstrate that the new government is an amplification of the old from the moment in which the president of the resigning government continues forming part of the new."

Caballero succinctly enough summarized his government's program to the Cortes:

> This government was constituted, all those forming it previously renouncing the defense of our principles and particular tendencies, in order to remain united on one sole aspiration: to defend Spain in her struggle against fascism. (*Claridad*, October 1, 1936.)

Certainly, Caballero had renounced his principles, but not the bourgeoisie and the Stalinists. For the common ground on which they joined with Caballero to form the government was the continuation of the old bourgeois order.

The programmatic declaration of the new cabinet had nothing in it which the previous government could not have signed. Point II is its essence:

> The ministerial program signifies essentially, the firm decision to assure triumph over the rebellion, co-ordinating the forces of the people, through the required unity of action. To that is subordinated every other political interest, putting to a side the ideological differences, since at present there can be no other task than that of assuring the smashing of the insurrection. (*Claridad,* September 5, 1936.)

Not one word about the land! Not one word about the factory committees! And, as "the representatives of the people," these "democrats" convened the former Cortes elected on February 16 by the electoral agreement which had given a majority to the bourgeoisie on the joint slate!

A few weeks before assuming the premiership, Caballero had been inveighing (through *Claridad*) against separating the revolution from the war. He had protested against the displacement of the militias. Now he became the leader in reconstructing the bourgeois state. What had happened?

We need not speculate on what went on in his mind. The observable change, reflected in *Claridad,* was that instead of depending on the working class of Spain and on international working class aid, Caballero now put his hopes on winning the aid of the "great democracies," Anglo-French imperialism.

On September 2, in an interview with the Havas Agency, Prieto had declared himself "pleased that the French government had taken the initiative in the proposals for non-intervention," although "it had not had the full value that France wishes to give it." "Each day is more urgent for France to work with great energy to avoid dangers for all."

"Why does the CNT act as if we were finding ourselves before a completed revolution?" complained *El Socialista:*

> Our geographic law is not that of immense Russia, by no means. And we have to take into account the attitude of the states that surround us, in order to determine our own attitude. Let not everything rest on spiritual force nor on reason, but on knowing how to renounce four in order to gain a hundred. We still hope that the estimate of the Spanish events made by certain democracies will be changed, and it would be a pity, a tragedy, to compromise these possibilities by pushing the velocity of the revolution, which at present does not conduct us to any positive solution. (*El Socialista,* October 5, 1936.)

The classical social democrats of the Prieto school could thus say, quite plainly, what the "Spanish Lenin," Caballero, and the ex-Leninists, the Stalintern, had to obscure: they were currying favor with Anglo-French imperialism by strangling the revolution. As late as August 24, Caballero had hoped that Hitler's intransigence would block the formation of the non-intervention committee. But with Hitler's "embargo" on arms shipments on that date, and the Soviet's declaration of adherence, it was clear that the Spanish blockade would be of long duration. The question was sharply posed: either fight the non-intervention blockade and denounce Blum and the Soviet Union for backing it, or accept the Stalinist perspective of gradually winning away France and England from the blockade by demonstrating the bourgeois respectability and stability of the Spanish Government. In other words, either accept the perspective of proletarian revolution and the necessity of arousing the international proletariat to aid Spain and spread the revolution to France, or accept class collaboration in Spain and abroad. When the alternatives became inescapable, Caballero chose the latter. Within a few days, his comrade, Alvarez del Vayo, was off to grovel at the feet of the imperialists in the League of Nations.

Caballero understood quite well that to arouse the Spanish masses to supreme efforts, it was necessary to offer them a program of social reconstruction. A circular order to the political commissioners at the front from Caballero's War Ministry emphasizes:

> It is necessary to convince the fighters who are defending the republican régime with their lives that at the termination of the war the organization of the state will undergo a profound modification. From the present we shall go on to a structure, socially, economically, and juridically, all for the benefit of the working masses. We should try to imbue such conceptions in the spirit of the troops by means of simple and plain examples. (*Gaceta de la Republica,* October 17, 1936.)

But the masses, Caballero presumably hoped, could be inspired with words, while the hard-headed imperialists of England and France would be content only with deeds.

*To rouse the peasantry to struggle,* to provide their best sons for the war, not as sullen, demoralized conscripts but as lion-hearted soldiers, to raise the food and fibres necessary to feed and clothe the army and the rear—that could only be done by giving the land to the peasantry, land to those who till it, the land as a national possession given in usufruct to the working farmer. Propaganda for liberty, etc., is absurdly insufficient. These are not your American or French farmers, who have already some land, enough to live on without being hungry:

> Misery is still appalling in Estremadura, Albacete, Andalusia, Caceres and Ciudad Real. It is by no means a figure of speech when it is said that peasants are dying of hunger. There are villages in Hurdes, in La Mancha, where the peasants, in absolute despair, revolt no longer. They eat roots and fruit. The events in Yeste [land seizures] are dramas of hunger. In Navas de Estena, about thirty miles from Madrid, forks and beds are unknown. The vil-

lagers' chief diet consists of a soup made from bread, water, oil and vinegar.

These words are not those of a Trotskyist agitator but the involuntary testimony of a Stalinist functionary ( *Inprecorr,* August 1, 1936). How can one seriously hope to rouse these depths, except by the one act which can convince them of a new era: give them the land. Can one expect them to "defend the republic"—that republic of Azaña—that had shot them like dogs for seizing land or stored grain?

Now the peasants and agricultural workers had seized land— not everywhere yet—but still had no assurance that the government was not permitting it merely as a provisional measure for the war which it would attempt to annul afterward. What the peasants wanted was a general decree nationalizing the land throughout Spain, giving it in usufruct to those who till it, so that no usurer can ever take it away from them. Equally, the tillers of the soil wanted the power to assure their land tenure, and that could only be a government of their flesh and blood—a workers' and peasants' régime.

Does it require much insight to see what effect such a land decree would have on the fascist forces? Not only on the land-hungry peasants in the fascist areas but, above all, among the sons of the peasants who constituted the ranks of the fascist armies, deceived by their officers as to the causes of the conflict. A few airplane loads of leaflets spread on the fascist fronts, announcing the land decree, would be worth an army of a million men. No single other move of the Loyalist side could sow more demoralization and decomposition in the fascist forces.

But thirty years as a "responsible leader" had left its mark too deeply. The inner forces of the masses had been too long an object of concern and fear to Caballero, something which he had to curb and channelize into safe boundaries. The land decree of October 7, 1936, merely sanctioned division of estates belonging to known fascists; other wealthy landowners, peasant exploiters, etc., remained untouched. The aroused hopes of the peasantry were smothered.

The UGT workers in the factories, shops, and railroads were setting up their factory committees, taking over the plants. What would Caballero have to say to them? In Valencia and Madrid, the government swiftly intervened, placing government directors in charge who confined the factory committees to routine activity. Not until February 23, 1937, was a comprehensive decree on the industries adopted (issued over the name of Juan Peiró, the anarchist Minister of Industry). It gave the workers no security for the future régime in industry; established strict intervention by the government. "Workers' control," by its terms, proved little more than a collective contract, such as for example, operates in shops dealing with the Amalgamated Clothing Workers Union in America—that is, no real measure of workers' control at all.

Caballero had denounced the Giral cabinet for building an army outside the workers' militias and for re-building the old Civil Guard. (The great "Caballero" column on the Madrid front, in its uncensored paper, had called for direct resistance to Giral's proposal.) Now Caballero put his prestige behind the Giral plans. The conscription decrees followed the traditional forms, gave no place to soldiers' committees. That meant reviving the bourgeois army, with supreme power in the hands of a military caste.

Freedom for Morocco? Delegations of Arabs and Moors came to the government, pleading for a decree. The government would not budge. The redoubtable Abd-el-Krim, exiled by France, sent a plea to Caballero to intervene with Blum so that he might be permitted to return to Morocco to lead an insurrection against Franco. Caballero would not ask, and Blum would not grant. To rouse Spanish Morocco might endanger imperialist domination throughout Africa.

Thus Caballero and his Stalinist allies set their faces as flint against revolutionary methods of struggle against fascism. In due time, at the end of October, came their reward: a modicum of army supplies from Stalin. In the ensuing months, came more supplies, particularly after great defeats: after the encirclement of Madrid, after the fall of Málaga, after the fall of Bilbao, supplies enough to save the Loyalists for the moment, but never enough to permit them to carry through a really sustained offensive which might lead to the total collapse of Franco.

What was the political logic behind this careful turning-off-and-on of the spigot of supplies? If it were a question of Soviet Russia's limited resources, that still does not explain, for example, why all the planes that were to go to Spain could not have been massed for a decisive struggle in one period. The explanation of the spigot is not technical but political. Enough was given to prevent early defeat of the Loyalists and the consequent collapse of Soviet prestige in the international working class. And this fitted in, at bottom, with Anglo-French policy, which did not desire an immediate Franco victory. But not enough was given to facilitate a victorious conclusion from which might issue—once the spectre of Franco was gone—a Soviet Spain.

Such was the program of the "provisional revolutionary government" of Caballero. Nothing was added or subtracted from it with the entry of the CNT ministers on November 4, 1936. By then the "great democracies" had had an opportunity, observing the CNT in the Catalonian government formed on September 26, to be reassured about the "responsibility" of these anarchists.

There was one troublesome point: the anarchist-controlled Council of Defense of Aragon, comprising the territory wrested from the fascists by the Catalonian militias on the Aragon front, had a fearsome reputation as an arch-revolutionary body. The price of four cabinet seats for the CNT was some reassurance on Aragon. Accordingly, on October 31, the Aragon Council met with Caballero. "The object of our visit," declared the Council's president, Joaquim Ascaso, "has been to pay our respects to the head of the government and to assure him of our attachment to the government of the people. We are disposed to accept all the laws it passes and we, in our turn, ask the Minister for all the help we need. The Aragon Council is formed of elements from the Popular Front so that all the forces upholding the government are represented in it." "Interviews with President Azaña, with President Companys, and with Largo Caballero," added a Generalidad statement of November 4, "have destroyed any suspicions that might have arisen that the government which has been constituted [in Aragon] was of an extremist character, unrelated to the other governmental organs of the republic and opposed to the government of Catalonia." That day the anarchists took their seats in Caballero's cabinet.

# 7

## The program of the
## Catalonian coalition government

On September 7, 1936, in a speech criticizing the Madrid coalition with the bourgeoisie, Nin had raised the slogan: "Down with the bourgeois ministers," and the crowd had gone wild with enthusiasm. But by September 18, *Batalla* published a resolution of the Central Committee of the POUM, accepting coalitionism:

> The Central Committee believes now, as always, that this government must be exclusively composed of representatives of the workers' parties and trade union organizations. But if this point of view is not shared by the other workers' organizations, we are willing to leave the question open, the more especially as the [Catalonian] left republican movement is of a profoundly popular nature—which distinguishes it radically from the Spanish left republican movement—and the peasant masses and workers' sections on which it is based are moving definitely toward the revolution, influenced by the proletarian parties and organizations. The important thing is the program, and the hegemony of the proletariat, which must be guaranteed. On one point there can be no doubt: the new government must make a declaration of

unquestionable principles, affirming its intention of turning the impulse of the masses into revolutionary legality, and directing it in the sense of the socialist revolution. As for proletarian hegemony, the absolute majority of workers' representatives will make it fully certain.

The *Esquerra* leadership, hardened bourgeois politicians of twenty–thirty years' struggle against the proletariat, was thus transformed overnight by the POUM into a movement "of a profoundly popular nature." And to this piece of legerdemain the POUM added the hitherto unknown principle of strategy, that the way to win the leftward-moving workers and peasants in the Esquerra was by collaborating in a government with their bourgeois leaders!

"The working class cannot simply lay hold of the ready-made state machinery and wield it for its own purposes," declared Marx. This was the great lesson learned from the Paris Commune: "not, as in the past, to transfer the bureaucratic and military machinery from one hand to the other, *but to break it up;* and that is the precondition of any real people's revolution on the Continent. And this is what our heroic party comrades in Paris have attempted." What is to replace the shattered state machinery? On this, the fundamental question of revolution, the meagre experience of the Commune was fully developed by Lenin and Trotsky. Parliamentarism was to be destroyed. In its place rise the workers' committees in the factories, the peasants' committees on the land, the soldiers' committees in the army, centralized in local, regional and, finally, the national soviets. Thus, the new state, a workers' state, is based on industrial representation, which automatically disfranchises the bourgeoisie, except as, after the consolidation of workers' power, they individually enter productive labor and are permitted to participate in electing the soviets. Between the old bourgeois state and the new workers' state lies a chasm over which the bourgeoisie cannot return to power except by overthrowing the workers' state.

It was this fundamental tenet, the essence of the accumulated experience of a century of revolutionary struggle, which the POUM violated in entering the Generalidad.* They received their ministry from the hands of President Companys. The new cabinet merely continued the work of the old and, like the old, could be dismissed and replaced by a more reactionary one. Behind the protective covering of the POUM-CNT-PSUC-Esquerra cabinet, the bourgeoisie would weather the revolutionary offensive, gather its shattered forces, and, with the aid of the reformists, at the ripe moment, return to full power. To this end, it was not even necessary for the bourgeoisie to participate in the cabinet. There had been "all-workers" cabinets in Germany, Austria, England, which had thus enabled the bourgeoisie to weather critical situations, and then kick out the workers' ministers.

The workers' state, the dictatorship of the proletariat, cannot exist until the old bourgeois state is destroyed. It can only be brought into existence by the direct, *political* intervention of the masses, through the factory and village councils (soviets) at that point where a majority in the soviets is wielded by the workers' party or parties which are determined to overthrow the bourgeois state. Such was the basic theoretical contribution of Lenin. Precisely this conception, however, was bowdlerized by the POUM. The same speech of Nin calling for the dismissal of the bourgeois ministers developed a conception which could only lead to preservation of the bourgeois state:

> Dictatorship of the proletariat. Another conception which is an object of difference with the anarchists. The proletarian dictatorship means the authority exercised by the working class. In Catalonia we can affirm that the dictatorship of the proletariat already exists. (Applause) . . . Not many days ago the FAI launched a manifesto which said that it would oppose all dictatorships exercised by whatever party. We are in agreement with

---

* Those who defended this violation—Lovestoneites, Norman Thomas socialists, I.L.P. etc.—thereby indicate their own future conduct in the revolutionary crisis.

them. The dictatorship of the proletariat cannot be exercised by one single sector of the proletariat, but by all, absolutely all. No workers' party or union center has the right to exercise a dictatorship. Let those present know that if the CNT or the Communist Party or the Socialist Party would wish to exercise a dictatorship of a party it would confront us. The dictatorship of the proletariat must be exercised by all. (*La Batalla*, September 8, 1936.)

For the dictatorship of the proletariat, as a state form, resting on the broad foundations of the network of workers', peasants' and combatants' councils throughout industry, the land and the fields of battle, Nin was here substituting an entirely different conception: an agreement among the top-leaderships of the workers' organizations jointly to assume governmental responsibility. False, and having nothing whatever in common with the Marxist conception of proletarian dictatorship! How could the proletarian dictatorship be wielded jointly with the Stalinist-democrats and the social democrats who stood for bourgeois democracy? How could party agreements be the substitute for the necessary vast network of workers' councils?

The Leninist prediction that every real revolution gives rise to organs of dual power had been confirmed on July 19: the militia committees, supply committees, workers' patrols, etc., etc. Leninist strategy called for the centralization of these organs of dual power into a national center, and the taking of state power through it. The dissolution of the organs of dual power, as in Germany 1919, was called by Lenin, "the liquidation of the revolution."

Uneasy memories of this led the POUM leaders, in announcing entry into the Generalidad, to end:

> We are in a transition state in which the force of events has obliged us to collaborate directly in the Council of the Generalidad, along with other workers' organizations. . . . From the committees of workers, peasants and soldiers, for the formation of which we

are pressing, will spring the direct representation of the new proletarian power.

But this was the last swan song of the committees of dual power.
For one of the first steps taken by the new cabinet of the Generalidad
was to *dissolve all the revolutionary committees which arose on July 19.*
The Central Committee of the Militias was dissolved and its powers turned over to the Ministries of Defense and Internal Security.
The local militia and anti-fascist committees, almost invariably proletarian in composition, which had been ruling the towns and villages, were dissolved and replaced by municipal administrations
composed in the same proportion as the cabinet (Esquerra 3, CNT
3, PSUC 2, Peasants Union, POUM, and Accio Catala, the right-
wing bourgeois organization, 1 each). Then to make sure that no
revolutionary organ had been overlooked, an additional decree was
passed which deserves full quotation:

> *Article* 1. There are dissolved in all Catalonia the local com-
> mittees, whatever be the name or title they bear, as well as all those
> local organisms which may have risen to down the subversive
> movement, with cultural, economic or any other species of aims.
> *Article* 2. Resistance to dissolving them will be considered as
> a fascist act and its instigators delivered to the Tribunals of Popu-
> lar Justice. (Decreed October 9, 1936.)

The dissolution of the committees marked the first great advance
of the counter-revolution. It removed the nascent soviet danger and
enabled the bourgeois state to begin retrieving in every sphere the
power which had fallen from its hands on July 19. Completely disoriented, the POUM made no attempt to harmonize its previous
call for committees with its sanction for their dissolution two weeks
later. On the other hand, there remained in the hands of the bourgeoisie its traditional lever, the parliament. For the POUM did not
even get, in return for participation in the government, a decree
dissolving the parliament. On the contrary, the financial decrees of

the new cabinet carried the usual article requiring an accounting to the Catalan parliament. Parliament is dead, the POUM assured the workers, but the government it sat in did not say so. True, unlike Caballero, Companys dared not convene parliament for many months, but this legal instrument of bourgeois domination remained intact. The meeting of the parliamentary deputation on April 9, 1937, during a ministerial crisis, scared the CNT back into the government. And after the May days, having defeated the workers, Companys convened the parliament which the POUM had sworn was dead!

One more important step for consolidating the power of the bourgeoisie state was carried out on October 27, 1936: a decree disarming the workers:

> *Article* 1. All long arms [e.g. rifles, machine guns, etc.] to be found in the hands of citizens shall be delivered to the municipalities or recovered by them, in a period of eight days after publication of this decree. Such arms shall be deposited in the Artillery Headquarters and the Ministry of Defense in Barcelona, in order to take care of the needs of the front.
>
> *Article* 2. At the end of the cited period those who retain such armament will be considered as fascists and judged with the rigor which their conduct deserves. (*La Batalla*, October 28, 1936.)

The POUM and CNT published this decree without a single word of explanation to their following!

Thus the salvation of the bourgeois state was achieved. The POUM, having been utilized during the critical months, was kicked out of the government in a cabinet reorganization, December 12, 1936. The CNT with its great following was utilized longer, particularly since it increasingly adapted itself to the domination of the bourgeoisie, and was, therefore, kicked out only in July of the next year. But the power which the POUM and CNT had enabled the government to arrogate to itself remained in the government's hands.

## The economic program of the coalition

Apart from the "workers majority," the POUM justified entry because of the "socialist orientation" of the government's economic program. This criterion was utterly false, for revolutionary Marxism has always made clear that the necessary precondition to socialist economics is the dictatorship of the proletariat.

The Bolsheviks in 1917 were even prepared, on the basis of a workers' state, to permit the continued existence, for a period, of private industry in certain fields, modified by workers' control of production. Precisely in those fields of economic life in which the Bolsheviks acted first, however, the Catalan coalition did not act: nationalization of the banks and of the land.

Finance capital, even in backward Spain as elsewhere, dominates all other forms of capital. Yet, all that the coalition agreed to, in point 8 of its economic program, was: "Workers' control of banking enterprises until arriving at the nationalization of banking." "Workers' control" in practice meant merely guarding against disbursements of funds to fascist sympathizers and unauthorized persons. "Until" put off nationalization of banking indefinitely—nothing was ever done about it. This vast lever meant, as the next months proved, that the collectivized industries were at the mercy of those who could withhold credits. Precisely through this means, the bourgeois state, month by month, was to whittle down the economic power of the working class.

The Bolsheviks had *nationalized* the land and granted control of it to the local soviets: that meant *the end of private property in land*. The peasant need not enter the collectives; he was, however, no longer able to buy and sell land, and no creditor could seize it.[*]

The "radical" Catalan program, "the collectivization of great rural properties and respect for small agrarian property," concealed a

---

[*] Louis Fischer, with ignorance fortified by impudence, argues against the Spanish collectives that in Russia collectivization came many years after the revolution. He leaves out the little "detail" that Lenin's first decree was the nationalization of the land and the end of private property in land.

reactionary perspective: land could still be bought and sold. Even more important: according to the Catalan autonomy statute, the central government had the last word on economic questions involving all Spain, and it had only authorized seizure of *fascist-owned estates.* The coalition "ignored" the discrepancy between the two decrees. The POUM did not have sense enough to bring the discrepancy out into the open and force the central government to formally recognize the Catalan decree, or have the Generalidad declare its full autonomy in economic questions. That meant: once the bourgeoisie recovered its strength, the Madrid decree on the land would prevail.

On October 24, a long and intricate decree was promulgated, concretizing the government's conception of "collectivization of the great industries, public services and transport." Before entry into the government, the POUM had criticized industrial "collectivization," pointing out that the unions, and even the workers in individual factories, were treating them as their own property. "Syndicalist capitalism" was making of the factories merely a form of producers' cooperatives, in which the workers divided the profits. But industry could be run efficiently only as a national entity, together with all banking facilities and a monopoly of foreign trade. Now the POUM accepted "collectivization," which was nothing more than producers' cooperatives, though real planning was impossible without banking and trade monopolies. The "control of foreign trade" which was promised never materialized. The POUM's proposal to include in the decree an "Industrial and Credit Bank of Catalonia to attend to the needs and requirements of collectivized industry," was rejected. Thus, the foundations were laid for cutting to pieces the industries seized by the workers.

Another deadly blow to the "collectivized" factories was the arrangement for compensation to their former owners. Contrary to popular thought, the question of compensation for confiscated property is not excluded in advance for revolutionary Marxists. If the bourgeoisie would not resist, Lenin offered to arrange for partial compensation. The POUM correctly concluded that the Spanish bourgeoisie had either gone over to Franco already or were—those in the Loyalist area—in no position except "opportunity to work, or if unable to work, social insurance, under the same conditions as other workers." (The question of compensation to foreign capitalists was not at issue, since all correctly agreed this had to be recognized; but under cover of this abstractly correct formula, the government was soon to "compensate" foreigners—by giving them back their factories!) The rest of the coalition, including the anarchists, rejected the POUM proposal. Nor did they arrange for definite norms of compensation. Nor did compensation—as it did in the case of foreign capital—rest on the government. Instead, "the inventoried credit balance of any firm" would "be placed at the credit of the beneficiary [former owner] 'as a social compensation'," and "the compensation for Spanish owners shall be suspended for later determination." In plain English, this meant that compensation would be a charge on the collectivized enterprise, i.e., on the workers involved, and the amount of it was left for a later time; with the re-construction of the bourgeois power, the bourgeoisie would levy against the workers' enterprises in favor of the former owners on the sole criterion of how far the bourgeoisie dared saddle the workers with enforced payments of interest on capital debt. If the government grew strong enough, the former owners would go on clipping their coupons and receiving their dividends, just as before. The POUM correctly termed this question "fundamental"; but stayed in the coalition government, nevertheless.

The collectivization decree provided for intervention in each factory of a government agent as part of the Factory Council. In all enterprises employing over 500, its director had to be approved by the government. Once elected by the workers in the factory, the Factory Council remained for two years in office, except for outright dereliction of duty, thus "freezing" the political composition of the councils and making it impossible for a revolutionary party to win control of the factories. The General Councils, embracing a whole industry, were even less flexible, eight out of twelve members being appointed by the leaders of the UGT and CNT, and presided over by representatives of the government. These measures, ensuring no "revolt from below," were approved by all, including the POUM.

Is it not obvious that the economic program of the Generalidad merely accepted some of the gains already made by the workers themselves, and combined them with a series of political and economic measures which would eventually wipe out those gains? Yet, for this and a seat in the cabinet, the POUM sold its chance to lead the Spanish revolution. By its blanket acceptance of the governmental program, the CNT revealed the complete bankruptcy of anarchism as a road to the social revolution.[*]

### International policy of the coalition

Like their counterparts in Madrid, the Esquerra and PSUC looked to the League of Nations and the "great democracies" for succor. Nor was the CNT much better. Juan Peiró, after the fall of the Caballero government, naively declared that the CNT had been assured that the moderate government program was meant for foreign consumption only.[†]

This undoubtedly explains why the CNT sent no organized delegations abroad to campaign among the workers.

The POUM too fell victim to this opportunist policy. Despite its abstractly correct understanding of the reactionary international rôle of the Soviet bureaucracy, and its criticism of the failure of Stalin to sell arms to Spain during the first three crucial months, the POUM failed to understand the fact that the Soviet note of

---

[*] After the May days the Generalidad repudiated the legality of the decree collectivizing industry.

[†] ". . . the International bourgeoisie refused to supply us with those requirements (arms). It was a tragic moment: we had to create the impression that the masters were not the revolutionary committees but rather the legal government; failing that, we should not have received anything at all. . . . We must needs adapt ourselves to the inexorable circumstances of the moment, that is to say, accept governmental collaboration . . ." (Garcia Oliver, ex-Minister of Justice, speech in Paris, text published by the anarchist *Spain and the World*, July 2, 1937)

"Spain offers all liberal and democratic nations of the world the opportunity

October 7, 1936—"if violation is not halted immediately, it will consider itself free from any obligation resulting from the agreement"—did not mean leaving the non-intervention committee, and in no sense guaranteed sufficient arms shipments to turn the tide. "There is no doubt that the recent step of the Soviet Government in breaking the non-intervention pact will be of extraordinary political consequence. It is probably the most important political event since the commencement of the civil war," said *La Batalla*. Even worse, the POUM's perspective was that French imperialism would send arms: "How will the French Government reply to this new situation? Will it keep its attitude of neutrality? This would mean utter unpopularity and discredit. Blum would fall from power in the midst of general condemnation. . . . We do not believe that Léon Blum would commit such a colossal blunder. Seeing that the only obstacle in the way of the correction of his policy was the Soviet Government's attitude, the change in the latter should determine a complete change in Blum's policy." (*La Batalla*, October 11, 1936.) Here, as everywhere, the POUM had lost its bearings. It is not accidental that during its ministerial months, it sent no delegations abroad to campaign among the advanced workers.

---

of undertaking a strong offensive against the fascist forces, and if this means war, they must accept it before it is too late. They must not wait until fascism has perfected its war machine." (Official English Edition No. 107, Dec. 8, 1936, Generalidad Commissariat of Propaganda) Federica Montseny (outstanding CNT leader): "I believe that a people of such great intelligence (England) will realize that the establishment of a fascist state to the south of France . . . would be directly against its interests. The fate of the world as well as the outcome of this war depends on England . . ." (Ibid, No. 108, Dec. 10, 1936.)

# 8

# Revival of the bourgeois state

September 1936–April 1937

The economic counter-revolution

The eight months after the workers' representatives entered the Madrid and Barcelona cabinets saw the proletarian conquests in the economic field slowly whittled down. Controlling the treasury and the banks, the government was able to force its will on the workers by the threat of withdrawing credits.

In Catalonia, the chief industrial center, the process moved more slowly but to the same end. Some fifty-eight financial decrees of the Generalidad in January sharply restricted the scope of activity of the collectivized factories. On February 3, for the first time, the Generalidad dared decree illegal the collectivization of an industry— dairy products. During the April ministerial crisis, the Generalidad annulled workers' control over the customs by refusing to certify workers' ownership of material that had been exported and was being tied up in foreign courts by suits of former owners; henceforth the factories and agricultural collectives exporting goods were at the mercy of the government.

Comorera, PSUC chieftain, had taken over the Ministry of Supplies on December 15, when the POUM was ousted from the cabinet. On January 7, he decreed dissolution of the workers' supply committees which had been purchasing food from the peasants. Into this breach poured the speculators and traders of the GEPCI (Corporation and Units of Petty Merchants and Manufacturers)— holding UGT cards!—and the resultant hoarding and rise of food prices led to widespread malnutrition. Each family received ration cards but supplies were not rationed according to the number of persons served by each depot. In the workers' suburbs of Barcelona long queues stood throughout the day, supplies often exhausted before the end of the queues was reached, while in the bourgeois districts there was plenty. The privately owned restaurants had ample supplies for those who could pay the price. Milk was unobtainable for workers' children but purchasable in the restaurants. Though bread (at a fixed price) was often not to be had, cake (price uncontrolled) was always to be bought. On the sixth anniversary of the republic (April 14, boycotted by FAI, CNT, and POUM), the Esquerra and Stalinist demonstrations were overshadowed by women's demonstrations against the food prices. Yet the Stalinists put to political use even their crimes. The masses were given to understand that PSUC and UGT membership would get them better rations. Anonymous stickers blamed the collectivized farms and transportation for the price rises.

Vicente Uribe, Stalinist Minister of Agriculture, played the same rôle here as a Stalinist minister of agriculture had played in the Wang Ching-wei régime of 1927, in Wuhan, in fighting the peasants. Uribe's department dismantled collectives, organized former landowners to whom their lands were returned as state "co-administrators," prevented the collectives from selling their produce without the use of middlemen.

A national campaign for "state control" and "municipalization" of industry laid the basis for wresting all control from the factory committees.

The economic counter-revolution proceeded, however, comparatively slowly. For the bourgeois-Stalinist bloc understood, as the anarchists did not, that the necessary pre-condition for destroying the workers' economic conquests was the crushing of the workers' militias and police, and the disarming of the workers in the rearguard. But force alone was insufficient to achieve this end. Force had to be combined with propaganda.

## Censorship

To facilitate the success of their own propaganda, the bourgeois-reformist bloc resorted, through the government, to systematic curtailment of the CNT-FAI-POUM press and radio.

The POUM was the chief victim. While it was still in the Generalidad, the Catalan *Hoja Official* boycotted all mention of POUM meetings and radio broadcasts. On February 26, the Generalidad forbade a CNT-POUM mass meeting in Tarragona. On March 5, *La Batalla* was fined 5,000 pesetas and refused a bill of particulars on the charge of disobeying the military censor. On March 14, *Batalla* was suspended for four days, this time openly for a political editorial. At the same time the Generalidad refused to the POUM use of the official radio station for broadcasts. The POUM dailies in Lerida, Gerona, etc., were constantly harassed.

The deadliest blows to the POUM in this period, however, were delivered outside Catalonia. The Stalinist-controlled Madrid Defense Junta in January permanently suspended *POUM,* a weekly. The same authority suspended and confiscated the presses of *El Combatiente Rojo,* POUM militia daily, on February 10, and shortly thereafter suspended the POUM radio station, closing it permanently in April. The Junta also refused to permit the POUM Youth (Juventud Comunista Iberica) to publish *La Antorcha,* the official prohibition cynically stating that "the JCI needs no press." *Juventud Roja,* Valencian POUM Youth organ, was submitted to severe political censorship in March. The only POUM organ untouched was *El Comunista* of Valencia, weekly organ of the ferociously anti-Trotskyist, half-Stalinist right wing.

Another important field of work among the masses was closed to the POUM when the POUM Red Aid was excluded at the demand of the PSUC from the Permanent Committee of Aid for

Madrid. The CNT, in the name of unity, agreed to this criminal act, which became national in scope in April, when the POUM Red Aid was excluded from participating in Madrid Week.

This sketchy outline of governmental outlawry of POUM activities *before May* conclusively refutes the Stalinist claim that the POUM was persecuted for its participation in the May events.

The censorship against the POUM was carried out by cabinets in which sat CNT ministers. Only the Anarchist Youth, Juventud Libertaria, publicly protested. But the CNT press also was systematically harassed. Does history record another instance of cabinet ministers submitting to repression of their own press?

The FAI daily, *Nosotros* of Valencia, was suspended indefinitely on February 27 for an article attacking Caballero's war policy. On March 26, the Basque Government suspended *CNT del Norte,* arrested the editorial staff and the CNT Regional Committee—and gave the presses to the Basque Communist party. Various issues of *CNT* and *Castilla Libre,* both of Madrid, were suppressed April 11–18. *Nosotros* was again suspended on April 16.

Censorship and suspension were formal measures. At least equally efficacious were the "informal" measures whereby the CNT-FAI-POUM newspaper packets "failed" to arrive at the front or arrived weeks late. Meanwhile enormous editions of the Stalinist and bourgeois press, untouched by the censor and always delivered, were distributed free to the CNT, UGT and POUM militias. The government radio stations were always at the service of the Nelkens and Pasionarias. Almost all the so-called political commissioners at the front were Stalinists and bourgeois. Thus deceit supplemented naked force.

### The police

In the first months after July 19, police duties were almost entirely in the hands of the workers' patrols in Catalonia and the "militias of the rearguard" in Madrid and Valencia. But the opportunity permanently to dissolve the bourgeois police slipped by.

Under Caballero, the Civil Guard was re-christened the National

Republican Guard. The remnants of this and the Assault Guards were gradually withdrawn from the front. Those who had gone over to Franco were more than replaced by new men.

The most extraordinary step in reviving the bourgeois police was the mushroom growth of the hitherto small customs force, the Carabineros, under Finance Minister Negrin, into a heavily armed pretorian guard of 40,000.[*]

On February 28, the Carabineros were forbidden to belong to a political party or a trade union or to attend their mass meetings. The same decree was extended to the Civil and Assault Guards thereafter. That meant quarantining the police against the working class. The hopelessly disoriented anarchist ministers voted for this measure on the ground that it would stop Stalinist proselytizing!

By April the militias were finally pushed out of all police duties in Madrid and Valencia.

In the proletarian stronghold of Catalonia, this process ran into the determined opposition of the CNT masses. There was also an "unfortunate incident" which slowed up the bourgeois scheme. The first Chief of Police for all Catalonia, appointed by the cabinet—Andre Reberter—proved to be one of the ringleaders in a plot to assassinate the CNT leaders, establish an independent Catalonia and make a separate peace with Franco.[†] Its exposure strengthened the position of the workers' patrols, largely manned by the CNT.

---

[*] "A reliable police force is being built up quietly but surely. The Valencia government discovered an ideal instrument for this purpose in the Carabineros. These were formerly customs officers and guards, and always had a good reputation for loyalty. It is reported on good authority that 40,000 have been recruited for this force, and that 20,000 have already been armed and equipped . . . The anarchists have already noticed and complained about the increased strength of this force at a time when we all know there's little enough traffic coming over the frontiers, land or sea. They realize that it will be used against them." (James Minifie, New York *Herald Tribune,* April 28, 1937.)

[†] CNT's intelligence service had discovered the plot and *Solidaridad Obrera* published the facts on November 27 and 28. At first it was scoffed at by the Stalinists and the Esquerra; but they were forced to order an investigation. As a result, it was

But then the patrols were attacked from within. The PSUC ordered its members to withdraw (most of them did not, and were expelled from the PSUC). The Esquerra also withdrew from the patrols. Thereafter all the usual Stalinist methods of defamation were directed at the patrols, loudest when the patrols arrested PSUC and GEPCI businessmen for hoarding and profiteering on food.

On March 1, a Generalidad decree unified all police into a single state-controlled corps, its members prohibited from association with trade unions and parties and to be chosen by seniority. This meant abolition of the workers' patrols and the barring of their members from the unified police. Apparently the CNT ministers voted for the decree. But the resultant outcry of the Catalan masses led the CNT to join the POUM in declaring they would refuse to submit to it. On March 15, nevertheless, the Minister of Public Order, Jaime Ayguade, attempted unsuccessfully to suppress forcibly workers' patrols in the outlying districts of Barcelona. This question was one of those leading to the dissolution of the Catalan cabinet on March 27. But there was no change when the new cabinet, again with CNT ministers, convened on April 16. Ayguade continued his attempts to disarm the patrols, while the CNT ministers sat in the cabinet, their papers contenting themselves with warning the workers against provocation.

## Liquidation of the militias

There could, of course, be no hope of reviving a stable bourgeois régime so long as the organization and administrative responsibility for the armed forces was in the hands of the unions and workers' parties, which presented payrolls, requisitions, etc., to the Madrid

---

found that the chief forces in the plot were those of the separatist *Estat Catala*, a khaki-shirt organization, a split-off from the Esquerra, and its secretary-general and over a hundred leading members were arrested. Chief of Police Reberter, *Estat Catala* member, was executed upon conviction. Casanovas, President of the Catalan Parliament, "at first toyed with the plot, then rejected it," said an official explanation. Casanovas was permitted to go to France—and to return to political life in Barcelona after the May days!

and Catalan governments, and stood between the militias and the governments.

The Stalinists early sought to set an "example" by handing their militias over to government control, helping to institute the salute, supremacy of officers behind the lines, etc. "No discussion, no politics in the army," cried the Stalinist press, meaning of course no working-class discussion or politics.

The example was wasted on the CNT masses. At least a third of the armed forces were CNT members, suspicious of the officers sent by the government, relegating them to the status of "technicians" and barring them from interfering in the social and political life of the militias. The POUM had 10,000 militiamen who acted likewise. The POUM reprinted for distribution in the militias the original Red Army Manual of Trotsky, providing for a democratic internal régime and political life in the army. The Stalinist campaign for wiping out the internal democratic life of the militias, under the slogan of "unified command," was countered by the simple and unanswerable question: why does a unified command necessitate reestablishing the old barracks régime and the supremacy of a bourgeois officer caste?

But the government eventually had its way. The militarization and mobilization decrees passed in September and October with CNT and POUM consent provided conscription of regular regiments ruled by the old military code. Systematic selection of candidates for the officers' schools gave preponderance to the bourgeoisie and Stalinists, and these manned the new regiments.

When the first drafts of the new army were ready and sent to the front, the government pitted them against the militias, demanding reorganization of the militias in a similar mold. By March the government had largely succeeded on the Stalinist-controlled Madrid front. On the Aragon and Levante fronts, manned chiefly by CNT-FAI and POUM militias, the government prepared the liquidation of the militias by a ruthless, systematic policy of withholding arms. Only after reorganization, the militias were informed, would they be given adequate arms for an offensive on these fronts. Yet the sheer mass of the CNT militias prevented the government from attaining its objectives until after the May days, when Azaña's ex-Minister of War, General Pozas, took over the Aragon front.

In the last analysis, however, the government's final success came not from its own efforts so much as from the politically false character of the CNT-POUM demand for a "unified command under control of the workers' organizations."

The Stalinists and their "non-party" publicists of the stripe of Louis Fischer and Ralph Bates have deliberately perverted the facts of the controversy between the POUM-CNT and the government on army reorganization. The Stalinists make it appear that the POUM-CNT wanted to retain the loosely organized militias as against an efficiently centralized army. This is a lie made out of whole cloth, as may be demonstrated by a thousand articles in the POUM-CNT press of the time calling for a disciplined army under unified command. The real issue was: who will control the army? Bourgeoisie or working class? Nor did the POUM-CNT alone raise this question. In opposing Giral's original scheme for a special army, the UGT organ, Claridad, had declared: We "must take care that the masses and the leadership of the armed forces, which should be above all the people in arms, should not escape from our hands." (August 20, 1936)

That was the real issue. The bourgeoisie won out because the UGT, POUM, and CNT-FAI made the hopeless error of seeking a proletarian-controlled army within a bourgeois state. So much were they for centralization and unified command that they voted for the governmental decrees which in the ensuing months served to wipe out all workers' control of the army. UGT, POUM, and CNT consent to these decrees was not the least of their crimes against the working class.

Their slogan for a unified command under control of the workers' organizations was false because it provided no method of achieving that goal. The demand which should have been raised, from the first day of the war, was for amalgamation of all the militias and the few existent regiments into a single force, with democratic election of soldiers' committees in each unit, centralized in a national election of soldiers' delegates to a national council. As new regiments were conscripted, their soldiers' committees would have entered the local and national councils. Thus, in drawing the armed masses into daily political life, bourgeois control of the armed forces could have been effectively prevented.

The POUM had a wonderful opportunity to demonstrate the efficacy of this method. On the Aragon front it had for eight months direct organizational control over some 9,000 militiamen. It had an unparalleled opportunity to educate them politically, to elect soldiers' committees among them as an example to the rest of the militias, then to demand amalgamation in which its trained forces would have been a powerful leaven. *Nothing* was done. The POUM press carried stories of representatives of the Aragon front meeting in congress. These meetings were nothing but gatherings of appointees of the national office. In fact, the POUM *forbade* election of soldiers' committees. Why? Among other reasons was the fact that opposition to the POUM's opportunist politics was rife in the ranks and the bureaucracy feared that creation of the committees would provide the necessary arena in which the Left Opposition might conquer.

The simple, concrete slogan of elected soldiers' committees was the only road for securing proletarian control of the army. This slogan, moreover, could only be a *transitional step*. For a worker-controlled army could not exist indefinitely side by side with the bourgeois state. If the bourgeois state continued to exist, it would inevitably destroy workers' control of the army.

The POUM-CNT-UGT proponents of workers' control raised neither the concrete slogan nor had they any program for displacing the bourgeois state. Their basic orientation, therefore, doomed to impotence their opposition to bourgeois domination of the army.

### Disarming of the workers in the rear

In the revolutionary days following July 19, the Madrid and Catalan governments had perforce sanctioned the arming of the workers who had already armed themselves. Workers' organizations were empowered to issue arms permits to their members. For the workers it was not only a question of guarding against the counter-revolutionary attempts of the government, but the daily necessity of protecting the peasants' committees against reactionaries, guarding the factories, railroads, bridges, etc., against fascist bands, protecting the coast from raids, ferreting out hidden fascist nests.

In October came the first disarming decree providing for delivery of all rifles and machine guns to the government. In practice, it was interpreted to allow the workers' organizations to continue issuing permits for long arms to industrial guards and peasant committees. But it set the fatal precedent.

On February 15, the central government ordered the collection of *all* long arms as well as all small arms not held by permission. On March 12, the cabinet ordered the workers' organizations to collect large *and* small arms from their members and to surrender them within forty-eight hours. This order was applied directly to Catalonia on April 17. National Republican Guards began officially to disarm workers on sight in the streets of Barcelona. Three hundred workers—CNT members holding organization permits—were thus disarmed by police during the last week in April.

The pretext that the arms were needed at the front was a barefaced lie, as any worker could see with his own eyes. For while the workers were being deprived of rifles and revolvers, some of them in the possession of the CNT since the days of the monarchy, the cities were being filled with the rebuilt police forces, armed to the teeth with new Russian rifles, machine guns, artillery, and armored cars.

## Extra-legal methods of repression: The Spanish G.P.U.

On December 17, 1936, *Pravda,* Stalin's personal organ, declared: "As for Catalonia, the purging of the Trotskyists and the Anarcho-Syndicalists has begun; it will be conducted with the same energy with which it was conducted in the U.S.S.R."

The "legal methods," however, moved too slowly. They were

supplemented by organized terrorist bands, equipped with private prisons and torture chambers, termed "preventoriums." The worthies recruited for this work beggar description: ex-members of the Fascist CEDA, Cuban gangsters, brothel-racketeers, passport forgers, sadists.[*] Spawned by the petty-bourgeois composition of the Communist party, nurtured by its counter-revolutionary program, these organized bands of the Spanish G.P.U. exhibited toward the workers the ferocity of Hitler's bloodhounds, for like them, they were trained to exterminate revolution.

Rodriguez, CNT member and Special Commissioner of Prisons, in April formally charged José Cazorla, Stalinist Central Committee member and Chief of Police under the Madrid Junta, and Santiago Carillo, another Central Committee member, of illegally seizing workers arrested by Cazorla but acquitted by the popular tribunals, and "taking said acquitted parties to secret jails or sending them into communist militia battalions in advanced positions to be used as 'fortifications.'" The CNT in vain demanded a formal investigation of its charges. Only when it was established that Cazorla's gang, as a side-line, was working with racketeers who were releasing important fascists from prison without official sanction,

---

[*] *Cultura Proletaria*, N.Y. anti-fascist paper, published a report from Cuba: "The C.P. . . . sent 27 ex-officers of the old army who have nothing in common with workers and are mercenaries formerly in Machado's service . . . On its last trip the 'Mexique' took an expedition of these fake militia (with a few exceptions), among them went the three Alvarez brothers, former Machado gunmen active in breaking the Bahia strike. On the 29th of this month . . . 'Sargento del Toro' sails, too, as a communist militiaman. He is a full-fledged assassin of the Machado days, bodyguard of the President of the Senate in that period. He was one of those who helped massacre workers in a demonstration here on August 27." The former Valencia Secretary of the CEDA is now in the C.P. Even Louis Fisher admits that "bourgeois generals and politicians, and many peasants who approve the C.P.'s policy of protecting small property holders have joined . . . essentially their new political affiliation reflects a despair of the old social system as well as a hope to salvage one or two of its remnants." An apt description, as Anita Brenner points out, of the social group which swelled Hitler's ranks. For further details on the Spanish G.P.U. and the repressions, see Anita Brenner's excellent article and "Dossier of Counter-revolution." *Modern Monthly*, September, 1937.

was Cazorla removed. He was simply replaced by Carrillo, another Stalinist, and the extra-legal G.P.U. and its private prisons continued as before.

"It is becoming clear that the Chekist* organizations recently discovered in Madrid . . . are directly linked with similar centers operating under a unified leadership and on a preconceived plan of national scope," wrote *Solidaridad Obrera* on April 25, 1937. On April 8, the CNT, armed with proofs, had finally forced the arrest of a gang of Stalinists in Murcia, and the removal of the civil governor for maintaining private prisons and torture chambers. On March 15, sixteen CNT members had been murdered by Stalinists in Villanueva de Alcardete in Toledo Province. The CNT demand for punishment was countered by *Mundo Obrero's* defense of the murderers as revolutionary anti-fascists. The subsequent judicial investigation established that an all-Stalinist gang, including the Communist party's mayors of Villanueva and Villamayor, operating as a "Defense Committee," had murdered political enemies, looted, levied tribute, and forcibly raped the defenseless women of the area. Five of the Stalinists were condemned to death, eight others sentenced to prison.

The organized gangsterism of the Spanish G.P.U. has been established in the Spanish Government's own courts of law. We limit ourselves here to juridically established instances. But the CNT press is filled with hundreds of instances in which the "legal" counter-revolution was supplemented by the G.P.U. in Spain.

---

* The anarchists refer to the G.P.U. In general, they blind themselves to the vast gulf between the "Cheka," which ruthlessly suppressed the White Guards and their associates in the early period of the Russian revolution, and the Stalinist G.P.U. which ruthlessly suppresses and assassinates proletarian revolutionists.

# 9

## The counter-revolution
## and the masses

It would be a libel on the socialist and anarchist-led masses to think that they were not alarmed by the advance of the counter-revolution. Discontent, however, is not enough. It is necessary also to know the way out. Without a firm, well-developed strategy for repelling the counter-revolution and leading the masses to state power, discontent can accumulate indefinitely and only issue in sporadic, desperate lunges which are doomed to defeat. In other words, the masses require a revolutionary leadership.

Especially in the ranks of the CNT and FAI the discontent was enormous. It seeped out in hundreds of articles and letters in the anarchist press. Though the anarchist ministers in Valencia and the Generalidad voted for the governmental decrees or submitted to them without public protest, their press did not dare defend the governmental policies directly. As governmental repressions increased, the pressure of the CNT workers on their leadership increased.

On March 27, the CNT ministers withdrew from the Catalonian government. The ensuing ministerial crisis lasted three whole weeks. "We cannot sacrifice the revolution to unity," declared the CNT press. "No more concessions to reformism." "Unity has been maintained until now on the basis of our concessions." "We can retreat no further."

Precisely what the CNT leadership now proposed, however, was a mystery. Companys neatly punctured their postures by a summary of the ministerial course since December, demonstrating that the CNT ministers had voted for everything—the disarming of the workers, the army mobilization and reorganization decrees, dissolution of the workers' patrols, etc. Stop this humbug and come back to work, Companys was saying. And as a matter of fact, the CNT ministers were ready to come back at the end of the first week. At this point, however, the Stalinists demanded a further capitulation: the organizations providing ministers should sign a joint declaration pledging themselves to carry out a stated series of tasks. The CNT ministers protested that the usual ministerial declaration after constituting the new cabinet would be sufficient—the Stalinist proposal would have left the CNT ministers absolutely naked before the masses. Thus the ministerial crisis dragged out two more weeks.

There then ensued a little by-play which amounted to nothing more than a division of labor, whereby the CNT leaders were bound more strongly than ever to the Generalidad. Companys assured the CNT that he agreed with them and not with the Stalinists, and offered his services to "force" the Stalinists to relinquish their demand. At the same time, Premier Tarradellas, Companys' lieutenant, defended the administration of the war industries (run by the CNT) against an attack in the PSUC organ, *Treball,* which he termed the "most arbitrary falsehoods." For these little services, the CNT abjectly gave Companys unconditional political support:

> We declare publicly that the CNT is to be found at the side of the President of the Generalidad, Luis Companys, whom we have accorded whatever facilities have been required for the solution of the political crisis. We stand by the president who, without any kind of servile praise—a proceeding incompatible with the morale of our revolutionary movement—knows that he can

count on our most profound respect and our most sincere support. (*Solidaridad Obrera,* April 15, 1937, p. 12.)

Companys, of course, managed to persuade the Stalinists to relinquish the demand for a pact, and on April 16, the ministerial crisis was "resolved." The new cabinet, like its predecessor, provided a majority for the bourgeoisie and the Stalinists, and, of course, differed in nothing from the previous one.

The masses of the CNT could not be so "flexible." They had a heroic tradition of struggle to the death against capitalism. Even more insistently, the revival of the bourgeois state was taking place on their backs. Inflation and the uncontrolled manipulation of prices by the businessmen "mediating" between the peasantry and the city masses now led to perpendicular price rises. In this period the rise of prices is the *leit-motif* of all activity. The press is full of the problem. The condition of the masses was growing daily more intolerable, and the CNT leaders showed them no way out.

Many voices now cried for a return to the traditional a-politicism of the CNT. "No More Governments!" Local CNT papers broke discipline and took up this refrain. It was counsel of unthinking despair.

Far more significant was the rise of the Friends of Durruti. In the name of the martyred leader, a movement rose which had assimilated the need for political life, but rejected collaboration with the bourgeoisie and reformists. The Friends of Durruti were organized to wrest leadership from the CNT bureaucracy. In the last days of April, they plastered Barcelona with their slogans—an open break with the CNT leadership. These slogans included the essential points of a revolutionary program: all power to the working class, and democratic organs of the workers, peasants and combatants, as the expression of the workers' power.

The Friends of Durruti represented a deep ferment in the libertarian movement. On April 1, a manifesto of the Libertarian Youth of Catalonia (*Ruta,* April 1, 1937) had denounced the "United Socialist Youth [Stalinists], who first assisted the revaluation of the

Azaña stock—fallen so low in the first days of the revolution when he tried to flee the country—and who called to the Unified Catholic Youth and even to those who were sympathetic to fascism;" stigmatized the bourgeois-Stalinist bloc as "supporting openly all the intentions of the English and French governments to encircle the Spanish revolution;" excoriated the counter-revolutionary assaults on the publishing houses and radio station of the POUM in Madrid. It pointed out that "arms are denied to the Aragon front because it is definitely revolutionary, in order to be able afterward to throw mud at the columns operating on that front"; "the Central Government boycotts Catalan economy in order to force us to renounce our revolutionary conquests"; "the sons of the people are sent to the front, but for counter-revolutionary ends the uniformed forces are being kept in the rear"; "they have gained ground for a dictatorship—not proletarian!—but bourgeois."

Clearly differentiating the Anarchist Youth from the CNT ministers, the manifesto concluded: "We are firmly decided not to be responsible for the crimes and betrayals of which the working class is being made the object. . . . We are ready to return, if that is necessary, to the underground struggle against the deceivers, against the tyrants of the people and the miserable merchants of politics." An editorial in the same issue of *Ruta* declared: "Let not certain comrades come to us with appeasing words. We shall not renounce our struggle. Official automobiles and the sedentary life of the bureaucracy do not dazzle us." This from the official organization of the anarchist youth!

Not in a day or a month, however, does a regroupment take place. The CNT had a long tradition and the discontent of its masses would evolve only at a slow pace into an organized struggle for a new leadership and a new program. Particularly was this true because no revolutionary party existed to encourage this development.

### The POUM's answer to the counter-revolution

An abyss was opening up between the CNT leaders and the masses within the CNT movement. Would the POUM step into the breach and place itself at the head of the militant masses?

The prevalence of a wide tendency in CNT ranks to go back to traditional a-politicism was an annihilating criticism of the POUM, which had done nothing to win these workers to revolutionary-political life. Also with no aid from the POUM leadership, a genuinely revolutionary current was crystallizing in the Friends of Durruti and the Libertarian Youth. If the POUM was ever to strike out independently of the CNT leadership, this was the moment!

The POUM did nothing of the sort. On the contrary, in the ministerial crisis of March 26–April 16, it revealed that it had learned nothing whatever from its earlier participation in the Generalidad. The Central Committee of the POUM adopted a resolution declaring:

> There is needed a government that would canalize the aspirations of the masses, giving a radical and concrete solution to all the problems by way of the creation of a new order that would be guarantor of the revolution and of the victory at the front. This Government can only be a government *formed by representatives of all the political and trade-union organizations of the working class* which would propose as immediate tasks the realization of the following program. (*La Batalla,* March 30.)

The proposed fifteen-point program is not a bad one—for a revolutionary government. But the absurdity of proposing it to a government which by definition includes the Stalinists and the Esquerra-controlled Union of Rabassaires (independent peasants) is indicated immediately by the last point on the program: the convocation of a congress of delegates of the unions, peasants, and combatants which will in turn elect a permanent workers' and peasants' government.

For six months the POUM had been saying that the Stalinists were organizing the counter-revolution. How, then, could the POUM propose to collaborate with them in the government and in convoking the congress? From this proposal the workers could only conclude that the POUM's characterization of the Stalinists had been so much factional talk, and would henceforth take no POUM charges against the Stalinists as being seriously meant.

And Companys and his Esquerra? A new cabinet must receive a mandate from Companys, and the POUM proposed no break with this law. Was it conceivable that Companys would agree to a government which would convoke such a congress? Here, too, the masses could only draw the conclusion that the POUM's declaration of the necessarily counter-revolutionary rôle of the Esquerra of Companys was not seriously meant.

As a matter of fact, the workers could not feel that the POUM attached fundamental importance to the congress. Much more important seemed the entry of the POUM into the Generalidad. *La Batalla* (March 30) published side by side two columns headed: "Balance of two periods of government." One, "the government in which the POUM participated"; the other, "the government in which the POUM did not participate." The government of September 26–December 12 is described lyrically as a period of revolutionary construction. Thus, the POUM still refused to understand how the government in which it had participated had taken the first giant steps in reviving the bourgeois state. From these tables, the worker could draw only one logical conclusion: all that was needed was that the POUM should be re-admitted into the government.

The POUM's proposal was indeed nothing but a shamefaced formulation for a return to the government of September 26. This is borne out by the POUM's *Adelante* of Lerida (April 13) which, more outspokenly, writes of a government in which the workers' organizations will have first place and the bourgeoisie second place. All the lessons of eight months had been lost upon the POUM leadership!

Let us look more closely at the POUM's proposed congress of delegates of unions, peasants, and combatants. It sounds "almost" like soviets; and indeed it was proposed precisely to delude the restless left wing of the POUM. But it has nothing whatever in common with the Leninist conception of soviets.

One must never forget—what the Stalinists have completely buried—that soviets *do not begin* as organs of state power. They arise in 1905, 1917, in Germany and Austria in 1918, rather as powerful strike committees and representatives of the masses in dealing with immediate concrete problems and with the government. Long before they can seize state power, they carry on as organs defending the workers' daily interests. Long before the workers', peasants' and soldiers' deputies have united in an all-national congress there must have been formed the city, village, regimental soviets which are later to be united in a national organ. The way to begin getting such a congress is to begin electing factory, peasants' and combatants' committees wherever the workers can be taught to function through their own committees. The example of a few committees in a few factories and regiments will win the masses to this form, the most democratic method of representation known to mankind. Then, only, can one organize an all-national congress in a bid for power.

At that point, moreover, the congress will inevitably be a reflection, even if a more accurate one than other organs, of the political level of the masses. If the Stalinist, anarchist, and other reformist organizations are still powerful, then the congress will reflect their political line. There is, in a word, no magic in the soviet form: it is merely the most accurate, most quickly reflecting and responsively changing form of political representation of the masses.

The mere convocation of the congress would not solve the basic political task of the POUM: *to wrest from the Stalinists and the anarchists the political leadership of a majority of the working class.* The congress would concentrate the political thoughts and yearnings of the masses as no other organ could. It would provide the arena in which the revolutionary party can win the support of the working class—but only in the sharpest struggle against the false political lines of the reformists of all varieties.

Were the POUM leadership serious about the proposed congress, it would not have asked the government to convoke it, but would immediately have sought election of committees wherever possible. But the POUM did not even elect such committees in the factories or militias under its own control. Its ten thousand militiamen were controlled bureaucratically by officials appointed by the Central Committee of the party, election of soldiers' committees being expressly forbidden. As the internal life of the party grew more intense, with the left wing workers demanding a new course, more and more bureaucratic became the control of the leadership over the factories and militiamen. Here was scarcely an example to inspire the workers elsewhere to create elective committees!

The soviet form bases itself directly on the factories, by direct representation from each factory in the localities. This provides direct contact with the factories, enabling the soviet through recall and new elections to renew itself and reduce the time-lag of political development to a minimum. This characteristic of soviets also enables the revolutionists to converse directly with the factories, without the intervention of the trade union bureaucrats. Yet, precisely in this basic characteristic, the congress proposed by the POUM differs from the soviet form: the POUM proposes representation of the *unions*. This was simply another concession to the prejudices of the CNT leadership, who conceive the unions, and not the far broader workers', peasants' and soldiers' soviets, as the governing form of industry in a socialist society and—incidentally!—object to the revolutionists reaching the workers in the factories.

Thus, the utopian project of the POUM was a fraud, a counterfeit, doomed to a paper existence—an empty concession to the left wing.

One seeks in vain, in the POUM documents, for a systematic defense of its opportunist course. One finds only a paragraph here and there, which may be presumed to be the germ of a new theory. For example, Nin appeared to think that the only genuine form of the dictatorship of the proletariat must be based on the leadership of more than one workers' party:

> The dictatorship of the proletariat is not that of Russia, for that is a dictatorship of one party. The reformist workers' parties

within the soviets worked for armed struggle against the Bolsheviks and this created the circumstances for the taking of power by the Bolshevik party. In Spain, nobody can think of a dictatorship of a party, but of a government of full workers' democracy . . . (*La Batalla*, March 23, 1937.)

Nin thus wipes out the soviet democracy of the first years after the October Revolution, and the history of the process of reaction, resulting from the isolation of the revolution from Europe, which in the end led in Russia, not to the dictatorship of a party but the dictatorship of a bureaucracy. If his words are to be taken seriously, Spain could not have a dictatorship of the proletariat, no matter how wide the influence of the POUM became, unless other organizations (FAI and CNT) agreed to work for it; if they did not, then Spain is doomed to capitalist domination! Thus Nin rationalized his refusal to let go of the coat-tails of the CNT leaders.

The crux of the matter is that Nin had abandoned the Leninist conception of soviets. This he did explicitly:

> In Russia there was no democratic tradition. There did not exist a tradition of organization and of struggle in the proletariat. We do have that. We have unions, parties, publications. A system of workers' democracy.
>
> One understands, therefore, that in Russia the soviets should have developed the importance that they did. The soviets were a spontaneous creation that in 1905 and 1917 took on an entirely political character.
>
> Our proletariat, however, had its unions, its parties, its own organizations. For this reason, the soviets have not risen among us. ("The Fundamental Problem of Power," *La Batalla*, April 27, 1937.)

Once embarked on a false, opportunist course, revolutionists will decompose politically at a fearful rate. Who would have believed, a few years ago, that Nin would be capable of speaking these lines?

The gigantic "tradition of organization and of struggle" amassed by the Russian proletariat in the Revolution of 1905, the study and analysis of which developed the cadres which made the October Revolution, "escapes" him. What was peculiarly Russian about the soviet form? In 1918, in countries with a far richer proletarian tradition than Spain—Germany and Austria—the soviets rose. As a matter of simple fact, what were the factory committees, the militia committees, the village committees, the workers' supply committees, the workers' patrols, the investigation committees, etc., etc., which surged up in Spain in July, 1936—were these not the foundation stones, which required only deeper politicalization and coordination, direct representation of the masses instead of the organizations, in order to form the soviet power? Nin's rationalization is pitiful; it will not stand up for a moment; he had joined with the Stalinists and the bourgeoisie, in September, explicitly to abolish the soviet dual power as "unnecessary duplication"—and nine months later could say, "the soviets have not risen among us."

Thus, the POUM leadership stood at the tail of the CNT. Instead of assimilating the lessons of Leninism, they denounced it as . . . Trotskyism. Why do the Stalinists call us Trotskyists?—this is the perennial complaint of the POUM leadership. The following is typical, from an article by Gorkin:

> In any case Trotsky has given no basis for our being called Trotskyists. In 1931 he published two articles upon the then Workers and Peasants Bloc and its chief Maurin. For him [Trotsky] our political line was a "mixture of petty-bourgeois prejudices, of ignorance, of provincial 'science' and of political knavery." . . .
>
> With the Spanish Civil War, we have seen manifested once more the sectarianism of Trotsky . . . The representative today of the Fourth International in Spain, within two hours of arriving, and a quarter of an hour of talking with us, drew from his pocket a program prepared a priori, giving us advice concerning the tactic that we ought to apply. Courteously, we advised him to take a walk through Barcelona and to study a little better the

situation. This citizen . . . is the perfect symbol of Trotskyism: of a sectarian doctrinairism, of a great sufficiency, certain that he possessed the revolutionary philosopher's stone. (*La Batalla*, April 24, 1937.)

This provincial smugness, the heritage of Maurin, had not only been criticized by Trotsky. Nin himself, in August, 1931, had declared that the greatest danger for the Workers and Peasants Bloc was Maurin's contempt for the lessons of the Russian Revolution. In inheriting Maurin's mantle, however, Nin had taken over this tradition of provincial blindness.

Not all those who had agreed with Nin in 1931 followed him in his renunciation of Leninism. Bearing the chief brunt of bourgeois-Stalinist repressions, the Madrid section of the POUM gave an overwhelming majority to an oppositional program based on the Leninist course. The main section of the party, Barcelona, voted for the immediate organization of soviets on April 15, 1937. Bureaucratic measures were resorted to by Nin and Gorkin to prevent the growth of the left wing. Dissidents were brought back from the front under guard, and expelled. Fraction organizations were forbidden. More important than the repressions by the leadership were those of the government which fell most heavily, naturally, on those workers who stood out in the ranks and in the factories. The left wing workers of the POUM—those expelled constituting themselves the Spanish Bolshevik-Leninists (Fourth Internationalists)—established close contacts with the anarchist workers, especially the "Friends of Durruti." But the regroupment took place too slowly. Before the revolutionary forces could come together and win the confidence of the masses, transform their discontent into the positive drive for power, substitute the objective strategy of leadership for the subjective desperation of the masses, the bitterness of the leaderless workers had already overflowed: the barricades went up on May 3.

# 10

## The May days:
## Barricades in Barcelona

Even more than before the civil war, Catalonia was the chief economic center of Spain; and these economic forces were now in the
hands of the workers and peasants (so they thought). The entire
textile industry of Spain was located here. Its workers now provided clothing and blankets for the armies and the civilian population, and the vitally needed goods for export. With Bilbao's iron
and steel mills virtually cut off from the rest of Spain, the metal and
chemical workers of Catalonia had, by the most heroic diligence,
created a great war industry to equip the anti-fascist armies. The
agricultural collectives, raising the greatest crops in Spanish history, were feeding the armies and cities and providing citrus fruit
for export. The CNT seamen were carrying away the exports which
gave Spain credits abroad and were bringing home precious car-
goes for use in the struggle against Franco. The masses of the CNT
were holding the Aragon and Teruel fronts; they had sent Durruti
and the pick of their militias to save Madrid in the nick of time. The
Catalonian proletariat, in a word, was the backbone of the anti-
fascist forces, and knew it.

What is more, its power had been acknowledged, after July 19, even by Companys. The Catalan president, addressing the CNT-FAI in the July days, had said:

> You have always been severely persecuted and I, with much pain but forced by political realities, I, who was once with you, later saw myself obliged to oppose and persecute you. Today you are the masters of the city and of Catalonia, because you alone vanquished the Fascist soldiers. I hope you will not find it distasteful that I should now remind you that you did not lack the aid of the few or many men of my party and of the Guards . You have conquered, and all is in your power. If you do not need or want me as President tell me now, and I shall become another soldier in the anti-fascist fight. If, on the contrary, you believe me when I say that I would abandon this post to victorious fascism only as a corpse, perhaps, with my party comrades and my name and prestige, I can serve you.

Consequently, the alarm and rage of the Catalonian masses at the counter-revolutionary inroads were the emotions of freed men and masters of their fate in danger again of enslavement. Submission without a fight was out of the question!

On April 17—the day after the CNT ministers rejoined the Generalidad—a force of Carabineros arrived in Puigcerda and demanded that the CNT worker-patrols there surrender control of the customs. While CNT top-leaders hurried to Puigcerda to arrange a peaceful solution—i.e., to cajole the workers into surrendering control of the border—Assault and Civil Guards were sent to Figueras and other towns throughout the province to wrest police control from the workers' organizations. Simultaneously, in Barcelona, the Assault Guards proceeded to disarm workers on sight, in the streets. During the last week of April they reported three hundred thus disarmed. Collisions between the workers and the Guards took place nightly. Truckloads of Guards would disarm solitary workers. The workers retaliated. Workers who refused to submit were shot. Guards were picked off in turn.

On April 25, a PSUC trade union leader, Roldan Cortada, was assassinated in Molins de Llobregat. Who killed him is not known to this day. The CNT denounced the murder and proposed an investigation. The POUM pointed out that, significantly enough, Cortada had been a supporter of Caballero before the fusion and had been known to disapprove of the pogrom-spirit being generated by the Stalinists. But the PSUC squeezed the opportunity dry, denouncing the "uncontrollables," "hidden fascist agents," etc. On April 27, the CNT and POUM representatives appeared at Cortada's funeral—and found it a demonstration of the forces of the counter-revolution. For three and a half hours the "funeral"—PSUC and government soldiers and police gathered from far and wide and armed to the teeth—marched through the workers' districts of Barcelona. It was a challenge and the CNT masses were not blind to it. The next day the government dispatched a punitive expedition to Molins de Llobregat, seized the anarchist leaders there and brought them handcuffed back to Barcelona. That night and the next, CNT and PSUC-Assault Guard groups were disarming each other in the streets. The first barricades were erected in the workers' suburbs.

The Carabineros, reinforced and joined by the local PSUC forces, attacked the worker-patrols in Puigcerda. Antonio Martin, mayor and CNT leader, popular throughout Catalonia, was shot dead by the Stalinists.

May Day, oldest and dearest of proletarian holidays, dawned: the government prohibited all meetings and demonstrations throughout Spain.

In those last days of April, the Barcelona workers learned for the first time, through the pages of *Solidaridad Obrera*, what had happened to their comrades in Madrid and Murcia at the hands of the Stalinist G.P.U.

✳

The Telefonica, the main telephone building dominating Barcelona's busiest square, had been occupied by fascist troops on July 19, 1936, surrendered to them by the Assault Guards the government had sent there. The CNT workers had lost many comrades in re-conquering it. So much the dearer was possession of it. Since July 19, the red and black flag of the CNT had flown from its tower, visible to workers throughout the city. Since July 19, the exchange had been managed by a CNT-UGT committee, with a government delegation stationed in the building. The working staff was almost entirely CNT in allegiance and CNT armed guards defended it against fascist forays.

Control of the Telefonica was a concrete instance of the dual power. The CNT was in a position to listen in on government calls. The bourgeois-Stalinist bloc would never be master in Catalonia so long as it was possible for the workers to cut off telephonic co-ordination of the government forces.

On Monday, May 3, at 3 P.M., three lorry loads of Assault Guards arrived at the Telefonica under the personal command of the Commissioner of Public Order, Salas, a PSUC member.* Surprised, the guards on the lower floors were disarmed. But halfway up, a ma-

---

* The knotty problem of justifying the armed seizure of the Telefonica was "solved," in the Stalinist press, by giving at least four different explanations: 1. "Salas sent the armed republican police to disarm the employees there, most of them members of CNT unions. For a considerable time the telephone service had been run in a way which was open to the gravest criticism, and it was imperative to the whole conduct of the war that the defects of the service should be remedied." (*London Daily Worker,* May 11.) 2. The police "occupied the central telephone exchange. In so doing the police by no means intended to interfere with the rights of the workers as guaranteed by law (as alleged subsequently by the Trotskyist provocateurs). What the police wanted was to put all telephone connections under the immediate supervision of the Government." (*Inprecorr,* May 22.) What was "guaranteed by law," however, was the *workers' control* sanctioned by the collectivization decree of October 24, 1936! 3. A week later, a new story: "Comrade Salas went to the Telefonica which on the previous night had been occupied by 50 members of the POUM and various uncontrollable elements. The guard forced its way into the building and turned the occupants out of it. The affair was soon settled. Surprised by the rapid move on the part of the Government, the 50 people left the building and the Telephone Exchange was again (!!) in the hands of the Government." (*Inprecorr,* May 29.) 4. Is the final version, issued by the Catalan

chine gun barred further occupation. Salas sent for additional Guards. Anarchist leaders pleaded with him to withdraw from the building. He refused. The news spread like wild fire to the factories and workers' suburbs.

Within two hours, at 5 P.M., the workers were pouring into the local centers of the CNT-FAI and POUM, arming and building barricades. From the dungeons of the Rivera dictatorship until today, the CNT-FAI have always had their local defense committees, with a tradition of local initiative. So far as there was leadership in the coming week, these defense committees provided it. There was almost no firing the first night, for the workers were overwhelmingly stronger than the government forces. In the workers' suburbs, many of the government police, with no stomach for the struggle, peacefully surrendered their arms. Lois Orr, an eyewitness, wrote:

---

section of the Comintern as Salas' own story: "In the first place there was no occupation of the Telefonica, nor was there any question of the occupation of the Telefonica. I received a signed order from Ayguade, Minister for Public Order, that a Government delegate was to be installed and that I was to be responsible for seeing that he was so installed. Accordingly, I, with Captain Menendez, and a personal escort of four men, entered the Telephone Building. I explained my business, and said that I wished to speak with some responsible member of the Committee. We were told that there was no one in the building. However, we waited downstairs while they went to look. Two minutes later some individuals started shooting at us from the stairs. None of us was hit. Immediately I phoned for the guards to come, not to occupy the building in which we were already but to cordon off the building and prevent anyone from entering . . . I and Eroles (Anarchist police functionary) went up to the top of the building, where they had established themselves with a machinegun, hand grenades and rifles. We went up together without escort, and without arms. At the top I explained the purpose of my visit. They came down. The delegate was installed according to orders. The forces were withdrawn. There were no casualties and arrests." The CNT account brands this story a lie: Salas began by disarming the guards and forcing the telephone workers to put their hands up; the guards on the upper floors withdrew only the next day as part of a general agreement for both sides withdrawing— which the Government promptly violated. The four different Stalinist versions testify to the difficulty of covering up the simple truth: they wanted to end workers' control of the Telefonica and they did.

By the next morning (Tuesday, May 4), the armed workers dominated the greatest part of Barcelona. The entire port, and with it Montjuich fortress, which commands the port and city with its cannon, was held by the anarchists; all the suburbs of the city were in their hands; and the government forces, except for a few isolated barricades, were completely outnumbered and were concentrated in the center of the city, the bourgeois area, where they could easily be closed in on from all sides as the rebels were on July 19, 1936.

CNT, POUM, and other accounts substantiate this fact.

In Lerida the civil guards surrendered their arms to the workers Monday night, as also in Hostafranchs. PSUC and Estat Catala headquarters in Tarragona and Gerona were seized by POUM and CNT militants as a "preventive measure." These overt steps were but the beginning of what could be done, for the masses of Catalonia were ranged overwhelmingly under the banner of the CNT. The formal seizure of Barcelona, the constitution of a revolutionary government, would have, overnight, led to working-class power. That this would have been the outcome is not seriously contested by the CNT leaders nor by the POUM.[*]

That is why the left wingers in the CNT and POUM ranks, sections of the Libertarian Youth, the Friends of Durruti and the Bolshevik-Leninists called for a seizure of power by the workers through the development of democratic organs of defense (soviets). On May 4, the Bolshevik-Leninists issued the following leaflet, distributed on the barricades:

LONG LIVE THE REVOLUTIONARY OFFENSIVE

No compromise. Disarmament of the National Republican Guard and the reactionary Assault Guards. This is the decisive

---

[*] Even the I.L.P. leader, Fenner Brockway, always to the right of the POUM, in this case concedes that "for two days the workers were on top. Bold and united action by the CNT leadership could have overthrown the Government."

moment. Next time it will be too late. General strike in all the industries excepting those connected with the prosecution of the war, until the resignation of the reactionary government. Only proletarian power can assure military victory.

Complete arming of the working class.

Long live unity of action of CNT-FAI-POUM.

Long live the revolutionary front of the proletariat.

Committees of revolutionary defense in the shops, factories, districts.

*Bolshevik-Leninist section of Spain (for the Fourth International)*

The leaflets of the Friends of Durruti, calling for "a revolutionary *Junta,* complete disarmament of the Assault Guards and the National Republican Guards," hailing the POUM for joining the workers on the barricades, estimated the situation in conceptions identical with those of the Bolshevik-Leninists. Still adhering to the discipline of their organizations, and issuing no independent propaganda, the POUM Left, the CNT Left and the Libertarian Youth agreed on perspective with the Bolshevik-Leninists.

They were undoubtedly correct. No apologist for the CNT and POUM leaders has adduced any argument against the seizure of power which stands up under analysis. None of them dares deny that the workers could easily have seized power in Catalonia. They adduce three main arguments to defend the capitulation: that the revolution would have been isolated, limited to Catalonia, and defeated there from the outside; that the fascists would have been able at this juncture to break through and win; that England and France would have crushed the revolution by direct intervention. Let us closely examine these arguments:

1. *Isolation of the Revolution:* The most plausible, most radical, form given to this argument is that based on an analogy with the "armed demonstration" of July, 1917, in Petrograd. "Even the Bolsheviks in July, 1917, did not decide to seize power and limited themselves to the defensive, leading the masses out of the line of fire with

as few victims as possible." Ironically enough, the POUM, I.L.P., Pivertists, and other apologists who use this argument are precisely those who have been incessantly reminding "sectarian Trotskyists" that "Spain is not Russia," and that, therefore, the Bolshevik policy is not applicable.

The Trotskyist, i.e., Bolshevik analysis of the Spanish Revolution, however, has always based itself on the concrete conditions of Spain. In 1931, we warned that the rapid rhythm of the developments of Russia in 1917 would not be duplicated in Spain. On the contrary, we then used the analogy of the great French Revolution which, beginning in 1789, passed through a series of stages before attaining its culmination in 1793. Just because we Trotskyists do not schematize historic events, we cannot take seriously the analogy with July 1917.[*]

The armed demonstration broke out in Petrograd only four months after the February revolution, only three months after Lenin's April Theses had given a revolutionary direction to the Bolshevik party. "The overwhelming mass of the population of the gigantic country was only just beginning to emerge from the illusions of February. At the front was an army of twelve million men who were only then being touched by the first rumors about the Bolsheviks. In these conditions the isolated insurrection of the Petrograd proletariat would have led inevitably to their being crushed. It was necessary to gain time. It was these circumstances that determined the tactic of the Bolsheviks."

In Spain, however, May 1937 came after six full years of revolution in which the masses of the whole country had amassed a gigantic experience. The democratic illusions of 1931 had been burned out. We can cite testimony from CNT, POUM, socialist leaders that the refurbished democratic illusions of the People's Front never caught hold of the masses—they voted in February, 1936 not for the People's Front but against Gil Robles and for the release of the

---

[*] Leon Trotsky, *The Revolution in Spain,* April 1931; *The Spanish Revolution in Danger,* 1931—Pioneer Publishers, New York.

political prisoners. Again and again the masses had shown that they were ready to go through to the end: the numerous anarchist-led armed struggles, the land seizures during six years, the October, 1934, revolt, the Asturian Commune, the seizure of the factories and land after July 19! The analogy with Petrograd of July, 1917, is childish.

Twelve million Russian soldiers, scarcely touched by Bolshevik propaganda, were available to be used against Petersburg in 1917. But in Spain more than a third of the armed forces carried CNT membership cards; nearly another third UGT cards, most of them left socialists or under their influence. Even grant that the revolution would not immediately spread to Madrid and Valencia. But that is entirely different from asserting that the Valencia government would have found troops with which to smash the Workers' Republic of Catalonia! Immediately after the May events, the UGT masses showed their determined hostility to repressive measures against the Catalonian proletariat. That was one reason Caballero had to leave the government. All the more could they not have been used against a victorious workers' republic. Not even the Stalinist ranks would have provided a mass army for that purpose: it is one thing to get backward workers and peasants to limit their struggle to one for a democratic republic; it is something entirely different to get them to crush a workers' republic. Any attempt by the bourgeois-Stalinist bloc to gather a proletarian force would have simply precipitated the extension of the workers' state to all Loyalist Spain.

We can assert more than this: that the example of Catalonia would have been followed elsewhere immediately. Proof? The Stalinist-bourgeois bloc, while seeking to consolidate the bourgeois republic, nevertheless, was compelled by the revolutionary atmosphere to raise the slogan: "Let us finish Franco first and make the revolution afterward." It was a clever slogan, well designed to keep the masses in check. But the very fact that the counter-revolution needed this slogan demonstrates that it based its hopes for victory over the revolution, *not* on the agreement of the masses but on the masses' *embittered toleration.* Gritting their teeth, the masses were saying, "we must wait until we finish off Franco, then we shall finish off the bourgeoisie and their lackeys." This feeling, undoubtedly widespread, would have disappeared in the face of the example of Catalonia. That example would have ended the feeling—"we must wait."

Nor would the example of Catalonia have affected only Loyalist Spain. For a workers' Spain would have embarked on a revolutionary war against fascism which would have disintegrated the ranks of Franco, more by political weapons than by military ones. All the political weapons against fascism which the People's Front had refused to permit to be used, which could only be used by a workers' republic, would now confront Franco. Trotsky wrote a few days after July 19:

> A civil war is waged, as everybody knows, not only with military but also with political weapons. From a purely military point of view, the Spanish Revolution is much weaker than its enemy. Its strength lies in its ability to arouse the great masses to action. It can even take the army [of Franco] away from its reactionary officers. To accomplish this it is only necessary seriously and courageously to advance the program of the socialist revolution.

> It is necessary to proclaim that, from now on, the land, the factories, and shops will pass from the capitalists into the hands of the people. It is necessary to move at once toward the realization of this program in those provinces where the workers are in power. The fascist army could not resist the influence of such a program: the soldiers would tie their officers hand and foot and hand them over to the nearest headquarters of the workers' militia. But the bourgeois ministers cannot accept such a program. Curbing the social revolution, they compel the workers and peasants to spill ten times as much of their own blood in the civil war.

Trotsky's prediction proved all too true. Fearing the revolution more than Franco, the People's Front government conducted no propaganda aimed at the peasants in Franco's forces and behind his lines. The government absolutely refused to promise the land to these peasants, and that promise would have had no effect unless the government had actually decreed giving the land to the peasant committees in its own regions, from which, by a thousand roads, the news would have spread to the peasants in the rest of Spain. Fearing the revolution more than Franco, the government had rejected all proposals (including those of Abd-el-Krim and other Moors) to incite revolution in Morocco under a declaration of independence for Morocco. Fearing the revolution more than Franco, the government appealed to the international proletariat to get "their" governments to help Spain—but never appealed to the international proletariat to help Spain in spite of and against their governments.

We are not doctrinaires. We do not declare the revolution every day. We judge from our concrete analysis of the conditions in Spain in May, 1937: Had the workers' republic been established in Catalonia, it would not have been isolated or crushed. It would have been quickly extended to the rest of Spain.

2. *The Fascists Would Have Broken Through:* The second apology for not taking power in Catalonia overlaps the first to the extent that it implicitly denies the effect of the taking of power on Franco's forces.[*]

Admitting that a proletarian revolution in May would have ex-

---

[*] A well-known anarchist leader said to me: "You Trotskyists are worse utopians than we ever were. Morocco is in Franco's hands ruled by him with an iron hand. Our declaration of the independence of Morocco would have no effect." I reminded him that Lincoln's Declaration of Emancipation of the slaves was issued while the Confederacy still held all the South. Marxists, at least, should recall that Marx and Engels gave this political act enormous weight in the defeat of the South. Another anarchist said: "Our peasants have already seized much land, yet it has had no effect on the peasants under Franco." Under questioning, however, he admitted that the peasants feared that the government would try to recover the land after the war. In Russia, too, by November, 1917, the peasants seized much land. They tilled it, however, sullenly and fearfully. The Soviet decree nationalizing the land transformed the psychology of the peasants and made them overwhelmingly partisans of the Soviet regime.

tended itself throughout Loyalist Spain, the CNT leaders argue: "It is obvious that, had we so desired, the defense movement could have been transformed into a purely libertarian movement. This is all very well but . . . the fascists would have, without doubt, taken advantage of these circumstances to break all lines of resistance." (Garcia Oliver)[*]

Though ostensibly dealing with the immediate situation in May in Catalonia, this line of argument is, in actuality, much more fundamental: *it is an argument against the working class taking power during the course of the civil war.*

That was also the line of the POUM. The Central Committee held that, in the event the government refused to sign its own death warrant by convoking a Constituent Assembly (Congress of soldiers', peasants' and union delegates), it would be wrong to wrest the power forcibly from the government.

> It believed that the workers would in time protest against the counter-revolution which the government was carrying through and that the demand for such a Constituent Assembly would become so strong that the government would be compelled to submit. It held that an insurrection would be wrong and inadvisable until after the fascists were defeated, and there was a difference of opinion in its ranks whether even then an insurrection would be necessary.[†]

In other words, the CNT and POUM called for socialism through the government. But if the government would not yield, then we must wait until after the war at least. In practice, this came down to covert adaptation to the bourgeois-Stalinist slogan—"Let us finish Franco first and make the revolution afterward."

The POUM-CNT tactic of waiting until Franco was finished off

---

[*] Speech in Paris, *Spain and the World* (Anarchist) July 2, 1937.

[†] Fenner Brockway, Secretary of the Independent Labor Party, *The Truth About Barcelona,* London, 1937.

meant, concretely, the doom of the revolution. For, as we have already pointed out, the bourgeois-Stalinist slogan of "wait" was designed to check the masses until the bourgeois state was supreme. Precisely for this reason, the bourgeois-Stalinist bloc and its Anglo-French allies had no intention of finishing off Franco or (more likely) making an armistice with him, until the counter-revolution had securely consolidated its power in Loyalist Spain.

We have commented on the failure of the People's Front and its government to conduct revolutionary propaganda to disintegrate Franco's forces. But in the field of purely military struggle, too, the government failed to fight Franco conclusively. More accurately, there is no wall between political and military tasks in civil war. Fearing the revolution more than Franco, the government was massing huge forces of picked soldiers and police in the cities, thereby withdrawing men and arms needed at the front. Fearing the revolution more than Franco, the government was pursuing a dilatory war strategy which could provide no decisive conclusion, while the counter-revolution was carried through. Fearing the revolution more than Franco, the government was subordinating the Asturian and Basque workers to the command of the treacherous Basque bourgeoisie who were soon to surrender the Northern front. Fearing the revolution more than Franco, the government was directly sabotaging the Aragon and Levante fronts held by the CNT. Fearing the revolution more than Franco, the government was giving fascist agents (Asensio, Villalba, etc., etc.) the opportunity to betray Loyalist fortresses to Franco (Badajoz, Irun, Málaga).[*]

The counter-revolution dealt terrible blows to the morale of the anti-fascist troops. "Why should we die fighting Franco when our comrades are shot by the government." This mood, so dangerous to the struggle against fascism, was prevalent after the May days and was hard to fight.

In all these ways, therefore, the government policy was making easier the military inroads of Franco. The establishment of a work-

---

[*] The military policy of the government is analyzed in detail in chapters 15 and 16.

ers' republic would have put an end to all this treachery, sabotage, disruption of morale. Wielding the instrument of state planning, the Workers' Republic would utilize as no capitalist régime could the full material and moral resources of Loyalist Spain.

Far from enabling the fascists to break through, only workers' power could lead to the victory over Franco.

3. *The Menace of Intervention:* The CNT darkly referred to English and French warships appearing in the harbor on May 3, to plans for landing Anglo-French troops. "In the case of a triumph of libertarian communism, it would have been crushed some time later by the intervention of capitalistic and democratic powers." (Garcia Oliver).

CNT references to specific warships, to a specific plot, deliberately obscure the fundamental character of the issue: *every social revolution must face the danger of capitalist intervention.* The Russian Revolution had to survive both capitalist-financed civil war and direct imperialist intervention. The Hungarian Revolution was crushed by intervention as well as by its own mistakes. When, however, the German and Austrian Social Democrats justified stabilization of their bourgeois republics because the Allied Powers would intervene against socialist states, revolutionary socialists and communists the world over—and anarchists—denounced the Kautskys and Bauers as betrayers, and rightly so.

The Austrian and German proletariat, the revolutionists said then, must take account of the possibility of defeat at the hands of Anglo-French intervention because revolutions always face that danger, and to wait for that hypothetical moment at which the Allies would be too preoccupied to interfere, meant to lose the conjuncture favorable to revolution. But the social democrats prevailed . . . and ended up in the concentration camps of Hitler and Schuschnigg.

Neither CNT nor POUM circles dare argue that there was any specific conjunctural situation which made capitalist intervention in May, 1937, more threatening than at another time. The apologists merely refer to the intervention danger without adducing specific analysis. We ask: was intervention more dangerous in May, 1937 than, for example, it was at the time of the April, 1931 revolution? The advantages, for the workers, were all with May, 1937. In 1931 the European proletariat was prostrated at the bottom of the well of the world crisis. If the German workers were not yet betrayed to Hitler by their leaders—without a fight—the French proletariat was as dormant as if exhausted by a dictator. France, contiguous to Spain, is decisive for Spain. And in May, 1937, the French proletariat was beginning the second year of the upsurge which opened with the revolutionary strikes of June, 1936. It is inconceivable that the millions of socialist and communist workers of France, already chafing against neutrality, and kept in line by their leaders only with the greatest difficulty, would permit capitalist intervention in Spain, whether by the French or any other bourgeoisie. The transformation of the struggle in Spain, from one for the preservation of a bourgeois republic, to one for the social revolution, would fire the French, Belgian, and English proletariat even more than had the Russian Revolution—for this time the revolution would be at their own doors!

In the face of an alert proletariat, what would the bourgeoisie do? The French bourgeoisie would open its borders to Spain, not for intervention but for trade enabling the new régime to secure supplies—or face immediately a revolution at home. The Spanish Workers' Republic would not, like Caballero and Negrin, aid and abet "non-intervention"! England, irrevocably tied to the fate of France, would be held back from intervention both by the whole weight of France and by her own working class for whom the Iberian Revolution would open a new epoch. Portugal would face immediate revolution at home. Germany and Italy would, of course, seek to increase their aid to Franco. But Anglo-French policy must continue to be: neither a Socialist Spain nor a Hitler-Mussolini Spain. Hoping to whittle down both sides eventually, Anglo-French imperialism would be forced to keep Italo-German intervention within such bounds as to prevent the Rome-Berlin axis from dominating the Mediterranean.

We, least of all, need to be told that all capitalist powers have in common, and seek in common, to destroy any threat of social revolution. Nevertheless, it is clear that two factors which saved the Russian Revolution from destruction by intervention would operate in May, 1937: In 1917 the world working class inspired by the revolution, forced a halt to intervention, while the imperialists could not sink their differences sufficiently to unite on a single plan for crushing the workers' republic. With the European proletariat on the rise again, the imperialists would seek to quench the Spanish fire at their peril

Yes, above all, we invoke the aid of the workers of the world! You Stalinists for whom the masses are no longer anything but sacrificial carcasses which you offer at the altar of an alliance with the democratic imperialists; you bureaucrats whose contempt for the masses, on whose backs you stand, makes you forget that these same masses carried through the October Revolution and the victorious civil war, on the moral and material capital of which you are still living, and which shrinks under your incompetent mismanagement! We know you do not like to be reminded that in 1919–1922, the world working class saved the Soviet Union from the imperialists. The revolutionary capacities of the proletariat are a factor which you have come to hate and fear, for they threaten your privileges.

Not we, but the Stalinists, believe in possible peaceful co-habitation of capitalist and workers' states. Certainly, European capitalism could not indefinitely bear the existence of a Socialist Spain. But the specific conjuncture in May, 1937, was sufficiently favorable to enable a workers' Spain to establish its internal régime and *to prepare to resist imperialism by spreading the revolution to France and Belgium and then wage revolutionary war against Germany and Italy, under conditions which would precipitate the revolution in the fascist countries.* This is the *only* perspective of the revolution in Europe in this period before the next war, whether the revolution begins with Spain or France. Whoever does not accept this perspective, rejects the socialist revolution.

Risks? "World history would indeed be very easy to make if the struggle were taken up only on condition of infallibly favorable chances," wrote Marx while the Paris Commune still lived. Clear-eyed, he saw "the decisive, unfavorable accident . . . in the presence of the Prussians in France and their position right before Paris. Of this the Parisian workers were well aware. But of this the bourgeois *canaille* of Versailles were also well aware. Precisely for that reason they presented the Parisians with the alternative of taking up the fight or succumbing without a struggle. In the latter case the de-moralization of the working class would have been a far greater misfortune than the fall of any number of 'leaders.' The struggle of the working class against the capitalist class and its state has en-tered upon a new phase with the struggle in Paris. Whatever the immediate results may be, a new point of departure of world-historic importance has been gained." (Letter to Kugelmann, April 17, 1871.) Berneri had been right. Crushed between the Franco-Prussians and Versailles-Valencia, the commune of Catalonia could have struck a flame to light up the world. And under conditions so incomparably more favorable than those of the Commune!

We have sought to analyse as seriously as possible the reasons given by the centrist leadership for not waging a struggle for power against the counter-revolution. Being centrists and not brazen re-formists, they have sought to justify their capitulation by references to the "special," "specific" situation in Spain in the month of May, 1937 but without providing us with the precise details. Upon ex-amination we have found that, as usual in all such alibis, the refer-ences to the specific are false and conceal a fundamental retreat from the revolutionary path. Not mistakes in fact but differences in principle, in world and class outlook, separate the revolutionists from both the reformist and centrist leaders.

On Tuesday morning, May 4, the armed workers on barricades throughout Barcelona felt again, as on July 19, masters of their world. As on July 19, the terrified bourgeois and petty-bourgeois elements hid in their homes. The PSUC-led trade unionists remained pas-sive. Only part of the police, the armed guards of the PSUC, and the armed Estat Catala hooligans were on the government barri-

cades. These barricades were limited to the center of the city, surrounded by the armed workers. The state of affairs is indicated by
Companys' first radio address: a declaration that the Generalidad
was not responsible for the provocation at the Telefonica. Every outer
section of the city, directed by its local defense committees and aided
by POUM, FAI, and Libertarian Youth groups, was solidly in the
control of the workers. There was almost no firing Monday night,
so complete was the workers' control. All that remained to establish
supremacy was co-ordination and joint action directed from the
center . . . At the center, the Casa CNT, the leaders forbade all action and ordered the workers to leave the barricades.[*]

It was not the organizing of the armed masses that interested the
CNT leaders. What occupied them was interminable negotiation
with the government. This was a game which suited the government perfectly: to hold back the leaderless masses in the barricades
by deluding them with hopes that a decent solution would be found.
The meeting at the Generalidad Palace dragged on until six o'clock
in the morning. The government forces thus got enough breathing
space to fortify the government buildings and, as the fascists had
done in July, occupy the cathedral towers.

At eleven Tuesday morning, the functionaries met, not to organize the defense, but to elect a new committee to negotiate with the
government. Now Companys introduced a new wrinkle. Of course,
we can come to an amicable settlement; we are all antifascists, etc.,
etc., said Companys and Premier Tarradellas—but we cannot carry
on negotiations so long as the streets are not cleared of armed men.
Whereupon the Regional Committee of the CNT spent Tuesday
before the microphones calling the workers away from the barricades: "We appeal to all of you to put down your arms. Think of
our great goal, common to all . . . Above all else, unity! Put down

---

[*] For critical accounts of the events of the next days, I am indebted to two American comrades, Lois and Charles Orr (the latter was editor of the POUM's English
language *Spanish Revolution*) and to the long and documented report of the Spanish Bolshevik-Leninists, appearing in *La Lutte Ouvrière,* June 10, 1937.

your arms. Only one slogan: We must work to beat fascism!" *Solidaridad Obrera* had the effrontery to appear with the story of Monday's attack on the Telefonica on page 8—not to alarm the militiamen at the front to whom went hundreds of thousands of copies—with no mention of the barricades erected, and no directives except "keep calm." At five o'clock delegations from the National Committees of the UGT and CNT arrived from Valencia and jointly issued an appeal to the "people" to lay down their arms. Vasquez, CNT National Secretary, joined Companys in the radio appeal. The night was spent in new negotiations—the government was always ready to make agreements involving the workers leaving the barricades!—out of which came an agreement for a provisional cabinet of four: one each from the CNT, PSUC, Peasant Union and Esquerra. The negotiations were punctuated with calls for authoritative CNT leaders to go to points where the workers were on the offensive, as at Coll Blanch where the workers had to be persuaded from carrying out occupation of the barracks. Meanwhile other calls were coming in—from the Leather Workers' Headquarters, the Medical Union, the local center of the Libertarian Youth—asking the Regional Committee to send help, the police were attacking . . .

Wednesday: neither the numerous radio appeals, the joint appeal of the UGT-CNT, nor the establishment of a new cabinet, had budged the armed workers from the barricades. On the barricades, anarchist workers tore up *Solidaridad Obrera* and shook their fists and guns at the radios as Montseny—when Vasquez and Garcia Oliver had failed, she had been hurriedly called from Valencia—exhorted the barricades to disperse. The local defense committees reported to Casa CNT: the workers will not leave without conditions. Very well, we give them conditions. The CNT radioed the proposals it was making to the government: hostilities to cease, every party to keep its positions, the police and civilians fighting on the side of the CNT (i.e. non-members) to retire altogether, the responsible committees to be informed at once if the pact is broken anywhere, solitary shots not to be answered, the defenders of union quarters to remain passive and await further information. The government soon announced its agreement with the CNT proposals, and why not? The government's sole objective was to end the fighting of the masses, the better to break their resistance for all time. Furthermore, the "agreement" pledged the government to nothing. The control of the Telefonica, disarming of the masses, were—not accidentally—unmentioned. The agreement was followed during the night by orders from the local CNT and UGT (the latter Stalinist-controlled, remember) to return to work. "The anti-fascist organizations and parties in session at the Palace of the Generalidad have solved the conflict that has created this abnormal situation," said the joint manifesto. "These events have taught us that from now on we shall have to establish relations of cordiality and comradeship, the lack of which we all regretted deeply during the last few days." Nevertheless, as Souchy admits, the barricades remained fully manned Wednesday night.

But on Thursday morning, the POUM ordered its members to leave the barricades, many of them still under fire. On Tuesday, the manifesto of the Friends of Durruti, hitherto cool to the POUM, had hailed its joining the barricades as a demonstration that it was a "revolutionary force." Tuesday's *La Batalla* had remained within the limits of the theory that there should be no insurrectionary overthrow of the government during the civil war but had called for defense of the barricades, the dismissal of Salas and Ayguade, withdrawal of the decrees dissolving the worker-patrols. Limited as this program was, it contrasted so with the CNT Regional Committee's appeals to desert the barricades that the prestige of the POUM soared among the anarchist masses. The POUM had an unparalleled opportunity to come to the head of the movement.

Instead, the POUM leadership, once again, put its fate in the hands of the CNT leadership. *Not* public proposals to the CNT for joint action made before the masses, proposals which would give the inchoate rebellion a focus of specific steps to demand of their leaders—in a whole year the POUM had, fawningly deferential to the CNT leaders, not made a single united front proposal of this specific character—but a behind-the-scenes conference with the CNT Regional Committee. Whatever the POUM proposals were, they were rejected. You don't agree? Then we shall say nothing about them. And the next morning (May 5) *La Batalla* had not a word to say about the POUM's proposals to the CNT, about the cowardly behavior of the CNT leaders, their refusal to organize the defense, etc.[*] Instead, "the Barcelona proletariat has won a partial battle against the counter-revolution." And, twenty-four hours later, "the counter-revolutionary provocation having been repulsed, it is necessary to leave the streets. Workers, return to work." (*La Batalla*, May 6.)

The masses had demanded victory over the counter-revolution. The CNT bureaucrats had refused to fight. The centrists of the POUM thus bridged the gap between masses and bureaucrats by— assuring them that the victory had already been achieved!

The Friends of Durruti had forged to the front on Wednesday, calling upon the CNT workers to repudiate the desertion orders of Casa CNT and continue the struggle for workers' power. It had warmly welcomed the collaboration of the POUM. The masses were still on the barricades. The POUM, numbering at least thirty thousand workers in Catalonia, could tip the quivering scales either way.

---

[*] The English language bulletin of the POUM, *Spanish Revolution*, (May 19, 1937.) says: "Caught up in the reigns of the government, (the CNT) tried to straddle the fence with a 'union' of the opposing forces . . . The attitude of the CNT did not fail to bring forth resistance and protests. The 'Friends of Durruti' group brought the unanimous desire of the CNT masses to the surface but it was not able to take the lead . . . The workers, who were deeply wounded by the capitulation of their trade union federation, are now looking for a new lead in other directions. The POUM should provide it for them." These radical words were for export purposes only. Nothing like them appeared in the regular press of the POUM. In general, *Spanish Revolution* has given English readers, who could not follow the POUM's Spanish press, a distorted picture of the POUM's conduct; it has been a "left face." This is said without any intention of reflecting on the revolutionary integrity of Comrade Charles Orr, its editor, who can scarcely be held responsible for the disparity between the English bulletin and the voluminous Spanish press of the POUM.

Its leadership tipped the scales for capitulation.

One more terrible blow against the embattled workers: The Regional Committee of the CNT gave to the entire press—Stalinist and bourgeois included—a denunciation of the Friends of Durruti as *agents-provocateurs;* it was, of course, prominently published everywhere on Thursday morning. The POUM press did not defend the left-wing anarchists against this foul slander.

✳

Thursday was replete with instances of the "victory" in the name of which the POUM called the workers to leave the barricades.

In the morning the shattered body of Camillo Berneri was found where it had been tossed by the PSUC guards who had seized the frail man in his home the night before. Berneri, spiritual leader of Italian anarchism since the death of Malatesta, leader of the Ancona revolt of 1914, escaped from Mussolini's clutches, had fought the reformists (including the CNT leaders) in his influential organ, *Guerra di Classe.* He had described the Stalinist policy in four words: "It smells of Noske." In ringing words he had defied Moscow: "Crushed between the Prussians and Versailles, the Commune of Paris initiated a fire that lit up the world. Let the General Godeds of Moscow remember this." He had declared to the masses of the CNT: "The dilemma 'war or revolution' has no longer any meaning. The only dilemma is: either victory over Franco, thanks to the revolutionary war, or defeat." How terribly true had been his identification of Noske and the Stalinists! As Noske, the Social Democrat, had Rosa Luxemburg and Karl Liebknecht kidnapped and murdered, so the Stalinist-democrats had assassinated Camillo Berneri.

Honor our comrade, Camillo Berneri. Let us remember him with the love we bear our Karl and Rosa. As I write, comrades, I cannot help weeping, weeping for Camillo Berneri. The list of our martyrs is as long as the life of the working class. Fortunate were those among them who fell fighting the open class enemy, fell in the midst of battle with their comrades beside them. Most terrible of all is it to

die alone at the stiletto-point of those who call themselves socialists or communists, as Karl and Rosa died, as our comrades are
dying in the execution chambers of Siberian exile. A special anguish was that of Camillo Berneri. He died at the hands of "Marx-
ists-Leninists-Stalinists," while his closest friends, Montseny, Garcia
Oliver, Peiro, Vasquez, were handing over the Barcelona proletariat
to his executioners. *Thursday, May 6, 1937.* Let us remember that
day.

Government and anarchist leaders had gone to Lerida on Wednesday to stop a picked force of 500 POUM and CNT troops speed-
ing from Huesca, with light artillery. Valencian and Generalidad
representatives had promised that if the workers' troops did not
advance, the government would not try to bring any more of its
troops into Barcelona. Upon this promise and the urging of the
anarchist leaders, the workers' troops had stopped. On Thursday,
however, came telephone calls from the CNT militants in towns
along the road from Valencia to Barcelona: 5,000 Assault Guards
are on their way. Shall we stop them? ask the CNT workers. The
CNT leaders ordered the Guards to be let through, sent no word to
the workers' troops waiting in Lerida, and suppressed the news that
the Guards were on the way.

Thursday at three o'clock, Casa CNT ordered its guards to va-
cate the Telefonica. The government and the CNT had made an
agreement: both sides should withdraw their armed forces. As soon
as the CNT guards had left, the police occupied the entire building
and brought in government supporters to take over the technical
work from the CNT workers. You have broken your promise, the
CNT complained to the government. The Generalidad replied: the
*fait accompli* cannot be recalled. "Had the workers in the outlying
districts been informed immediately of this development," admits
the CNT spokesman, Souchy, "they would surely have insisted upon
taking firmer measures and turned to the attack." So—the ultra-
democratic, anarchist leaders of the CNT simply suppressed the
news!

Under the orders of Casa CNT, the telephone workers had serviced all calls during the fighting: revolutionary and counter-revolutionary. Once the government took over, however, the FAI and CNT locals were cut off from the center.

On the streets through which the workers had to come and go in returning to work as the CNT-UGT had instructed, police and PSUC guards were searching the passers-by, tearing up CNT cards, arresting CNT militants.

At four o'clock, the main railroad station of Barcelona, in the hands of the CNT since July 19, was attacked by PSUC and Assault Guards, with machine guns and hand-grenades. The small CNT force guarding it tried to telephone for help . . . At four o'clock General Pozas presented himself to the Ministry of Defense of Catalonia (a CNT ministry) and politely informed the comrades-ministers that the post of the Catalan Ministry of Defense had ceased to exist, that the Catalan armies were now the Fourth Brigade of the Spanish Army with Pozas as chief. The Valencian cabinet had made this decision by authority of the military decrees for a unified command signed by the CNT ministers. The CNT, of course, surrendered control to Pozas.

Terrible news from Tarragona. Wednesday morning a large police force had appeared and seized the telephone exchange. The CNT had thereupon asked for the inevitable conference. While negotiations went on the Republicans and Stalinists were arming; the next day they assaulted the Libertarian Youth headquarters. Whereupon the CNT asked for another conference at which they were informed that the Generalidad had sent explicit instructions to destroy the anarchist organizations if they did not surrender their arms. (Let us remember that these instructions came from a government in which sat anarchist ministers.) The CNT representatives agreed to surrender their arms, if the government would set free all arrested, replace the police and PSUC guards with regular army men, and guarantee immunity of attack of CNT members and their headquarters.

Captain Barbeta, the government delegate, agreed, of course. The CNT laid down its arms and during the night the Assault Guards occupied the CNT buildings and killed a score of anarchists, among them Pedro Rua, the Uruguayan writer, come to fight against fascism and risen to commandant of the militias. Casa CNT noted that this was "breaking the word of honor given the evening before by the authorities." Not a word of this was meanwhile transmitted to the Barcelona masses, though Casa CNT-FAI knew hourly of the developments.*

Thursday, 6 P.M.: Word arrived at Casa CNT: the first detachment from Valencia, 1,500 Assault Guards, had arrived at Tortosa on the way to Barcelona. Casa CNT had sent word ahead not to oppose them, everything was arranged, etc. The Assault Guards occupied all CNT-FAI-Libertarian Youth buildings of Tortosa, arresting all found, taking some, handcuffed, along to the Barcelona jails.

The masses knew nothing of the events at Tarragona, Tortosa, the Telefonica, Pozas, the coming of the Valencian Guards. But the attacks on workers in the streets, on the railroad station, the renewed firing at the barricades, spurred many who had left to return to the barricades.

In response to these cataclysmic events of Thursday, the Casa CNT "sent a new delegation to the government to find out what they intended doing" (Souchy) but without waiting to learn, issued a new, calming manifesto. While the barricades still resounded, Casa CNT declared:

> Now that we have returned to normal, and those responsible for the outbreak have been dismissed from public office, when all the workers have returned to their jobs, and Barcelona is once more calm . . . the CNT and FAI continue to collaborate loyally as in the past with all political and trade union sectors of the anti-fascist front. The best proof of this is that the CNT continues to collaborate with the central government, the government of the Generalidad and all the municipalities . . . The press of

---

* They only released the story on May 15–16, *Solidaridad Obrera*.

the CNT appealed for calm and called upon the population to return to work. The news issued by radio to the unions and the defense committees was nothing but appeals for calm.

A further proof that the CNT did not want to break and did not break the anti-fascist front is that when the new government of the Generalidad was formed, on the 5th of May, the representatives of the CNT of Catalonia offered it every facility, and the secretary of the CNT formed part of the government . . .

The members of the CNT who controlled the Defense Council (Ministry) of the Generalidad, gave orders to all their forces not to intervene on either side in the conflict. And they also saw to it that their orders were carried out.

The Defense Committee of the CNT also gave orders to every district of Barcelona that no one should come from there to the center to answer the provocations. These orders, too, were carried out because no one actually did come to the center to answer the provocations.

. . . Many were the traps laid for the CNT up to the very end but the CNT remained firm in its position and did not allow itself to be provoked . . .

Thursday evening: The PSUC and Assault Guards continued their raids, arrests, shootings. So . . . the Casa CNT-FAI sent a new delegation to the government with new proposals to cease hostilities: All groups to obligate themselves to remove their armed guards and patrols from the barricades, to release all prisoners; no reprisals.

News from Tarragona and Reus, "where members of the PSUC and Estat Catala, taking advantage [!] of the presence of some Assault Guards passing through on their way to Barcelona, used their temporary advantage to disarm and kill the workers" (Souchy).

"The CNT tried to get a promise from the government in Valencia and Barcelona that the Assault Guards would not enter the city immediately [!], but should be detained outside the city limits until the situation had cleared up . . . They were somewhat skeptical regarding the assurances that the coming troops would be loyal to the workers." But that skepticism (when did it arise?) had not been shared by the CNT ministers in the Valencia and Catalonian cabinets *who had voted for the central government to take over control of public order in Catalonia.* The Ministry of Public Order of Catalonia had, therefore, ceased to exist on May 5.

The night of May 6–7: "Again and again the anarchists offered to negotiate, eager to end the conflict." The government, of course, was always ready to negotiate while its forces broke the back of the working class under the cover provided by Casa CNT. The near-by anarchist workers had rallied to defend Tortosa and Tarragona. At four o'clock the Provincial Committee—the leadership of the CNT in Catalonia outside Barcelona—informed Casa CNT-FAI that they were prepared to hold up the guards from Valencia. No, you must not, said Casa CNT. At 5:15, the government and Casa CNT make another agreement: armistice, all to leave barricades, both parties to release their prisoners, the worker-patrols to resume their functions . . . Again the Regional Committee radioed the workers: "Having reached an understanding . . . we wish to notify you . . . establishment of complete peace and calm . . . keep that calm and presence of mind . . ."

Friday: Under orders from Casa CNT-FAI some workers began to tear down barricades. But the barricades of the Assault Guards, Estat Catala, PSUC, remained intact. The Assault Guards systematically disarmed workers. Again, as the workers saw the government forces continue the offensive, they returned to the barricades, against the will of both the CNT and the POUM. But disillusionment and discouragement set in: many of the anarchist workers had maintained faith in Casa CNT-FAI up to the last, others as their faith ebbed, had looked for leadership to the POUM workers until these were ordered off the barricades. The Friends of Durruti and the Bolshevik-Leninists were able to bring the workers back to the barricades for Thursday and Friday night, but not strong enough, not sufficiently rooted in these masses, to organize them for a long struggle.

The Valencian Guards came in Friday night. They immediately seized the press and leaders of the Friends of Durruti. Groups of guardsmen patrolled all streets to overawe the workers. "The Government of the Generalidad has suppressed the uprising with its own forces," announced Companys. See here, cried the CNT leaders, you know it wasn't an uprising, you said so. "We must root out the uncontrollables," answered Companys. . . .

The promise to release prisoners was not kept; on the contrary mass arrests began. No reprisals was another promise; but the next weeks came brutal reprisals against towns and suburbs which had dared resist. The government, of course, retained control of the Telefonica—that was why they had begun the struggle. The control of the police was now in Valencia—soon to be turned over to the Stalinists! The Ministry of Defense and the army of Catalonia had become the property of Valencia—soon to come under the control of Prieto. The worker-patrols were to be dissolved shortly, with the application of Ayguade's public order decree. Catalan autonomy had ceased to exist as Valencia's armed forces poured in. Ayguade, "dismissed" said the CNT, was in a week to go to Valencia to sit in the central government as the representative of the Generalidad . . . in which the CNT continued to sit.

After the Assault Guards entered Barcelona, *La Batalla* complained: "This is a provocation. By a demonstration of force they are attempting to convert our victory into a defeat." And, whiningly: "It was the POUM that counselled ceasing the struggle, abandoning the streets, returning to work; it was it—no one can doubt—that was one of those who most contributed to bring the situation back to normal." The tameness of the Poumist lamb didn't, however, save it from the wolf. Pitiful politicians, indeed, who cannot distinguish victory from defeat!

"We did not feel ourselves spiritually or physically strong enough to take the lead in organizing the masses for resistance," a member of the POUM Central Executive had said to Charles Orr on Tuesday. So . . . they had rationalized their impotence into a "victory", to justify ending the struggle.

Suppose the POUM had come to the fore and, in spite of the CNT, had sought to lead the workers at least to a real armistice, i.e., with the workers remaining armed in the streets and factories ready to resist any further offensive. Suppose even this had not come about, that the POUM and the workers would have been conquered by sheer force of arms. "In the worst case," the POUM opposition pointed out, "there could have been organized a central committee of defense, based on representation from the barricades. For this it would have been sufficient to hold first a meeting of delegates from each of the POUM barricades and such others of the CNT, to name a provisional central committee. During Tuesday afternoon the local POUM committee was working along this line. But it met with no enthusiasm from the central leadership to carry this out." At the least, such a central body directly rooted in the masses would have been able to organize resistance to the subsequent raids, arrests, suppression of the press, outlawry of the Friends of Durruti and the POUM.

Certainly the attempt to organize resistance would have resulted in no more victims than were produced by capitulation: 500 dead and 1,500 wounded, almost all after the CNT began the retreat Tuesday afternoon; hundreds more killed and wounded during the "mopping up" of the following weeks; the "cleansing" of the POUM and anarchist troops by sending them during the next weeks into the line of fire without protecting aviation and artillery; Nin, Mena, other POUM leaders murdered, thousands and tens of thousands jailed in the ensuing period. Capitulation took at least as many victims as struggle and defeat would have taken.

The POUM opposition—and it is not a Trotskyist opposition—were more than right when they said in their Bulletin of May 29:

> This retreat, ordered without conditions, without obtaining the control of public order, without the guarantee of workers patrols, without practical organs of the workers' [united] front, and without a satisfactory explanation to the working class, placing all the struggling elements—revolutionary and counter-revo-

lutionary—in the same sack, is one of the greatest capitulation and treason to the workers' movement.

The iron logic of politics is inexorable. The wrong course carries its supporters to undreamed-of depths. Determined to continue the policy of collaboration with the bourgeois state, the anarchist leadership—it seems only yesterday that these men defied the monarchy to the death—were sacrificing the lives and future of their following in the most cowardly fashion. Hanging on to the coattails of the CNT, the POUM leaders were chasing workers off barricades still under fire. They, least of all, would have believed themselves, a year ago, capable of falling so low. . . . Leaders who have betrayed the workers as these have are irrevocably lost to the revolutionary movement; they cannot turn back, admit their terrible complicity . . . But they are also pitiful, for on the morrow of their betrayal, the bourgeoisie, thus reinforced, will dispense with them too.

Let us remind the apologists for the POUM of one other respect in which their analogy with Petersburg of July, 1917 does not hold. The failure of the "armed demonstration" was followed by a savage hunt of the Bolsheviks: Trotsky was imprisoned, Lenin and Zinoviev went into hiding; the Bolshevik papers were suppressed. The cry went up: the Bolsheviks are German agents. Within four months, however, the Bolsheviks had carried through the October Revolution. I write six months after the May days, and the POUM is still crushed, dead. The analogy does not hold on this point because the difference is: the Bolsheviks fearlessly placed themselves at the head of the July movement and thereby became flesh and blood of the masses, while the POUM turned its back on the masses, and the masses, in turn, felt no urge to save the POUM.

# 11

# The dismissal of Largo Caballero

The defeat of the Catalonian proletariat marked a new stage in the advance of the counter-revolution. Hitherto, the reaction had developed under cover of collaboration with the CNT and UGT leaders, and even from September to December in the Generalidad with the POUM leaders. Thus, the gap between the openly bourgeois program of the bourgeois-Stalinist bloc and the revolutionary aspirations of the masses had been obscured by the centrists.* Now the moment arrived for the bourgeois-Stalinist bloc to dispense with the centrists.

The process is a familiar one in recent history. When blows to the left have sufficiently strengthened the right, the latter are then enabled to turn against the centrists whose services, heretofore, had been indispensable in crushing the left. The result of the suppression of the revolutionary workers is a government far to the right of the régime that suppressed them. Such was the result of the bloody

---

* This is the Marxian term employed to describe the variety of political formations which are not revolutionary but which also do not proclaim the class-collaboration doctrines of classical reformism.

suppression of the Spartacists in 1919 by Noske and Scheidemann. Such was the aftermath of the "stabilization" of Austria by Renner and Bauer. It was now the turn of the Spanish centrists to pay the price for having abetted the crushing of the Catalonian proletariat.

The first item of the bill presented by the Stalinists to the Valencia cabinet was the complete suppression of the POUM. Why the POUM? Like all renegades, the Stalinists understand the dynamics of revolutionary development better than their allies who have always been reformists. In spite of its vacillating policies, the POUM had in its ranks many revolutionary fighters for the interests of the proletariat. Even the POUM leaders, unready for revolution, would be driven to resist the naked counter-revolution. Stalin has understood that even the capitulators, the Zinovievs and Kamenevs, will be a danger on the day the masses rebel. Stalin's formula is: wipe out every possible focus, every capable figure, around whom the masses can rally. That bloody formula, already carried out in the August and January trials in Moscow, was now applied to Spain and the POUM.

The left socialists recoiled. One of their organs, *Adelante* (of Valencia) said editorially on May 11:

> If the Caballero government were to apply the measures of repression which the Spanish section of the Comintern is trying to incite, it would approximate a Gil Robles or Lerroux government; it would destroy working-class unity and expose us to the danger of losing the war and wrecking the revolution . . . A government composed in its majority of people from the labor movement cannot use methods reserved for reactionary and fascist-like governments.

The cabinet convened on May 15, and Uribe, the Stalinist Minister of Agriculture, bluntly put the question to Caballero: was he prepared to agree to the dissolution of the POUM, confiscation of its broadcasting stations, presses, buildings, goods, etc., and imprisonment of the Central Committee and local committees which had

supported the Barcelona rising? Federica Montseny awoke sufficiently to the occasion to present a dossier to prove that a plan had
been prepared, both in Spain and abroad, to strangle the war and
revolution. She accused Lluhi y Vallesca and Gassol (Esquerra), and
Comorera (PSUC), together with a Basque representative, of having participated in a meeting in Brussels at which it was agreed to
annihilate the revolutionary organizations (POUM and CNT-FAI)
in order to prepare for ending the civil war by the intervention of
"friendly powers" (France-England).

Caballero declared he could not preside over repression against
other workers' organizations, and that it was necessary to smash
the false theory that there had been a movement against the government in Catalonia, much less a counter-revolutionary movement.*

As the Stalinists continued to press their demands, Montseny
sent for a package containing hundreds of scarves adorned with
the shield of the monarchy. Thousands of these had been found in
the hands of the PSUC provocateurs and Estat Catala members,
who were to have planted them in POUM and CNT buildings. The
two Stalinist ministers rose and rushed out of the meeting, and the
ministerial crisis had begun.

Caballero looked at the others. He wanted them to state their
positions. The bourgeois and Prieto ministers solidarized themselves
with the Stalinists and went out. Such was the last meeting of the
Caballero cabinet.

✳

Outlawry of the POUM was the first demand of the counterrevolution, but the Stalinists followed it up with other basic demands which

---

* On May 4, the Valencia *Adelante* (obviously speaking for Caballero) solved the
problem of which side of the barricades to support by denying the real meaning
of the struggle: "We understand that this is not a movement against the legitimate
power. . . . And even if it were a revolt against the legitimate authority, and we do
not admit that such was the case, instead of being merely an inopportune and

Caballero and the left socialists would not accept responsibility for.

Friction between the Stalinists and left socialists had, indeed, been developing for some months. A stealthy campaign against Caballero himself had been waged in the Stalinist press since March, when the flow of adulatory telegrams to the "leader of the Spanish people" from "the workers of Magnitogorsk" had been turned off like a faucet. The Stalinist campaign had been the subject of comment in the organs of the CNT and POUM, and of resentful polemics in the left socialist press. The befuddled anarchists interpreted the Stalinist campaign in terms of the original sin of politics; this was the way political parties acted toward each other. The POUM sought to make easy capital among socialist workers by berating the Stalinists for attempting to absorb the socialists. Juan Andrade, the POUM commentator, saw more clearly, recognizing that Caballero was resisting the Anglo-French directives in their fullest implications. But the main POUM line of shouting "absorption" lost it the opportunity to make use of the real conflicts between Caballero and the bourgeois-Stalinist bloc. For there *were* real conflicts. Not, of course, as basic as the conflict between reform and revolution; but important enough so that a bold revolutionary policy could have driven a wedge between the Stalinists and Caballero's mass base, could have aroused the UGT workers to the meaning of the road which Caballero had followed for eight months.

Stalinist inroads into Caballero's ranks were a fact. It is a familiar enough phenomenon in the labor movement that when two organizations follow the same policy, the one with the stronger apparatus will proceed to absorb the other. By holding identical views with the Stalinists on the People's Front, winning the war before making the revolution, conciliating foreign opinion, building a regular bour-

poorly prepared collision between the organizations with different orientations and political and trade union interests opposed to each other within the general anti-fascist front in which the proletarian groups of Catalonia move, the responsibility for the consequences would have to be charged, naturally, to those who provoked the collisions."

geois army, etc., Caballero had ceased to differ from Stalinism in the eyes of the masses. With the native Stalinist apparatus tremendously reinforced by Comintern functionaries and funds—the International Brigades came in with hundreds of such functionaries attached to them—the Stalinists were in a position to recruit at Caballero's expense.

Particularly was this true in the youth. The socialist youth had been Caballero's strongest support but its fusion with the Stalinist youth had left him the loser, although the latter had not had one tenth the membership of the socialist youth. The usual Stalinist methods of corruption—trips to Moscow, adulatory relationships with the Russian and French YCL, the offer of posts in the Central Committee of the party, etc.—had been successful. Shortly after fusion, the socialist youth leadership had entered the Communist party and the "united" youth organization came under rigidly Stalinist control. Dissenting locals were "reorganized" and left wingers expelled as Trotskyists. Caballero was scarcely in a position to protest at the outcome, having himself connived at the bureaucratic method of fusion, without a congress of the socialist youth having been held to pass on the decision. Under the slogan of "unifying the whole youth generation," the Stalinist leadership bulwarked itself by recruiting indiscriminately anyone who could be persuaded to accept a card. Santiago Carrillo at a Central Committee Plenum of the Communist party shamelessly advocated recruiting of "fascist sympathizers" among the youth. Leaning on backward elements, including many Catholics, the Stalinists were able for a time to muzzle the thousands of left wingers still in the youth organization.

Nevertheless, Caballero's losses to the Stalinists had not led him to break with them. Absorption of his following only made him feel weaker and make further concessions.

Only when Caballero discovered that Stalinist inroads were less serious than he had supposed, and that he was more likely to lose his following to the left than to Stalinism, did he come into serious conflict with the Stalinists. The two biggest sections of the socialist youth, the Asturian and Valencian organizations, denounced the Stalinist top leadership and refused to accept seats in the "united" National Committee. In the delegates' meeting of the Madrid UGT, the Caballero ticket carried all eight seats on the Municipal Council allotted to the UGT, against a Stalinist ticket. In the Asturian Congress of the UGT, the Caballero group held 87,000 votes against 12,000 for the Stalinists. These indices, shortly before the government crisis, showed that Caballero could have the dominant following in the UGT, and that he would have to pacify his following and not the Stalinists in the coming period.

There was one step, above all, which Caballero could not accept responsibility for: the final moves in smashing the workers' control of the factories. Whatever else happened, the UGT masses were firmly convinced; they would never give up the factories. The Madrid organ of the UGT declared repeatedly: "The ending of the war must signify also the ending of capitalism."

> That the exploiters of all life cease to be masters of all the means of production, it has sufficed that the people take up arms in the struggle for national independence. From the great financial establishments to the smallest shops, they are, in actual fact, in the hands and under the direction of the working class . . . What vestiges remain of the old economic system? The revolution has eliminated all the privileges of the bourgeoisie and the aristocracy. (*Claridad*, May 12, 1937.)

*Claridad*,[*] indeed, continually studded its pages with quotations from Lenin. That these quotations were often enough damning commentary on Caballero's political conceptions hardly requires documentation. Quotations appeared from *The State and Revolution*, while Caballero strengthened and rebuilt the bourgeois state

---

[*] With the Negrin cabinet, *Claridad* passed into Stalinist control still continuing to call itself "organ of the UGT", although twice repudiated by the National Executive Committee.

apparatus which would inevitably attempt to wrest the factories from the workers. But, unless he was prepared to lose the support of the masses of the UGT, Caballero could not himself participate in wresting the factories from the workers. Caballero was just enough of a labor politician to recognize that the state he had himself revived was alien to the workers and that the bourgeois-Stalinist slogan of "state control of the factories" meant smashing the power of the factory committees.

We may sum up the fundamental differences between Caballero—i.e., the bureaucracy of the UGT—and the bourgeois-Stalinist bloc in this way: Caballero wanted a bourgeois democratic republic (with some form of workers' control of production co-existing with private property), victorious over Franco. The bourgeois-Stalinist bloc was ready to accept whatever Anglo-French imperialism proposed, which, at the stage of the overthrow of Caballero, was a stabilized bourgeois régime based on participation in the régime of the capitalist-landlord forces behind Franco, parliamentary in form, but actually Bonapartist since unacceptable to the masses.

Caballero's perspective was not so fundamentally different from that of the bourgeois-Stalinist bloc that they could not go along together for a considerable distance. They had gone along together for eight months. Was May 15 the correct moment for the rightists to break with Caballero? Should not the bourgeois-Stalinist bloc have bided its time for a few more months while the army and police were still further strengthened as bourgeois institutions? Should they not have carried the CNT ministers deeper and deeper into the swamp? Were they not risking a regroupment of forces by forcing the two mass labor organizations out of the cabinet? Were not the Stalinists too nakedly revealing their reactionary rôle by becoming the only labor group, apart from the long hated Prieto group, to participate in the government?

The Stalinists probably overestimated their ability to secure expressions of support for the new cabinet from enough UGT unions to obscure the fact that the labor unions as a whole were opposed to the new government. Even in the bureaucratically controlled UGT of Catalonia, the Stalinists proved unable to prevent many of the most important unions from declaring support for Caballero. Elsewhere the Stalinists got only a handful of unions to sanction the dismissal of Caballero.

If, however, the Stalinists miscalculated their ability to provide a labor "front" for Negrin, they were undoubtedly correct in other calculations. For them, the Barcelona events revealed that the CNT ministers were no longer of use in keeping the CNT masses in line; the fighting of May 3–8 had revealed the chasm between the leaders and the masses of the CNT. Further governmental participation of the CNT would provide little brake to the resistance of the masses and, on the other hand, could only speed up a split between these leaders and the masses. For the next period, the Olivers and Montsenys were more useful as a "loyal opposition" outside the government. As oppositionists they could regain control over their following, yet their opposition would be of a kind that would not unduly embarrass the Negrin Government.

As for the opposition from Caballero, its temper and quality had already been experienced: his "revolutionary criticism" of the People's Front government of February–July, 1936, and his even more radical declarations during the first war cabinet of July 19–September 4, 1936. In those periods Caballero had channelized discontent— and then had entered the government himself. If unforeseeable obstacles arose to endanger the government, the bourgeois-Stalinist bloc could always return to the status of May 15, for the centrists were demanding nothing more than that: "One cannot govern without the UGT and CNT" was the slogan of Caballero and the CNT leaders. Meanwhile, it was safe to predict that Caballero's opposition would not take the form of revival of the network of workers' committees and the co-ordinating of them into soviets—and only along that road did the bourgeois-Stalinist bloc have anything serious to fear.

If dropping the UGT and CNT involved no serious dangers, it offered immediate and far-reaching advantages for the bourgeois-

Stalinist bloc. Their immediate requirements were:

1. Complete control of the army. The mobilization and army re-organization decrees had been carried out by Caballero, as Minister of War, to a considerable extent. The regiments formed of drafted soldiers were built entirely on the old bourgeois model, largely officered by old army officers or the handpicked graduates of the government-controlled training schools. Any attempts among the conscripts at election of officers' and soldiers' committees had been stamped out. But the workers' militias which had carried the brunt of the struggle during the first six months were not yet all "reorga-nized"; their masses resisted fiercely any systematic replacement of their officers, most of whom came from their own ranks. Even on the Madrid front the CNT and UGT militias, despite partial reor-ganization, retained most of their former officers and continued to print their own political papers at the front. On the Catalan fronts, the anarchist militias refused to honor the decrees which the CNT ministers had signed. Equally important, Caballero became alarmed enough, after the loss of Málaga, to arrest General Asensio and the Málaga commander, Villalba, for treason, and cleaned out of the staffs many bourgeois friends of Prieto and the Stalinists. Caballero's caution thereafter in army reorganization was a serious obstacle to the Prieto-Stalinist program. For a ruthless reorganization of the militias into bourgeois regiments, officered by bourgeois appoin-tees in consonance with the old military code, and a purge of radi-cal army leaders thrown up by the July days, it was necessary to wrest the army entirely from Caballero.

2. The War Ministry offered the best vantage point from which to begin wresting control of the factories from the workers. In the name of the exigencies of the war, the ministry could step in and break the hold of the workers in the most strategic industries: rail-road and other transportation, mining, metals, textiles, coal and oil. The Stalinists had already begun to prepare for this in April by a barrage against the war-supply factories. Unfortunately for the Stalinists, they had organized this campaign (a persistent weakness of campaigns carried out obediently under orders of Comintern

representatives from Moscow) at a time when the atmosphere was not yet propitious for a pogrom. Their charges were refuted by joint statements of the CNT *and* UGT organizations in the Catalonian factories involved and, as we have seen, were disavowed even by Premier Tarradellas who, as Minister of Finance, disbursed to the factories the funds received from the Valencia treasury. It was clear, then, that this campaign could not be successfully consummated from outside but that the bourgeois-Stalinist bloc needed the Ministry of War to further their inroads into workers' control of the factories.

3. In Caballero's cabinet the Ministry of the Interior, which controlled the two main police bodies (Assault and National Republican Guard) and the press, was presided over by Angel Galarza, a member of the Caballero group. The revolutionary workers had sufficient reason to denounce his policies. Above all, Caballero and Galarza had sanctioned the decree forbidding police to join political and trade union organizations; and quarantining the police against the labor movement could only mean, inevitably, pitting them against the labor movement.

Nevertheless, the Caballero group recognized that repression of the CNT would be a fatal blow to the Caballero base, the UGT, and Caballero needed the CNT as a counterweight to the bourgeois-Stalinist bloc. Galarza had sent five thousand police to Barcelona, but had refused to carry out the Prieto-Stalinist proposals for complete liquidation of the POUM and reprisals against the FAI-CNT. Here again the Caballero group had built the instrument for hostilities against the workers, but drew back at carrying out its complete implications. Once Caballero and Galarza had induced the Generalidad, during the Barcelona fighting, to extend control of public order by the central government to Catalonia, the moment was ripe to oust Galarza, in order for the Stalinists to secure control of the police and press in Catalonia and elsewhere.

4. The Prieto-Stalinist program for conciliation with the Catholic Church—halfway house to conciliation with Franco—was being resisted by Caballero. Backbone of the monarchy and of the

*bienio negro,* the two black years of Lerroux-Gil Robles, the churches had been the fortresses of the fascist uprising. To be a member of a labor organization has always, in Spain, had to mean to be against the church, for the official catechism has declared it to be mortal sin to "vote liberal." The masses had spontaneously forced the closing of all the Catholic churches in July. One could scarcely propose a more unpopular measure than to permit the church organization to operate freely again—and in the midst of civil war! Furthermore, it was actually dangerous to the anti-fascist movement; for with the Vatican on the side of the Franco régime, it would inevitably use the church organization to help Franco. Yet this was the proposal of the Basque Government and its allies, Prieto and the Stalinists. Caballero had done many things to curry favor with the Anglo-French imperialists; but to permit the church organization to operate freely in the midst of the civil war was too much for him.

※

These causes of conflict between Caballero and the reactionary bloc are clearly revealed in the demands expressed by the various parties on May 16, during the customary visits to President Azaña, to acquaint him with the position of each group on the ministerial crisis.*

Manuel Cordero, spokesman for the Prieto Socialists, piously declared his organization stood for a government including all factions—but "I have insisted very particularly on the necessity of an absolute change in the policy of the Ministry of the Interior."

Pedro Corominas, for the Catalan Esquerra, declared: "Whatever be the solution that is adopted, it will be necessary to strengthen it and do away with difficulties of personal origin, by greater and more frequent contact with the Cortes of the Republic." In other words, the government policy should be dictated by the remnants of the Cortes elected in February, 1936, under an electoral agree-

---

* The statements of the parties are published in the press.

ment which gave the overwhelming majority of the Cortes to the bourgeois parties!

Manuel Irujo, for the Basque capitalists, spoke fairly bluntly:

> I have advised His Excellency for a government of national concentration presided over by a socialist minister who has the confidence of the [bourgeois] republicans. Since Caballero . . . has lost the political confidence of the groups of the Popular Front, it would be advisable to form a government, in our opinion, of Negrin, Prieto, or Besteiro, with the cooperation of all the political and trade union organizations which would accept the proposed bases.
>
> As specific demands, I feel obliged to make two, at present. The first is the necessity of proceeding, with such guarantees and restrictions as the war and public order dictate, to the re-establishment of the constitutional régime of liberty of conscience and religion.
>
> The second demand refers to Catalonia. The Catalan republicans would have preferred earlier and effective intervention by the Government of the Republic in assuming control of public order in support of the Generalidad. What is more, in now carrying out these duties, I feel that it is an unescapable duty of the Government that it liquidate to the bottom the problem which disturbs Catalonian life, firmly doing away with the causes of the disorder and insurrection, be they circumstantial or endemic . . .

It was to this Irujo that the Prieto-Stalinist bloc were soon to intrust . . . the Ministry of Justice.

Salvador Quemades, for the Left Republicans, Azaña's own party, required that the next cabinet "must have a decided policy in the matter of public order and of economic reconstruction, and that the commands of war, marine and the air force be placed in a single hand." Prieto was already Minister of Marine and Air. This meant adding to his posts that of control of the army (as was done).

The Stalinists demanded:

a) The President of the Council (Premier) occupy himself exclusively with affairs of the Presidency. The War Ministry to be separately conducted by another minister.

b) Elimination of Galarza from the new cabinet because of "his lenity in the problems of Public Order."

c) The Ministers of War and of the Interior "should be persons who enjoy the support of all the parties and organizations which form the Government." Which meant that these key posts, essential to the further schemes of the Basque-Prieto-Stalinist bloc, should pass to them.

The CNT declared it would support no government not headed by Caballero as Premier and Minister of War. The UGT issued a similar declaration. President Azaña, knowing the cards were already stacked, delegated Caballero to form a new cabinet with all groups represented. Caballero, in true centrist fashion, proceeded to cut the ground from beneath himself. He had already weakened his chief ally, the CNT, by his conduct in the Barcelona events. He now offered to cut the representation of the CNT from four ministries to two, Justice and Sanitation. To the Prieto group he offered two ministries, but these were to combine Finance and Agriculture, Industry and Commerce. Education and Labor were the two ministries for the Stalinists. The bourgeoisie, which in the previous ministry had enjoyed no posts except ministries without portfolios, were to have the ministries of Public Works and Propaganda (Left Republicans), the ministry of Communications and Merchant Marine (Union Republican), and ministries without portfolios for the Esquerra and Basque Nationalists. Caballero's proposed government was thus decidedly to the right of its predecessor. Caballero's conciliationism to the right could only impress the masses as meaning that the intransigence of the right denoted superior strength, and paved the way for the Right assuming all power with impunity.

The Stalinists rejected Caballero's compromise, and refused to participate in his cabinet except on the terms they had laid down. The Prieto group promptly declared it would not participate if the

Stalinists refrained. The bourgeois parties followed suit. Caballero could now either form a government of the UGT-CNT or surrender the government to the bourgeois-Stalinist bloc.

Caballero conducted himself during the ministerial crisis according to the traditional rules of bourgeois politics, which is to say that he kept the masses completely in the dark about developments and made no attempt to rally the workers against the right. So, too, the CNT. Later it became known that the day the cabinet had collapsed, Caballero had assured the CNT he was ready, if necessary, to have the UGT and CNT assume power. However, he begged off within a few hours, on the grounds of opposition within the UGT. "During the government crisis the UGT played a double game," said an FAI manifesto afterward: "The bourgeois and communist influences are so strong within this organization that its revolutionary sector, that is, the one which is inclined to work with us, was paralyzed. . . . That meant a victory not only for the bourgeois-communist bloc but also for France, England, and Russia who had obtained what they wanted." In other words, the anarchists leaned on Caballero, he pointed to the opposition, and in the general paralysis of the masses induced by their leaders, the rightist government came to power.

Perhaps, indeed, in his numerous sessions with Azaña during the days of the crisis, Caballero had broached the subject of a UGT-CNT government—and been refused. For Azaña constitutionally had the power to reject cabinets which did not suit him. The 1931 constitution endows the president with truly Bonapartist powers. Azaña himself had experienced this as premier, when in 1933 his cabinet, though still wielding a majority in the Cortes, was dismissed by President Zamora to make way for the semi-fascist government of Lerroux. These Bonapartist powers had not been wiped out on July 19. Azaña had quietly retired to a country retreat in Catalonia, had remained quiescent for most of the period of Caballero's rule. When members of the Caballero group were reproached for not having done away with the presidency during these months, they had patronizingly explained that the constitution and the presidency no longer existed, it was purely formalism to say that they did and, on the other hand, it was very useful for securing aid from abroad to continue the pretense of constitutionalism . . . and now, here was a very lively President Azaña, condescendingly receiving the spokesmen for the various parties, receiving reports from Caballero on his progress in getting together a cabinet, while Azaña's party, the Left Republicans, were in the bourgeois-Stalinist bloc . . . In any event, Caballero saved this bloc the unpleasantness of a public controversy over the presidential prerogatives. He informed Azaña that he had failed to form a cabinet and Azaña promptly designated Negrin to form a government of the bourgeoisie, the Prieto group, and the Stalinists.

# 12

## 'El gobierno de la victoria'

La Pasionaria christened the new cabinet "the government of victory." "We have made up our minds," she said, "to win the war quickly, though that victory cost us an argument with our dearest comrades." The Stalinists launched a world-wide campaign to prove that victory had been held up by Caballero and that it would now be forthcoming.

The annals of the Negrin government, however, proved to be not the record of military victory, nor even of serious attempts at military victory, but of ruthless repression of the workers and peasants. That reactionary course was dictated to the government by the Anglo-French rulers to whom it looked for succor. The spokesman for the Quai d'Orsay, *Le Temps*, indicated the real meaning of the ministerial crisis:

> The republican government of Valencia has reached the point where it must decide. It can no longer remain in the state of ambiguity in which it has hitherto lived. It must choose between democracy and proletarian dictatorship, between order and anarchy. (May 17.)

The next day the Negrin cabinet was formed. *Le Temps* approved but peremptorily pointed the road the new régime must resolutely travel:

> It would be too early to conclude that the orientation in Valencia is toward a more moderate government determined to free itself finally from the control of anarcho-syndicalists. But this is an attempt which, in the end, will have to be made no matter what the resistance of the extremists may be.

Clear directives, indeed!

The government, wrote an ardent sympathizer with its reactionary course, the New York *Times* correspondent, Matthews:

> . . . intends to use an iron hand to maintain internal order . . . By so doing, the government hopes to win the sympathy of the two democracies that mean most to Spain—Great Britain and France—and to retain the support of the nation that has been most helpful, Russia. The government's main problem now is to pacify or squash the anarchist opposition. (May 19, 1937.)

"In a word, the government unloosed a completely repressive machinery without any regard for the state of the war, or the requirements of keeping up the morale of the war," as a FAI statement of July 6 put it. "Anarchists are being eliminated as an active factor. The Caballero Socialists, if they persist in their present tactics, may be outlawed within three months," wrote the Stalinist, Louis Fischer (The *Nation,* July 17.)

In Caballero's cabinet Garcia Oliver, the "one hundred per cent anarchist," had labored mightily, fashioning democratic tribunals and judicial decrees, while the counter-revolution advanced behind him. The Generalidad had used Nin for the same purpose during the early months of the revolution. Now the government named as its Minister of Justice, the Basque capitalist and devout Catholic, Manuel Irujo. That such a man could hold this office meant: the time for pretending is over. Irujo in 1931 had voted against adoption of the republican constitution as a radical and atheistic document. Was he not then just the man for the Minister of justice?

Irujo's first step was to dismantle the popular tribunals which, each constituted by a presiding judge and fifteen members designated by the different anti-fascist organizations, had been set up after July 19, 1936. The FAI members were now barred from the tribunals—by the device of decreeing that only organizations legal on February 16, 1936, could participate. The FAI, of course, had been outlawed by the *bienio negro!* Most of the presiding judges had been left-wing attorneys. Roca, former sub-secretary of the Ministry, has since told how, in September, 1936, the Ministry of justice had called a meeting of the old judges and magistrates and had asked for volunteers to go to the provinces and set up the tribunals. Not one would volunteer. They knew the fascists would have to be convicted. Now the tribunals were cleansed of the left-wing attorneys who were replaced by the once reluctant judges for the tribunals no longer were to ferret out fascists but to prosecute workers. *Daily bulletins* listing fascists and reactionaries put at liberty were issued by Irujo's Ministry.

The complaints on this score were absolutely ignored for months. Finally—after his party had betrayed Bilbao and Santander—*Frente Roja* (August 30) denounced Irujo for "sheltering fascists." "It is intolerably ridiculous that at the same time as the fascist conquest of Santander, there should be distributed in Valencia the shameful lists of fascists and reactionaries that have been absolved and put at liberty." But this was merely for the record. The Stalinist ministers continued to sit in the cabinet with this man.

On June 23, the government decreed special courts to deal with sedition. Among "seditious acts" were included: "giving military, diplomatic, sanitary, economic, industrial or commercial information to a foreign state, armed organization or private individual," and all offenses "tending to depress public morale or military discipline." The judges were to be appointed by the Ministries of Justice and Defense, empowered to sit in secret session and to bar any third parties. The decree concludes:

> Attempted or frustrated offenses, conspiracies and plans, as well as complicity in sheltering of persons subject to this decree may be punished in the same way as if the offenses had actually been committed. Whoever, being guilty of such offenses, denounces them to the authorities, shall be free of all punishment. Death sentences may be imposed without formal knowledge of the cabinet.

The confession clause, the punishment for acts never committed, the secret trials, were translated directly from Stalin's laws. The sweeping definition of sedition made treason of any opinion, spoken or written or indicated by circumstantial evidence, which was construable as critical of the government. Applicable to any worker who agitated for better conditions, to strikers, to any governmental criticism in a newspaper, to almost any statement, act or attitude other than adoration of the régime, this decree was not only unprecedented in a democracy, it was more brazen than Hitler or Mussolini's juridical procedure.

On July 29, the Ministry of Justice announced that trials under this decree were being prepared for ten members of the Executive Committee of the POUM. These men had been arrested on June 16–17—before the new decree. That meant that the decree, to cap everything else, *was an ex post facto law,* punishing crimes *allegedly committed before the law was passed!* Thus, the most unquestioned juridical principle of modern times was expressly repudiated.

Irujo sponsored another decree, adopted and issued by the government on August 12, which declared:

> Whoever censures as fascist, as traitor, as anti-revolutionary, a given person or group of persons, unreasonably or without sufficient foundation, or without the [court] authority having

pronounced sentence on [the accused] . . .

Whoever denounces a citizen for being a priest or for administering the sacrament . . . causes an unnecessary and disruptive disturbance of public order when not committing an irreparable crime worthy of penal punishment.

This decree not only outlawed sharp ideological criticism of anybody in the governmental bloc, but also put an end to ferreting out of fascists by the workers. It also ended all forms of surveillance of the Catholic priesthood—just after the Vatican had openly thrown full support to Franco. Denunciations "without the court authority having pronounced sentence" in practice applied only against criticism from the left. The Stalinists continued, of course, to denounce the POUM as fascists, though no sentence had been passed.

Press censorship operated under a system which not only destroyed free criticism but required that the very acts of censorship be concealed from the people. Thus, on August 7, *Solidaridad Obrera* was suspended for five days for disobeying censors' orders, the specific act of obedience being—according to Gomez, General Delegate of Public Order in Barcelona, who had given the order—"that they should not publish white spaces." That is, deletions by the censor who worked from galleys must be hidden from the masses by inserting other material! As a silent protest, the CNT press had been leaving censored spaces blank.

On August 14, the government issued a decree outlawing all press criticism of the Soviet government:

With repetitions that permit divining a deliberate plan of offending an exceptionally friendly nation, thereby creating difficulties for the government, various newspapers have occupied themselves with the U.S.S.R. unsuitably . . . This absolutely condemnable license should not be permitted by the council of censors . . . The disobeying newspaper will be suspended indefinitely, even though it may have been passed by the censor; in that case the censor who reads the proofs is to be held for the Special Tribunal charged with dealing with crimes of sabotage.

The censorship decrees no longer referred to the radio. For, on June 18, police detachment had appeared at all the radio stations belonging to the trade unions and political parties and closed them down. Thenceforward, the government monopolized radio broadcasting.

One of the most extraordinary uses of the press censorship came when the Stalinist-Prieto bloc on October 1 split the UGT by a rump meeting of some unions which declared the Caballero-led Executive Committee deposed. While the new "Executive" freely published a stream of abusive declarations, the statements of the Caballero Executive were cut to pieces, as were the headlines in the CNT press referring to it as the rightful Executive. Formal protests of the CNT press against the government, thus taking sides in the inner union fight were fruitless.

Despite terrible instances—in almost every city captured by the fascists—of Assault and Civil Guards in large numbers going over to the fascists during the siege, the Ministry of the Interior proceeded to cleanse the police, not of the old elements, but of the workers sent in by their organizations after July 19. Examinations were decreed for all who entered the services in the past year. The Security Councils, formed by the anti-fascists among the police to clean out fascist elements, were ordered dissolved. More, the director-general of the police, the Stalinist, Gabriel Moron, ordered the ranks not to make denunciations of fascist suspects in the police, on pain of dismissal (*CNT,* September 1.)

Held to a slower pace until the political pre-conditions had been more fully achieved, the economic counter-revolution was now speeded up. In agriculture, the road to be followed had been mapped by the very first decree, October 7, 1936, which merely confiscated estates of fascists, leaving untouched the system of private property in land, including the right to own large properties and to exploit wage labor.

Despite the decree, however, collectivized agriculture became widespread during the first months of the revolution. The UGT was at first unfriendly to the collectives, and changed its attitude only after the movement developed strong roots in its own ranks. Several factors explained the speedy development of collectivized farming. Unlike the old Russian moujik, the Spanish peasants and agricultural workers had built trade unions for decades, and had provided considerable sections of the membership of CNT and FAI, UGT, POUM and the Socialist Party. This political phenomenon flowed in part from the economic fact that the division of the land was even more unequal in Spain than in Russia, and almost the entire Spanish peasantry was dependent partially or wholly on wage labor on the big estates. Hence, even those with a bit of land were weakened in the peasants' traditional preoccupation with his own plot of ground. Collective labor also derived strength from the almost universal necessity for joint work in providing water for the dry land. To these factors were added the enthusiastic aid given to the collectives by many factories, providing equipment and funds, the equitable purchasing of produce from the collectives by the workers' supply committees and the cooperative markets, the friendly collaboration of the collectivized railroads and trucks in bringing the produce to town. Another important factor was the peasant's realization that he no longer stood alone. "If, in some locality, a crop is lost or greatly reduced because of a long drought, etc." wrote the head of the CNT agrarian federation in Castille, speaking for 230 collectives, "our peasants don't have to worry, don't have to fear hunger, for the collectives in the other localities or regions consider it their duty to help them out." Many factors thus joined to encourage the swift development of collective agriculture.

But with the Stalinist Uribe's assumption of the Ministry of Agriculture, first in Caballero's cabinet and then in Negrin's, the weight of the government was thrown against the collectives. "Our collectives did not receive any sort of official aid. On the contrary, if they received anything at all, it was obstruction and calumnies from the

Minister of Agriculture and from the majority of institutions that depend upon this Minister," reported the CNT's Castilian agrarian federation (*Tierra y Libertad*, July 17). Ricardo Zabalza, national head of the UGT's Peasant and Landworkers' Federation, declared:

> The reactionaries of yesterday, the erstwhile agents of the big landowners, are given all sort of assistance by the government while we are deprived of the very minimum of it or are even evicted from our small holdings . . .
>
> They want to take advantage of the fact that our best comrades are now fighting on the war fronts. Those comrades will weep with rage when they find, upon leave from the war fronts, that their efforts and sacrifices were of no avail, that they only led to the victory of their enemies of old, now flaunting membership cards of a proletarian organization [the Communist party].

These agents of the big landowners, the hated *caciques*—overseers and village bosses—had been the backbone of the political machine of Gil Robles and the landowners. Now they were to be found in the ranks of the Communist party. Even such an outstanding chieftain of Gil Robles' machine as the secretary of the CEDA in Valencia had survived the revolution . . . and joined the Communist party.

Uribe justified the assault on the collectives by claiming that unwilling peasants were being forced to join them. One need scarcely comment on the irony that a Stalinist should complain of forced collectivization, after the Draconian slaughters and exiles of the "liquidation" of the Russian kulaks! Uribe would undoubtedly have produced evidence on this score, had he been able to find it, but none was forthcoming. *Both* big peasant and landworkers' federations, the affiliates of the CNT and UGT, opposed forced collectivization, favored voluntary collectives, and denounced the Stalinists as supporters of the *caciques* and reactionary rich peasants. In June, the Socialist *Adelante* sent a questionnaire to the various provincial sections of the UGT peasants' organization: almost unanimously they defended the collectives, and to a man reported that the main opposition to the collectives came from the Communist party, which for this purpose recruited the *caciques* and utilized the governmental institutions. All declared the October 7 decree was creating a new bourgeoisie. In a letter of protest to Uribe, Ricardo Zabalza described the simple but effective system of the Stalinists in attacking the collectives: old *caciques,* kulaks, landowners, were recruited and organized by the Stalinists and thereupon demanded the dissolution of the local collective, making claims on its land, equipment, stores of grain. Every such controversy brought in its wake the "mediation" of Uribe's representatives who invariably decided in favor of the reactionaries, imposing "settlements" whereby the collectives were gradually deprived of their equipment and land. When asked to explain this strange behavior, said Zabalza, the government agents declared they were acting under specific orders from their superior: Uribe. It was not surprising then that the UGT Peasants' Federation of Levante Province denounced Uribe as "Public Enemy Number One." Irujo's wards, the ex-fascists recently released became, by the very fact of release, eligible to demand return of their lands. When one of these returned as landlord, peasants fiercely resisted—and the Assault Guards were sent against them.

In the cities and industrial towns, too, the government proceeded to destroy all elements of socialization. "It is unquestionably true that had the workers not taken over control of industry the morning after the insurrection, there would have been complete economic paralysis," wrote the Stalinist, Joseph Lash, "but the improved schemes of workers' control of industry have not worked out very well." (*New Masses,* October 19.) There was a half-truth in this but the whole truth leads not back to the old proprietors but forward to the workers' state. Planning on a national scale is obviously impossible through factory and union apparatus alone. What is needed is a centralized apparatus, i.e., a state. Had the CNT understood this, and initiated the election of militia and peasant and factory committees, joined in a national council which would have constituted the government—that would have been a *workers' state,* which would have given full scope to the workers' committees and yet achieved the necessary centralization.

Instead, the anarchist leaders fought a losing battle, arguing as to just how much authority the state should have. Peiró, ex-minister of industry, for example: "I was prepared to nationalize the electric industry in the only way compatible with my principles—leave its administration and direction in the hands of the trade unions and not in the hands of the state. The state has only the right to act as accountant and inspector." Formally correct: Lenin said that socialism was simply bookkeeping. But only a workers' state would faithfully accept the functions of accountant and inspector, while the existent Spanish state, a bourgeois state, *must* fight socialization. Here again the anarchists, continuing to make no distinction between a workers' and bourgeois state, yielded to the bourgeois state, instead of fighting for the workers' state.

Through the Ministry of Defense, factories were taken over one by one. On August 28, a decree gave the government the right to intervene in or take over any mining or metallurgical plant. Quite explicitly, the government stated that workers' control was to be limited to protection of working conditions and stimulation of production. Resisting factories found themselves without credits or, having made deliveries to the government, payment was not forthcoming until the government's will was accepted. In many foreign-owned plants, the workers had already been stripped of any form of authority. The Department of Purchases of the Ministry of Defense announced that on a given date it would make contracts for purchases only with enterprises functioning "on the basis of their old owners" or "under the corresponding intervention controlled by the Ministry of Finance and Economy." (*Solidaridad Obrera,* October 7.)

The next step, for which the Stalinists had been campaigning for months, was militarization of all industries necessary to war—transportation, mines, metal plants, munitions, etc. This barracks régime is reminiscent of Gil Robles under whom munitions workers were also militarized—strikes and trade union membership forbidden. The militarization decree is sugar-coated by being titled "militarization and nationalization decree." But to militarize factories already in workers' hands, coupled with government recognition of full indemnification of former owners, simply ends workers' control and prepares for returning the factories to their former owners.

✳

The long-delayed session of the Cortes opened October 1, and fittingly symbolized this government. Negrin made a dull, gray speech, notable, however, for a long passage declaring that "one must prepare for peace in the midst of war." (The perturbed CNT press was not allowed to analyze the meaning of this talk of peace.) Caballero did not appear, the ostensible reason being his pre-occupation with the crisis in the UGT. His followers were silent while Gonzales Peña, on behalf of the socialist delegation, declared unconditional support for the government as, of course, did the Stalinists. Angel Pestaña, once a CNT leader, and now just re-admitted to the organization, pledged unconditional support to the government on behalf of his Syndicalist party. Twice during his speech, however, he was peremptorily silenced by Barrio who presided. The first time he was attempting to complain of Stalinist use of intimidation in proselytizing the army; the second time he was criticizing the failure to cleanse the rear of fascists and espionage elements. Thus, not a hint of the spirit of the masses penetrated the chamber.

Above all, the government was symbolized by new-found friends—reactionary deputies—who now appeared for the first time in Spain since July, 1936.

Miguel Maura was there! Chief of the extreme right republicans, Minister of the Interior in the first republican government, an implacable enemy of the trades unions, the first minister of the republic to re-institute the dreaded "law of flight" to shoot political prisoners—Maura had fled the country in July. His brother, Honorio, a monarchist, had been shot by the workers; the rest of his family had gone over to Franco. In exile, Maura had made no contact with the Spanish Embassies.

Portela Valladares was there! Governor-general of Catalonia for

Lerroux after the crushing of Catalan autonomy in October, 1934, he had been the last premier of the *bienio negro,* just before the February, 1936 elections. He had fled Spain in July. What he had done in the interim was unknown. Now he rose in the Cortes: "This parliament is the *raison d'etre* of the Republic; it is the title to life of the Republic. My first duty before you, before Spain, before the world, is to assure the legitimacy of your power . . . Today is for me one of intimate and great satisfaction, in having contributed with you to seeing our Spain in transition to a serious and profound reconstruction." At the end of the session, he and Negrin embraced. To the press, Valladares praised "the prevailing atmosphere as he had observed it in Spain." He went back to Paris, while the Stalinist press proved statistically that the presence of Valladares and Maura, signifying the center's support of the régime, gave a statistical majority of the electorate to the government.[*]

The ardor of the Stalinist press was cut abruptly by the reproduction in the fascist *Diario Vasco,* October 8, 1937, of a letter of Valladares to Franco, dated October 8, 1936, offering his services to the "national cause."

The Stalinist welcome to Vallarades and Maura was "offset" by a passing reference of Pasionaria to the unwelcome presence in the Cortes of another reactionary, a minor figure, a member of Lerroux's ruling party of the *bienio negro.* The deputy, Guerra del Rio, was given the floor to answer, in effect, that if the government rested on the Cortes, here he was. La Pasionaria subsided. CNT attacks on Maura and Valladares were deleted by the censor.

Was it for this then that the masses had shed their blood?

But we have still to tell the story of the government's conquest of Catalonia and Aragon.

---

[*] This anti-Marxist criterion enabled the fascists, by the same criterion, to argue that the rightist vote, plus that of those center deputies now with them, constituted a majority of the people. The claims of both, of course, were based on the February, 1936 election figures. The Marxist criterion is that a revolution derives its justification from the revolutionary vanguard's representing a majority of the *working class,* supported by the peasantry. By the present Stalinist criterion, one could condemn the Russian Revolution!

# 13

# The conquest of Catalonia

On May 5, Catalan autonomy had ceased to exist. The central government had taken over the Catalan Ministeries of Public Order and Defense. Caballero's delegate in Barcelona had broadcast: "From this moment, all the forces are at the orders of the central government . . . These forces do not consider any union or anti-fascist organization as an enemy. There is no other enemy than the fascists." But a week later the Ministries of Defense and Public Order were surrendered by Caballero's delegate to the representatives of Negrin-Stalin, and the pogrom began in earnest. The POUM went down with hardly a ripple. The PSUC opened a monstrous campaign against it identical in language, slogans, etc. with the witch-hunts of the Soviet bureaucracy before the Moscow trials. "The Trotkyists in the POUM have organized the latest insurrection on orders from the German and Italian secret police." The POUM's answer to the PSUC was—to institute a libel suit against the Stalinist editors in a court filled with bourgeois and Stalinist judges and officials!

On May 28, *La Batalla* was suppressed permanently and the POUM radio seized. The Friends of Durruti headquarters were occupied and the organization outlawed. Simultaneously, the official anarchist press was put under iron political censorship. Yet the POUM and CNT did not join in a mass protest. "We formulate no protest. We only make public the facts," wrote *Solidaridad Obrera,* May 29. The POUM youth organ, *Juventud Communista* (June 3) grandly remarked: "These are cries of panic and of impotence against a firmly revolutionary party . . ." And: "The [libel] trial goes forward. The PSUC organ must appear before the Popular Tribunals and they shall be revealed before national and international labor for what they are: vulgar calumniators." Naturally, on a technicality the trial was soon dismissed.

On the night of June 3, the Assault Guards attempted to disarm one of the remaining workers' patrols. Shots were exchanged. There were dead and wounded on both sides. Here was the government's opportunity to finish off the patrols. But here, also, was the POUM's opportunity to force the CNT leaders to defend the workers elementary rights by demanding a united front for simple, concrete proposals—defense of free assembly, the press, the patrols, common defense of workers' districts against the Stalinist hooligans, freedom of political prisoners, etc. The anarchist leaders could have hardly rejected these proposals without compromising themselves irreparably before their membership. Even against the CNT leaders' will, united front committees could have been created in the localities to fight for such simple, concrete demands.

For the POUM leaders, however, to raise such simple demands meant: we have been wrong in estimating the May days as a defeat of the counter-revolution; it was a defeat of the workers and now we must fight for the most elementary democratic rights. Secondly, it meant: we have been wrong in leaning on the CNT leaders, limiting ourselves to the general, abstract proposal of a "revolutionary front" of CNT-FAI-POUM which implies that the CNT is a revolutionary organization with which we can have a common platform on fundamental policies.* We must say openly, that a united front

---

* Juan Andrade had justified the "revolutionary front" absurdity by the following argument: "The disillusioned worker, turning away from the democratic tenden-

for the most elementary workers' rights is the most that can be expected of the anarchist leadership, if even that.

*Not once* in the year had the POUM called for a united front with the CNT for concrete tasks of struggle! The whole policy of the POUM leadership essentially consisted of nothing but trying to curry favor with the CNT leadership. *Not once* did they characterize the capitulatory policy of the CNT leadership, not even when they expelled the Friends of Durruti and left them to the mercies of the Assault Guards!

In its darkest hour the POUM was completely isolated. On June 16, Nin was arrested in his office. The same night, widespread raids caught almost all the forty members of the Executive Committee. A few who escaped were forced to give themselves up because their wives were seized as hostages. The next morning the POUM was outlawed.

The Regional Committee of the CNT did not come to the defense of the POUM. *La Noche* (CNT) of June 22, published in boldface: "About the espionage service discovered in the last days. The

---

cies of the socialists and communists, inclines to join a powerful organization, such as, CNT-FAI, which holds radical positions *even if they are not applied in fact,* rather than join a minority party bothered by material difficulties. The workers already in the CNT see no need of leaving it to join a revolutionary Marxist party because in contrasting the *surface* revolutionary positions of the CNT-FAI with the simply democratic ones of the socialists and Stalinists, they believe the tactics of their organization still hold the guarantee for continued development of the revolution toward the building of a socialist economy. In this sense, all those who hold a strictly sectarian schematic concept of how a minority with a correct political line can rapidly become a decisive force, can learn a valuable lesson from the events in Spain. . . . The difficulties in the way of the rapid development of a great mass party which would assume the effective leadership of the struggle can be largely resolved by the establishment of the Revolutionary Front between these two organizations . . ." In other words, it is impossible to build the party of the revolution: the Revolutionary Front is a substitute. But the main obstacle to building the revolutionary party, beside the POUM's own false program, was that the CNT's *surface* radicalism was *not* systematically criticized before the masses by the POUM. The POUM had thus cut itself off from growth—and used its failure to justify continuing that failure.

principal ones implicated were found in the leading circles of the POUM. Andres Nin and other known persons arrested." There followed some general reflections on slander, with copious references to Shakespeare, Gorki, Dostoievski and Freud . . . If censorship was to be blamed, then where were the CNT's illegal leaflets? In Madrid, *CNT* did come to the defense of the POUM, and was followed by *Castilla Libre* and *Frente Libertario,* militia organ. On June 28, the National Committee of the CNT addressed a letter to the ministers and their organizations reminding them that Nin, Andrade, David Rey, Gorkin, etc., "had acquired their prestige among the masses by long years of sacrifice." "Let them solve their problem in the U.S.S.R. as they can or circumstances advise them. It is not possible to transplant to Spain the same struggle, prosecuted with blood and fire, internationally by means of the press and here by means of the law utilized as a weapon." The letter indicated an entire lack of understanding of the significance of the persecutions: "Before all it imports us to declare that the CNT, by its intact and powerful strength, today perfectly organized and disciplined, is above all fear that tomorrow this method of elimination can overcome us. Placed above this semi-internal struggle," etc. This pompous chest-beating meant that the CNT masses would not be aroused by their leaders to the counter-revolutionary meaning of the persecutions.

Above all, the great masses had not been prepared to understand the Stalinist system of frame-up and slander. Currying favor with Stalin, the anarchist leaders had been guilty of such statements as that of Montseny: "Lenin was not the true builder of Russia but rather Stalin with his practical realism." The anarchist press had preserved a dead silence about the Moscow trials and purges, publishing only the official news reports. The CNT leaders even ceased to defend their anarchist comrades in Russia. When the anarchist Erich Muehsam was murdered by Hitler, and his wife sought refuge in the Soviet Union, only to be imprisoned shortly after her arrival, the CNT leadership stifled the protest movement in the CNT ranks. Even when the Red Generals were shot, the CNT organs published only the official bulletins.

By mid-July, the POUM's leaders and active cadres were all in jail! Over its buildings flew the violet-yellow-red flags of the bourgeoisie. The Lenin barracks were occupied by the Republican "People's Army." Its presses had been destroyed or given to the PSUC. On the bulletin board of *Batalla* was a copy of *Julio,* PSUC youth organ, headlining: "Trotskyism is synonymous with counterrevolution." The POUM's dormitories, ex-Hotel Falcon, had become a prison for POUM members and the headquarters of the Spanish GPU. Its members were dispersed, disoriented, living in fear of nightly raids by the Assault Guards. "Small groups work on their own hook," wrote an authoritative eyewitness early in July. "It reminds one very much of the crumbling of the Communist Party of Germany in January, 1933. The working class remains passive and permits anything to happen. The CNT press prints only official notices. No protest! Nowhere even a word of protest! The POUM has been swept away like a speck of dust. 'Like under Hitler,' say the German comrades. The Russian Bolshevik-Leninists would add: 'Almost like under Stalin'."

In July, the local FAI committees began illegal propaganda. Unfortunately it did not center around rallying the workers to the concrete tasks of freeing the political prisoners. One typical leaflet recalled the German Social Democracy's propaganda on the eve of Hitler, demanding the help of the state—*Staat greif zu!*—against its own bands. Protesting Stalinist assaults on anarchist youth buildings, "How long? It is time for the Government Council to speak, or lacking that, the Delegate General of Public Order and the Chief of Police," read one pathetic leaflet.

Nor were the illegal POUM leaflets, which now began to appear, much better. They, who had always reproached the Bolshevik-Leninists for seeing only Stalinism as the enemy, became themselves anti-Stalinist and nothing more. One typical leaflet, for example, addressed itself to everybody on the left and on the right: to the anarchists as well as to the "young separatists" of the Estat Catala. "The men of the Left cannot betray their postulates. The Separatists cannot sell Catalonia by their silence." And the final slogan!

"Prevent the establishment of the dictatorship of a party behind the lines." What of the Estat Catala and Esquerra, Prieto and Azaña, accomplices of the Stalinists, indeed the main beneficiaries?

Thus, false policies facilitated the deadly advance of the counter-revolution. Only the small forces of the Bolshevik-Leninists, who had been expelled as "Trotskyists" from the POUM, and had formed their organization in the spring of 1937—only this small band, working under the three-fold illegality of the state, the Stalinist and the CNT-POUM leadership, clearly pointed the road for the workers. Not only the ultimate road of the workers' state but the immediate task of defending the democratic rights of the workers. That the CNT masses could be aroused was shown by the protection they accorded Bolshevik-Leninists distributing illegal leaflets. At one meeting (of the woodworkers' union), lorries of Assault Guards arrived and attempted to arrest the distributors. The meeting declared that the leaflet distributors were under their protection and would repulse with arms any attempt to break in. The police were forced to leave without our comrades.

A Bolshevik-Leninist leaflet of July 19 points the road: the united front of struggle of the CNT-FAI, POUM, the Bolshevik-Leninists and the dissident anarchists:

> Workers: demand of your organization and your leaders a united front pact which must contain:
>
> 1. Struggle for the freedom of the workers' press! Down with political censorship!
>
> 2. Liberation of all revolutionary prisoners. For the liberation of comrade Nin, transported to Valencia!
>
> 3. Joint protection of all centers and enterprises in the possession of our organizations.
>
> 4. Reconstitution of strengthened Workers' Patrols. Cessation of disarming the working class.
>
> 5. Equal pay for officers and soldiers. The return to the front of all the armed forces sent from Valencia. General offensive on all fronts.

6. Control of prices and distribution through committees of working men and working women.

7. Arrest of the provocateurs of May 3: Rodriguez Salas, Ayguade, etc.

To achieve this, all workers form the united front! Organize Committees of Workers, Peasants and Combatants in all enterprises, barracks and districts on the land and at the front!

But not in a day, or a month, does a new organization win the leadership of the masses. The road is long and hard—and yet the only road.

✳

By July, according to the official CNT figures, eight hundred of their members in Barcelona alone were imprisoned, and sixty had "disappeared"—euphemism for assassination. The left socialist press reported scores of its leading militants everywhere seized and jailed.

One of the most repulsive phases of the counter-revolution was its merciless persecution of the foreign revolutionists who had come to Spain to fight in the ranks of the militias. A single report to the CNT on July 24, counted 150 foreign revolutionists in a Valencia prison—arrested on "the charge of illegally entering Spain." Hundreds were expelled from the country and the CNT cabled the workers' organizations in Paris, appealing to them to prevent the German, Italian, Polish exiles from being delivered into the hands of their consulates.

But the foreigners arrested and expelled did not meet the worst fate. Others among them were selected to complete the amalgam between the POUM and the fascists. Maurin was in fascist hands, in danger of death. Nin, Andrade, Gorkin were too well known to the Spanish masses. The POUM had too many thousands of its best men at the front. Too many of its leaders had died fighting fascism: Germinal Vidal, the Youth Secretary, at the taking of the Atarazanas barracks on July 19; his successor, Miguel Pedrola, commandant on the Huesca front; Etchebehere, commandant at Siguenza; Cahué and Adriano Nathan, commandants on the Aragon front; Jesus Blanco, commandant on the Pozuelo front, etc. Among the POUM's military figures were men like Rovira and José Alcantarilla, famed throughout Spain. A few unknown foreigners, fighting in the POUM battalions, would serve to add to the credibility of the fantastic charges.

Georges Kopp, a Belgian ex-officer, serving in the POUM's Lenin Division, had just returned to Barcelona from Valencia, where he had been given a major's commission—the highest commission awarded foreigners—when the Stalinists arrested him. Then the Stalinist propaganda factory went to work. Robert Minor, American Stalinist leader, announced that the paucity of arms on the Aragon front—this was the first time the Stalinists admitted this charge of the CNT—was now explained: "The Trotskyist General Kopp had been carting enormous supplies of arms and ammunition across no-man's land to the fascists!" (*Daily Worker,* August 31 and October 5.)

The choice of Kopp, however, was a G.P.U. blunder of major proportions, comparable to the story of Romm's meeting with Trotsky in Paris or Piatakov's flight to Norway. For Georges Kopp, forty-five years old, was a militant of long standing in the Belgian revolutionary movement. When the Spanish war broke out, he was chief engineer in a large firm in Belgium. It had been usual for him to experiment at night. He circulated the story that he was trying out a new machine, perfecting it by the actual process of manufacture. What he manufactured, however, were the ingredients for millions of rounds of cartridges. Left socialists organized illegal transport to Barcelona. When Kopp discovered that he was under suspicion, he took leave of his four children and headed for the frontier. The very day he fled, the police raided his laboratory. *In absentia,* Kopp was sentenced by the Belgian courts to fifteen years at hard labor: five for making explosives for a foreign power, five for leaving the country without permission while a reserve officer in the Belgian Army, and five for joining a foreign army. Twice wounded on the Aragon front, he soon won the rank of commandant.*

Kopp cannot answer the Stalinist slanderers for they have killed him. He was in a Barcelona jail with our American comrade, Harry Milton. In the middle of the night, Kopp was dragged out. That was in July, and the last time he was ever seen.

On July 17, a group of POUM members were released from prison in Valencia. It is a fact that most of them were extreme right-wingers, such as, Luis Portela, editor of *El Comunista*, Jorge Arquer, etc. Consequently their subsequent testimony was particularly cogent. Upon release, they went to Zugazagoitia, Minister of Interior, who told them that Nin had been taken from Barcelona to one of the private prisons of the Stalinists in Madrid. Arquer thereupon requested a safe-conduct to search for Nin. The minister, a Prieto man, told him: "I guarantee you nothing; what is more, I advise you not to go to Madrid because with my safe-conduct or without you would endanger your life. These communists don't respect me and they do as they please. And there would be nothing strange if you were seized and shot immediately by them." Publicly, however, Zugazagoitia was still saying that Nin was in a government prison. On July 19, however, Montseny, for the CNT, publicly charged that Nin had been murdered. Embarrassed by the numerous inquiries from abroad about specific prisoners' whereabouts which the government was unable to answer for the simple reason that most of the prominent ones were in private Stalinist "preventoriums," it was arranged that the prisoners be transferred from the Stalinist jails in Madrid and Valencia to the formal keeping of the Ministry of Justice. Nin was not among them. Irujo issued a statement that Nin was "missing." Fled, the Stalinists said, toward the fascist lines. But the truth finally got out. On August 8, the New York *Times* reported that "nearly a month ago a band of armed men 'kidnapped' Nin from a Madrid prison. Although every effort has been made to hush up the affair, it is now a matter of common knowledge that he was

---

* The British *New Leader,* August 13, 1937, published two detailed articles on Kopp's record.

found dead on the outskirts of Madrid, a victim of assassination." As a personal friend of Nin and Andrade, the great Italian novelist, Ignazio Silone, had tried to save them. "But," he warned, "unless the revolutionary proletariat of other countries is watchful, the Stalinists are capable of every crime." Alvarez del Vayo, former Minister of Foreign Affairs in Caballero's cabinet, notoriously Stalin's agent in the Caballero group, had the effrontery to tell the wife of Andrade that Nin had been murdered by his own comrades. (It is only just to add that del Vayo has since been excluded by the Socialist organization—Caballero-led—of Madrid.) Premier Prieto shrived his soul for this and other crimes by dismissing the Stalinist Police Chief, Ortega . . . and replaced him with the Stalinist, Moron.

To cap the suppression of revolutionists with slander is scarcely a new invention. When, in Paris, the June, 1848, insurrection was drowned in blood, the National Assembly was assured by the left democrat, Flaucon, that the insurrectionists had been bribed by monarchists and foreign governments. When the Spartacists were shot down, Ludendorff charged that they—and indeed, the social democrats who shot them too!—were agents of England. When the counter-revolution got the upper hand in Petrograd, after the July days, Lenin and Trotsky were indicted as agents of the Kaiser. The destruction of the generation of 1917 is now carried out by Stalin under the charge that they have sold themselves to the Gestapo.

The parallel goes further. While Kerensky was shouting that Lenin and Trotsky were German agents, Tseretelli and Lieber—in the soviets—were, under questioning, dissociating themselves from the charge, limiting themselves to demanding the outlawry of the Bolsheviks for planning an insurrection. But, profiting from Kerensky's charge, the Mensheviks did not ascend the housetops to proclaim the Bolsheviks' innocence.

So, too, in Spain. The Stalinists were not even as successful as Kerensky: the indictment handed down against the POUM leaders made no mention of collaboration with Franco or the Gestapo. The charge was based on the May days and similar subversive and oppositional deeds. Prieto and other collaborators of the Stalinists told the I.L.P. delegation they did not believe the Stalinist linking of POUM to the fascists. They "merely" did not come to the defense of the POUM. Companys not only disavowed belief in the charges but made the fact public. Thus there was a division of labor: if you don't believe the slanders, then you must believe the POUM was organizing an insurrection, i.e., they were either counter-revolutionists or revolutionists, whichever you preferred. A narrower division of labor was that between the world Stalinist press, which repeated the "Trotskyist-fascist" slanders, and the anti-POUM-CNT propaganda of Louis Fischer, Ralph Bates, Ernest Hemingway, Herbert Matthews, etc. who "merely" repeated such myths as that the POUM militias played football in no-man's land with the fascists.

✳

Already by the end of June, Catalan autonomy, though guaranteed by statute, was completely suppressed. The authorities distrusted anybody who had any tie with the Catalan masses, no matter how tenuous. With the exception of the most reactionary sector, the old Civil Guards, all the police in Catalonia were transferred to other parts of the country. Even the firemen were transferred to Madrid. Parades were forbidden, and union meetings could be held only by permission of the delegate of public order and on three days notice—as under the monarchy!

The workers' patrols had been wiped out, their most active members imprisoned, their chiefs "disappeared."

Having done all this with the aid of the screen provided by CNT ministers still sitting in the Generalidad, the bourgeois-Stalinist bloc now dispensed with their services.

A June 7 bulletin of the FAI published a Stalinist communication which had been intercepted, saying:

> Based on the provisional composition of the government, our party will demand the presidency. The new government will have

the same characteristics as that of Valencia; a strong government of the People's Front *whose chief task* will be to calm the spirits and demand punishment for the authors of the last counter-revolutionary movement. The anarchists will be offered posts in this government but in such a manner that they will be compelled to refuse to collaborate, and in this manner we shall be able to present ourselves to the public as the only ones willing to collaborate with all sections.

The anarchists challenged the PSUC to deny the authenticity of this document, but there were no challengers.

At the end of June, came the ministerial crisis. The CNT agreed to whatever demands were made, and the new ministry was formed. Publication of the ministerial list on June 29, however, revealed to the CNT that, without their knowledge, a minister without portfolio had been added—an "independent" named Dr. Pedro Gimpera, a notorious reactionary and anarchist-baiter. Companys blandly refused to withdraw him. The CNT at last withdrew, leaving a government of the Stalinists and the bourgeoisie.

The only difference between the Stalinist bulletin exposed by the FAI and the actual course of the ministerial crisis was that the Stalinists had not asked for the presidency . . . But six weeks later, without any previous hint, the Stalinists clashed with President Companys.

In November, 1936, when the CNT intelligence service had seized Reberter, the Chief of Police, and had him tried and shot for organizing a *coup d'etat,* the investigation had implicated Casanovas, President of the Catalan parliament. But the Stalinists had supported Companys in prevailing upon the CNT to let Casanovas leave the country and Casanovas had fled to Paris. After the May days, he had returned to Barcelona with impunity. He spent the next three months pleasantly re-establishing himself in political life. During all these nine months, he had not been subject to a word of condemnation from the Stalinists. (Stalin has employed this method systematically in Russia: a bureaucrat is involved in a misdeed; he is permitted to go on because all the more servile for knowing that his crime is detected, then—sometimes years later—Stalin needs a scapegoat and the wretch is pilloried.) On August 18, the Catalan parliament opened. Without a previous word of warning to their allies—it could obviously have been settled behind closed doors—the PSUC delegation of four publicly attacked Casanovas as a traitor. The Esquerra had been tricked into a position where it had to reject Casanovas' offer to resign. With this excellent little whip, the Stalinists began to drive the Esquerra as they pleased, ending with the announcement of Companys' early resignation from the presidency, after the Stalinists had boycotted the October 1 session of the Catalan parliament.

Why did the Stalinists break with Companys? He had done their bidding in so much! Why, then, was Companys now slated to go?[*]

He had made one unforgivable break with the Stalinists. Companys had publicly declared that he had known nothing of the plans for outlawing the POUM; had protested transfer of the prisoners from Barcelona; and had sent to Madrid the chief of the Catalan press bureau, Jaime Miravittlles, to see the Stalinist Police Chief, Ortega, on behalf of Nin. When Ortega showed him the "crushing proofs"—a document "found" in a fascist center, linking one "N" to a spy ring, Miravittlles—by his own account—had burst out laughing, and declared the document was such an obvious forgery no one would dream of taking it seriously. Companys had then written to the Valencia government that Catalan public opinion could not believe Nin was a fascist spy.

Not that Companys was going to fight for the POUM prisoners. Having salved his conscience—and made the record for any future overturn!—Companys relapsed into silence. That his silence did not save him from attack indicated that the Stalinists could not forgive any ally who exposed their frame-ups: the frame-up is the very foundation-stone of Stalinism today.

---

[*] The speed with which the fascists broke through the Aragon front disrupted the Stalinists' plans, and Companys was not dropped.

But there was a more profound reason for the break with the Esquerra. The Nin incident merely indicated that Companys was not hardened enough for the future moves of the Stalinists. He was, after all, a nationalist, desiring a return to Catalan autonomy. And for Stalinism, Spain and Catalonia were merely pawns which they were ready to sacrifice, with which they were ready to do anything that Anglo-French imperialism dictated, in return for a military alliance for Stalin in the coming war. That is why there had to be a selection even from among the Prieto socialists and the Azaña republicans: only the most brutalized, most corrupt, most cynical could weather the coming storms created by the Stalinists, and remain in collaboration with them.

The economic counter-revolution in Catalonia advanced against the collectives. To the honor of the local sections of the libertarian movement, they stood their ground. For example, the strong anarchist movement in Bajo Llobregat (heart of armed struggles against the monarchy and the republic), declared in its weekly, *Ideas,* on May 20:

> Here is what we must do, workers! You have the opportunity to be free. For the first time in our social history the arms are in our hands: don't drop them. Workers and peasants! When you hear that the government, or anybody else, tells you that the arms should be at the front, answer them that that is certainly so, that the thousands of rifles, machine guns, mortars, etc. that are kept in the barracks, that are used by the carabineros, Assault and National Guards, etc. should be sent to the front because to defend your fields and factories, nobody can do that better than you.
>
> Remember always that airplanes, cannons and tanks are what are needed at the front quickly to crush fascism . . . that what the politicians are looking for is to disarm the workers, to have them at their mercy, and to take away from them what has cost so much proletarian blood and lives. Let nobody permit the disarming of anybody; let no village allow another to be disarmed;

let us all disarm those who try to disarm us. This should be, must be, the revolutionary slogan of the hour.

The gap between the pusillanimity of the central organs of the CNT and the fighting spirit of the local papers, close to the masses, was as wide as that between craven cowards and revolutionary workers.

But tens of thousands of Assault Guards, concentrated behind the lines, struck systematically at the collectives. Without centralized direction, the villages were overpowered, one by one. *Libertad,* one of the dissident illegal anarchist papers of Barcelona (incidentally, it paid its contemptuous respects to *Solidaridad Obrera,* which had denounced the illegal organs), described the situation in the countryside in its issue of August 1:

> It is useless that the censorship, in the power of one party, prevents a word being said about the thousands of blows inflicted on the workers' organizations, the peasant collectives. In vain that they prohibit mention of that terrible word, counter-revolution. The working masses know perfectly that the thing exists, that the counter-revolution advances under the protection of the government, and that the black beasts of reaction, the disguised fascists, the old *caciques,* are again raising their heads.
>
> And how should they not know it, if there is not a village in Catalonia where the punitive expeditions of the Assault Guards have not been, where they have not assaulted the CNT workers, destroying their locals or what is worse, destroyed those portentous works of the revolution, the collectives of the peasants, in order to return the land to the old proprietors, almost always known as fascists, *ex-caciques* of the black epoch of Gil Robles, Lerroux or Primo de Rivera?
>
> The peasants took the goods of the bosses—which in justice did not belong to them—to place them at the service of collective labor, permitting the old bosses to dignify themselves, if they wished, by work. They believed, the peasants, that so noble a

work was guaranteed by its own efficiency, if fascism were not triumphant, and it could not triumph. Scarcely did they suspect that in the midst of war against the terrible enemy, with the government being men of the left, the public forces [police] would come to destroy that which had been created with such fatigue and joy. For this inconceivable thing to happen, there had to come to power, by dirty means, those called communists. And the workers, ready always to make the greatest sacrifices to defeat fascism, do not end wondering how it is possible that they be attacked from behind, that they be humiliated and betrayed, when there still is so much lacking for conquering the common enemy . . .

The technique of repression is always the same. Lorries of Assault Guards that enter the village like conquerors. Sinister registrations in the locals of the CNT. Annulment of municipal councils where the CNT is represented. Plundering searches and arrests. Seizure of the food of the collectives. Return of the land to their old proprietors.

This movingly simple description was followed by a long list of villages, the dates on which they were assaulted, the names of those arrested or killed—and in the ensuing months the list grew longer and longer.

In industry and commerce, the juridical basis of the collectivized establishments rested on the insecure foundation of the collectivization decree of October 24, 1936. But immediately after the May days, the Generalidad repudiated the decree! The occasion was the attempt of the CNT to release the factories from the stranglehold of the customs officials, without whose certification of ownership of export goods arriving abroad were being sequestered under claims of emigrated former owners. The anarchist-led Council of Economy (of the Ministry of Industry) adopted on May 15 a proposed decree to record the collectivized establishments as the official owners in the Mercantile Register. But the bourgeois-Stalinist majority in the Generalidad rejected the proposal on the ground that the October 24 collectivization decree "was dictated without competency by the Generalidad" because "there was not, nor is there yet, legislation of the [Spanish] State to apply" and "article 44 of the [Spanish] Constitution declares expropriation and socialization are functions of the [Spanish] State," i.e., the Catalan autonomy statute had been exceeded! The Generalidad would now await action by Valencia. But Companys had signed the October decree! That was during the revolution . . .

The chief agency of economic counter-revolution was the GEPCI, the long-established businessman's organization taken bodily into the Catalan section of the UGT by the Stalinists but repudiated by the UGT nationally. With union cards in their pockets, these men did with impunity what they would never have dared before July 19 against the organized workers. Many of them were now no longer petty manufacturers but great entrepreneurs. They received preferential consideration in securing financial credits, raw materials, export services, etc., as against the factory collectives. One little item will destroy the Stalinist myth that these were petty little storekeepers, one-man establishments. In June, 1937, the UGT clothing workers drafted a scale of wages, identical with those in the clothing collectives, and sought to negotiate with the capitalist-owned clothing factories. The employers rejected the demands. But who were the employers? Members, to a man, of GEPCI, that is, like the employees whom they were refusing wage rises, they were members of the UGT in Catalonia! (*Solidaridad Obrera,* June 10.) Would the most reactionary trade union bureaucrat, of the stamp of Bill Green or Ernest Bevin, propose that bosses and workers be in one "union"? No, that vast step backward could come only from the Stalinists, aping Fascist Italy and Nazi Germany.

In June, under the slogan of "municipalization," the PSUC launched a campaign to wrest the transportation, electric, gas, and other key industries from workers' control. On June 3, the PSUC delegation formally proposed, in the Barcelona Municipal Council, that it municipalize public services. On the morrow, of course, the CNT councillors would be thrown out, and the Stalinists would have the public services in their hands for the next step in returning them to their former owners. But this time they were confronted, not merely by the temporizing CNT leaders—who proposed that municipalization was "premature" in this field, one ought to begin with housing—but with the mass response of the workers involved. The Transport Workers Union plastered every block of the city with huge posters: "The revolutionary conquests belong to the workers. The workers' collectives are the product of these conquests. We must defend them . . . To municipalize the urban public services, yes—but only when the municipalities belong to the workers and not to the politicians." The posters demonstrated that since the workers had taken control, there had been a thirty per cent increase in plant facilities, lowering of fares, additional workers employed, big donations to the agricultural collectives, subventions to the harbor workers, social insurance to families of deceased or wounded workers, etc. For the moment, the Stalinist advance was beaten in this field.

But the Stalinists continued toward their goal of destroying the worker-controlled factories. The Catalan Generalidad set September 15 as the deadline for proving the legality of collectivized factories. Since much of the collectivization was done overnight to speed the civil war against the fascists, few factories had established any juridical procedure. What, indeed, were the legalities involved in the expropriations? The original decree of October 24, 1936, we have discussed in our chapter on the first Generalidad cabinet. It was designed precisely to provide entering wedges for the future. And the Generalidad had now repudiated it! At leisure and at will, the Generalidad would now examine the legal title of the social revolution and find it undoubtedly full of legal flaws. What a preposterous business! But a tragic one.

It was in the food industries, distribution, markets, etc., that the Stalinists had gotten their first grip, holding the Ministry of Supplies in the Generalidad since December, when they had promptly dissolved the workers' supply committees, which then had been provisioning the cities under controlled prices. Even through the temporizing of the CNT press and the opacity of the censorship, the accounts now reflected what was happening here:

> ... Collectives, socialized undertakings and co-operatives, embracing both members of the UGT and CNT, have been made the target of attack on the part of those who hid in desertion on the 19th of July ... The dairymen of both unions are being arrested right and left. The cows and the dairy farms, organized legally on a co-operative basis, are being confiscated, although their statutes have been officially approved by the Generalidad for several months. These cows and dairy establishments are being handed over to their former owners ... The same thing is happening, although still on a small scale, in the bread industry ... Our markets, the central fish market, etc., although collectivized legally, are also suffering from these vicious attacks by the former bourgeoisie. They are being encouraged by the poisonous campaigns conducted daily in the press of the party that has constituted itself the Champion for the Defense of the GEPCI (Corporations and Units of Petty Merchants and Manufacturers). It is no longer merely a fight against the CNT collectives, but against all the revolutionary conquests of the UGT-CNT ...
>
> A hard fist against the fascists and counter-revolutionaries hiding behind a trade union card! (*Solidaridad Obrera*, June 29.)

"Is the Ministry of Supplies at the service of the people, or has it been transformed into a bigger merchant?" asked the CNT press. "The basic articles of food are: rice, string beans, sugar, milk, etc. Why are these not included among those items that the Committee of Distribution, recently formed by the UGT-CNT, distributes equally among all the stores of Barcelona, regardless of the organization to which they belong?" Instead, these basic articles were uncontrolled, left to the mercy of the GEPCI. *La Noche* (June 26) responding to the bitterness of the masses: "The death penalty for thieves! Scandalous abuses of the merchants at the expense of the people." And, after showing, from the official statistics, the precipitous rise of food prices between June, 1936 and February, 1937, *La Noche* said: "Nor would it have been so bad if the prices had remained at that level! One can speak to the housekeepers about the increase in the cost of living since February. It is reaching inaccessible figures. . . . We must create some form of protection for the interests of the people against the egoism of the merchants who are carrying on with full impunity."

Yes, it was in food supplies that the Stalinists had their grip longest. And the result: hunger, yes, actual hunger stalked Catalonia. The bitterness of the masses breaks through in *Solidaridad Obrera* (September 19):

> Proletarian mothers with sons at the front here suffer stoically of hunger together with their innocent little ones . . . We say that sacrifices ought to be by all and it is an inconceivable situation that in actuality there are places where, by paying prices outside the reach of any worker, it is possible to obtain all kinds of food. These luxurious restaurants are veritable foci of provocation and should disappear, as ought to disappear all privileges of any sector. Flagrant inequality, privilege, is in such cases a terrible dissolvent of popular cohesion. It must be eliminated at all costs . . . Protected . . . there has entered into action a repugnant caste of speculators and profiteers who traffic in the hunger of the people . . .
>
> We repeat that our people do not fear sacrifices but do not tolerate monstrous inequality . . . Respect the proletariat that fights and suffers!

Yes, the masses do not fear sacrifices. The workers of Petrograd suffered the most extreme privations—not even running water in the city during the civil war. But what there was belonged to all equally. It is not the bare pangs of hunger that contort the faces of the Barcelona workers and their women and children. It is that while they hunger, the bourgeoisie eat luxuriously—and this in the midst of civil war against fascism! But that is the inevitable consequence of not finishing with bourgeois "democracy."

To those who have been impressed by Stalinist "common sense" in modestly fighting for democracy: Do you begin to understand what it meant in the concrete, in the seared souls of the Spanish people?

# 14

# The conquest of Aragon

The fertile province of Aragon was the living embodiment of victorious struggle against fascism. It was the only province actually invested by the fascists and then conquered from them by force of arms. It was especially the pride of the Catalan masses, for they had saved Aragon. Within three days of the victory in Barcelona, the CNT and POUM militias were off for Aragon. The PSUC then was small and contributed little or nothing. Imperishable names of battles there—Monte Aragon, Estrecho Quinto, etc.—were associated solely with the CNT and POUM heroes who had won them. It was in the victorious conquest of Aragon that Durruti acquired his legendary fame as a military leader, and the forces he brought to the defense of Madrid in November were the picked troops whose victorious morale had been welded in Aragon victories.

Not the least of the reasons for the successes in Aragon had been that, under Durruti's leadership, the militias marched as an army of social liberation. Every village wrested from the fascists was transformed into a fortress of the revolution. The militias sponsored elections of village committees, to which were turned over all the large estates and their equipment. Property titles, mortgages, etc. went into bonfires. Having thus transformed the world of the village, the CNT-POUM columns could go forward, secure in the knowledge that every village behind them would fight to the death for the land that was now theirs.

Backed by their success in freeing Aragon, the anarchists met with little resistance there from the bourgeois-Stalinist bloc in the first months. Aragon's municipal councils were elected directly by the communities. The Council of Aragon was at first largely anarchist. When Caballero's cabinet was formed, the anarchists agreed to give representation to the other anti-fascist groups in the Council, but up to the last day of its existence the masses of Aragon were grouped around the libertarian organizations. The Stalinists were a tiny and uninfluential group.

At least three-fourths of the land was tilled by collectives. Of four hundred collectives, only ten adhered to the UGT. Peasants desiring to work the land individually were permitted to do so, provided they employed no hired labor. For family consumption, cattle were owned individually. Schools were subsidized by the community. Agricultural production increased in the region from thirty to fifty per cent over the previous year, as a result of collective labor. Enormous surpluses were voluntarily turned over to the government, free of charge, for use at the front.

Libertarian principles were attempted in the field of money and wages. Wages were paid by a system of coupons exchangeable for goods in the co-operatives. But this was merely pious genuflection to anarchist tradition, since the committees, carrying on sale of produce and purchase of goods with the rest of Spain, perforce used money in all transactions, so that the coupons were merely an internal accounting system based on the money held by the committees. Wages were based on the family unit: a single producer was paid the equivalent of 25 pesetas; a married couple with only one working, 35 pesetas, and four pesetas weekly additional for each child. This system had a serious weakness, particularly while the rest of Spain operated on a system of great disparity in wages between manual and professional workers, since that prompted trained technicians to migrate from Aragon. For the time being, however, ideological conviction, inspiring the many technicians and professionals in the libertarian organizations, more than made up for this weakness. Granted that with stabilization of the revolution, a transitional period of higher wages for skilled and professional workers would have had to be instituted. But the Stalinists who had the effrontery to contrast the Aragon situation with the monstrous disparity of wages in the Soviet Union, appeared to have forgotten completely that the family wage—which is the essence of Marx's "to each according to his needs"—was a goal toward which to strive, from which the Soviet Union is infinitely further away under Stalin than under Lenin and Trotsky.

The anarchist majority in the Council of Aragon led in practice to the abandonment of the anarchist theory of the autonomy of economic administration. The Council acted as a centralizing agency. The opposition was in such a hopeless minority within Aragon, and the masses were so wedded to the new order, that there was no record of a single Stalinist mass meeting in Aragon in direct opposition to the Council. Many joint meetings were celebrated, with Stalinist participation, including one as late as July 7, 1937. Neither at these meetings nor elsewhere *in Aragon* did the Stalinists repeat the calumnies which the Stalinist press elsewhere was spreading, in order to prepare the ground for an invasion.

Many workers' leaders from abroad saw Aragon and praised it: among them Carlo Rosselli, the Italian anti-fascist leader, serving as a commandant on the Aragon front (on leave in Paris when he and his brother were assassinated by the Italian fascists). The prominent French socialist, Juin, wrote strong praise of Aragon in *Le Peuple. Giustizia e Liberta,* the leading Italian anti-fascist organ, said of the Aragon collectives: "The manifest benefits of the new social system strengthened the spirit of solidarity among the peasants, arousing them to greater efforts and activity."

The manifest benefits of social revolution, however, scarcely weighed in the balance against the grim necessities of the bourgeois-Stalinist program for stabilizing a bourgeois régime and winning the favor of Anglo-French imperialism. The pre-condition of such favor was destruction of every vestige of social revolution. But the masses of Aragon were united. The destruction must, therefore, come from outside. Once the Negrin government came to power, a terrific barrage of propaganda against Aragon was laid down in the bourgeois and Stalinist press. And, after three months of this preparation, the invasion was launched.

On August 11, the government decreed the dissolution of the Council of Aragon. In its stead was appointed a Governor-General "with the faculties which the prevailing legislation attributes to civil governors"—legislation from the days of reaction. The Governor-General, Mantecón, proved only a figurehead, however. The real job was done by military forces under the leadership of the Stalinist, Enrique Lister.

One of the manufactured heroes of the Stalinists (*CNT* published his picture with the title, "Hero of many battles. We know it because the Communist party has told us so"—irony was the only way of getting past the censor—), Lister marched his troops into the rear of Aragon. The municipal councils elected directly by the population were forcibly dissolved. Collectives were broken up and their leaders jailed. As with the POUM prisoners in Catalonia, not even the Governor-General knew the whereabouts of the members of the CNT Regional Committee arrested by Lister's bands. They had, indeed, carried safe-conducts from the Governor-General but that did not save them. Joaquin Ascaso, President of the Council of Aragon, was jailed on the charge . . . of stealing jewels! The government censorship forbade the CNT press to publish the news of Ascaso's imprisonment, refused to divulge the place of his incarceration, and from their foully reactionary viewpoint, they were right. For Ascaso was flesh and blood of the masses, as the dead Durruti had been, and they would have torn the jail down with their bare hands.

Suffice it to say that the official CNT press—none too anxious to arouse the masses—compared the assault on Aragon with the subjection of Asturias by Lopez Ochoa in October, 1934.

To justify the rape of Aragon, the Stalinist press published fantastic tales. *Frente Rojo* wrote:

> Under the régime of the extinguished Council of Aragon, neither the citizens, nor property, could count on the least guarantee ... The government will find in Aragon gigantic arsenals of arms and thousands of bombs, hundreds of the latest model machine-guns, cannons and tanks, reserved there, not to fight fascism on the battle fronts, but the private property of those who wished to make of Aragon a bastion from which to fight the government of the republic ... Not a peasant but had been forced to enter the collectives. He who resisted suffered on his body and his little property the sanctions of terror. Thousands of peasants have emigrated from the region, preferring to leave the land than to endure the thousand methods of torture of the Council ... The land was confiscated, the rings, lockets, and even the earthen cooking pots were confiscated. Animals were confiscated, grain and even the cooked food and wine for home consumption ... In the Municipal Councils there were installed known fascists and Falangist chiefs. Holding union cards they officiated as mayors and councillors, as agents of the public order of Aragon, bandits by origin making a profession and a government régime of banditry.

Was anybody expected seriously to believe this nonsense? The police mentality of the Stalinists was evident in the alibi that an insurrection was preparing. Unfortunately, it was not true. The arms? The Aragon front had come under complete government control on May 6, with a Stalinist party member, General Pozas, in supreme command. Prior to that the CNT, POUM, FAI press from October, 1936, on had abounded in long and precise complaints that the Aragon front was being deprived of arms, and that the armed guard of the Aragon collectives—actually, with the front irregular and shifting, part of the front-line defenses—were dangerously stripped of arms. For eight months these charges had been made, from press, platform, and radio and with it the charge that Russian aid was being conditioned by Stalinist control of the disposition of incoming arms. The Stalinists had met these specific charges with dead silence. Now, in the pogrom atmosphere of August, 1937, their answer was that arms were there! No one was, nor could be expected to believe this poppy-cock, not even the party members.

But the charges do not require serious rebuttal. For on September 18, the man who presumably had been the chief culprit, who had terrorized, installed fascists, etc., etc., etc., Joaquin Ascaso, was released from prison. If the Stalinists were ready to prove their charges against Ascaso even in their corrupted courts, why did they not do so? The answer is: the charges were balderdash. What was terribly real, however, was the destruction of the Aragon collectives.

After the bourgeois-Stalinist bloc conquered Aragon and the story of their invasion began to seep out to the world labor movement where the Stalinists did not dare to attempt to repeat their fantastic charges, they adopted a new tack which sought to move away from these charges to the assertion that the dissolution of the Council was required in order to re-organize the Aragon front. Thus Ralph Bates wrote:

> . . . There have been exaggerated charges against the Council of Aragon, but I think the following can be substantiated by detailed evidence: the wholesale application of extreme measures in land and social reform had confused and even antagonized non-anarchist peasantry and workers; anarchist control of village military committees had undoubtedly hampered efficient conduct of operations . . . The problem, therefore, was to bring this strip of Aragon under the control of the Valencia government, as part of a campaign to reform the Aragon military forces. (*New Republic*, October 27, 1937.)

This latest alibi had two functions: first, to get away from the preposterous charges on which the dissolution had first been justified; second, to cover up the fact that, although the central government had been in complete control of the Aragon front since May, its so-called offensives had been fiascoes. The infinite infamy of all this will become apparent if we now turn to the military question itself and examine the Aragon front as part of the whole program of military strategy.

# 15

# The military struggle
# under Giral and Caballero

Military warfare is merely the continuation of politics by forcible means. A proclamation dropped over the enemy lines, expressing the aspirations of the landless peasants, is also an instrument of warfare. A successfully incited revolt behind enemy lines may be infinitely more efficacious than a frontal attack. Maintenance of the morale of the troops is as important as equipping them. To guard against treacherous officers is as important as training efficient officers. In sum, the creation of a workers' and peasants' government for which the masses will work and die like heroes is the best political adjunct of military struggle against the fascist enemy in civil war.

By these methods, the workers and peasants of Russia defeated imperialist intervention and White Guard armies on twenty-two fronts, despite the most rigid economic blockade ever imposed on any nation. In the organization and direction of the Red Armies under these adverse conditions, Trotsky seemed to perform miracles, but these were miracles compounded of revolutionary politics, of the capacities for sacrifice, labor and heroism of a class defending its newly-won freedom.

That reactionary political policies determined the false military policies of the Loyalist government can be demonstrated by surveying the course of the military struggle.

From July 19 until September 4, 1936—seven decisive weeks—the Giral cabinet of the People's Front was at the helm, with the unconditional political support of the Stalinists and the Prieto Socialists (Prieto, indeed, was unofficially part of the ministry, establishing an office in the government on July 20).

The Giral government had about $600,000,000 in gold at its disposal. Recall that the real embargo on the sale of munitions to Spain was not established until August 19, when the British Board of Trade revoked all licenses for export of arms and planes to Spain. Thus, the Giral régime had at least a month in which to purchase stores of arms—but the damning fact is that it bought almost nothing! The story of the treacherous attempt of Azaña-Giral to reach a compromise with the fascists has already been told. One further fact: Franco and his friends waited six days before forming their own government. Gil Robles later revealed that they waited in expectation of a satisfactory arrangement with the Madrid government. By that time the militias had emerged from the ranks of the workers and Giral no longer had the power to meet Franco's demands.

The most important gains of the first seven weeks were the successful march on Aragon by the Catalan militias, using socialization of the land as much as they used their rifles; and the attack of the loyalist warships on Franco's transportation of troops from Morocco to the mainland.

"The loyalty of a large part of the navy decisively prevented Franco from transporting large numbers of Moroccan troops to the mainland in the first two weeks of the war. The naval patrol in the south made transport by sea extremely hazardous. Franco was forced to resort to airplane passage, but this was slow work. In this respect, again, the government was given a chance to organize defense and take stock," wrote two Stalinists at the time.[*] What they failed to add was that the warships were under the command of elected sail-

---

[*] *Spain in Revolt*, by Gannes and Repard, p. 119.

ors' committees, which, like the militias, had no faith in the Giral government and carried on operations despite the passivity of the government. The significance of this fact will become apparent when we come to the naval policy of the Caballero-Stalinist-Prieto cabinet.

The terrible defeats of Badajoz and Irun finished the Giral cabinet. Why Irun fell was told in a moving dispatch by Pierre Van Paasen:

> They fought to the last cartridge, the men of Irun. When they had no more ammunition, they hurled packets of dynamite. When dynamite was gone, they rushed forward barehanded and tackled each their man, while the sixty times stronger enemy butchered them with bayonets. A girl held two armored cars at bay for half an hour by hurling glycerine bombs. Then the Moroccans stormed the barricade of which she was the last living defender and tore her to pieces. The men of Fort Martial held three hundred foreign legionnaires at a distance for half a day by rolling rocks down the hill on which the old fort is perched.

Irun fell because the Giral government had made no attempt to provide its defenders with ammunition. The Central Committee of Anti-fascist Militias of Catalonia, having already transformed the available factories into munition works, had sent several carloads of ammunition to Irun by way of the regular railroad from Catalonia to Irun. But that railroad runs part-way through French territory. And the government of "comrade" Blum, the ally of Stalin, had held up the cars at Behobia, just across the frontier for days . . . they rumbled across the bridge into Irun after the fascists had won.

The Giral cabinet gave way to the "real, complete" People's Front government of Caballero-Prieto-Stalin. Undoubtedly, it had the confidence of a large part of the masses. The militias and the sailors' committees obeyed its orders from the first.

There were three major military campaigns that the new government had to undertake. There were, of course, other tasks, but these were the most important, the most pressing, and essentially the simplest.

## Morocco and Algeciras

 Franco's military base during the first six months was Spanish Morocco. From here he had to bring his Moors and Legionnaires and military stores.

The first successes of the Loyalist navy under the sailors' committees in harassing Franco's communication lines with Morocco were followed by others. On August 4, the Loyalist cruiser *Libertad* effectively shelled the fascist fortress at Tarrifa in Morocco. It was a deadly blow at Franco. So deadly that it was answered by the first open Italian act of intervention: an Italian plane proceeded to bomb the *Libertad*. When Loyalist warships steamed into position for a large-scale shelling of Ceuta in Morocco while fascist transports were loading, the German battleship *Deutschland* brazenly steamed back and forth between the Loyalist warships and Ceuta to prevent the bombardment. A week later a Spanish cruiser stopped the German freighter *Kamerun,* found her loaded to the decks with arms for Franco, and prevented her from landing at Cadiz. Whereupon Portugal openly went over to the fascists, permitting the *Kamerun* to unload at a Portuguese port and forwarding the munitions by rail to Franco. German naval commanders received orders to fire on any Spanish vessel attempting to stop German munitions shipments. The Loyalist naval operations, if continued, were fatal to Franco, and his allies had to unmask completely to save him.

At this point the Caballero cabinet was formed and Prieto, now in the closest collaboration with the Stalinists, and always "France's man," became head of the Naval Ministry. He put an end to naval operations off Morocco and the straits of Gibraltar, and recalled the Loyalist forces which had held Majorca.

The task of the hour was to prevent the Moors and Legionnaires from landing at Algeciras and constituting that army which was soon to make that fearful march from Badajoz straight through to

Toledo, through Toledo and Talavera de la Reina to the gates of Madrid. The first line in that task belonged to the navy. *It was not used for this purpose.*

Instead, in mid-September, almost the whole fleet—including the battleship *Jaime I,* the cruisers *Cervantes* and *Libertad,* and three destroyers—were ordered to leave Málaga and go all the way around the peninsula to the Biscayan coast! They left behind the destroyer *Ferrandiz* and the cruiser *Gravina.* On September 29, two fascist cruisers sank the *Ferrandiz,* after having shelled and driven away the *Gravina.* What considerations determined that the naval forces go off to the Biscayan coast, while news dispatches reported—to quote but one instance—"an armed trawler conveying Moroccan troops from Ceuta and escorted by the *Canarias,* the *Cervera* and a destroyer and torpedo boat crossed the straits this evening. The convoy landed the troops at Algeciras without hindrance. It transported from Morocco a supply of field and other guns and abundant supplies of ammunition." (New York *Times,* September 29.) What considerations? Certainly not military ones, for the forces sent to Biscay were more than sufficient to hold their own with the fascists' armed convoy; and certainly barring communications from Morocco was the chief task of the navy.

The American military expert, Hanson W. Baldwin, writing (in the New York *Times* of November 21) on the naval question in Spain said:

> The Spanish navy has been to a great extent neglected, particularly in the recent troubled years of the republic's history, and it has never been properly led or manned. But with efficient, well-drilled crews, Spain's handful of cruisers and destroyers could be a force to be reckoned with, particularly in the narrow basin of the Mediterranean, *where well-handled ships long ago could have cut General Franco's line of communication to his reservoir of manpower in Africa . . .*
>
> Judging from the somewhat obscure reports, *most of the ships*—despite the officers' efforts—continued to fly the red, yel-

low and mauve of [Loyalist] Spain or else hoisted the Red flags at
their gaffs . . .

. . . but altogether the role of the navy in the civil war has to
date been a minor one. The occasional engagements in which
the ships have participated have had in most instances an opera
bouffe quality and have attested to the poor marksmanship and
seamanship of the crews.

The loyalist operations of September 27, at Zumaga near Bilbao,
however, demonstrated accurate firing. The real point, however, was
that it would have been a simple matter to equip the Loyalist warships with able crews. Toulon, Brest, and Marseilles were filled with
thousands of socialist and communist sailors, veterans of the navy,
including skilled gunners and officers. They could more than have
manned the fleet, and other ships that could have been built at the
main construction docks, in Cartagena in Loyalist hands.

Returning eventually from the northern coast, the fleet was an-
chored far from the strait, at Cartagena—and there it stayed, except
for a few pointless trips down the coast. That it existed at all, one
learned on November 22, when foreign submarines entered the port
of Cartagena and loosed torpedoes, one damaging the *Cervantes*.
The same day the Ministry of Marine announced reorganization of
the fleet to combat attempted blockades . . . and that was the last
heard of that project. Franco's transports moved at will from Ceuta
to Algeciras, bringing tens of thousands of troops and the arma-
ments they required.

In a letter to Montseny, demanding that the anarchist ministers
publicly fight against the false governmental policies, Camillo Berneri said of the navy: "The concentration of the forces coming from
Morocco, the piracy in the Canaries and the Balearics, the taking of
Málaga, are the consequences of this inactivity. If Prieto is incapable and inactive, why tolerate him? If Prieto is bound by a policy
which paralyzes the fleet, why not denounce this policy?"

Why did Prieto and the governmental bloc follow this suicidal
policy? It was simply one facet of the whole policy which rested on

securing the good will of England and France. What these were seeking is clear. An aggressive Loyalist naval policy, as the August incidents off Morocco had shown, would have precipitated the decisive stage of the civil war. It would have threatened to crush Franco immediately. Germany and Italy, their prestige involved in supporting Franco, would perhaps have been driven to desperate steps in his defense, such as, the open resort to use of the Italian and German navies in sweeping the Loyalists out of the straits. But England and France could not have tolerated Italo-German control of the straits (it might be retained thenceforward). That open war would thus begin was, of course, not a certainty. Especially prior to November 9, 1936, when Germany and Italy formally recognized the Burgos régime, Germany and Italy might have retreated before precipitating war. Had revolutionists been at the helm and boldly moved in August and September to a systematic naval campaign, and succeeded in cutting off Morocco from Spain, the probability was that Italy and Germany would have retreated as gracefully as they could. Anglo-French imperialism, however, was not interested in a Loyalist victory but in staving off a war crisis while resisting encroachments on their imperialist interests in the Mediterranean. And they had their way due to the Anglo-French orientation of the Loyalist government. Each month that passed thereafter, involving Germany and Italy more deeply, rendered more and more likely an international explosion if the Loyalist navy were activized. *It simply ceased to exist as a Loyalist weapon.*

Here is the first terrible instance of how anti-revolutionary politics hamstrung the military struggle.

The same Anglo-French orientation explains the failure to strike by land at Algeciras, the Spanish port at which the fascist forces were landing from Morocco. Málaga was strategically located to be the spearhead for this drive. Instead, Málaga itself was left defenseless. Chiefly defended by CNT forces, who pleaded in vain from August until February for the necessary equipment, Málaga was invaded by an Italian landing force, while the fleet which could have stopped them rode at anchor in Cartagena. Málaga fell on February 8. For two days before that, the militias had received no instructions from the military headquarters and then, the day before Málaga fell, they discovered that the headquarters had already been abandoned without a word to the defending militiamen. It was not a military defeat, but a betrayal. The basic treachery was not the last-minute desertion by the general staff but the political policy which dictated the inactivity of the navy and disuse of Málaga as a base against Algeciras.[*]

If not by sea or by land, there was still another way of striking at Franco's Moroccan base. We quote Camillo Berneri:

> The fascist army's base of operations is in Morocco. We should intensify the propaganda in favor of Moroccan autonomy on every sector of Pan-Islamic influence. Madrid should make unequivocal declarations, announcing the abandonment of Morocco and the protection of Moroccan autonomy. France views with concern the possibility of repercussions and insurrections in North Africa and Syria; England sees the agitation for Egyptian autonomy being reinforced as well as that of the Arabs in Palestine. It is necessary to make the most of such fears by adopting a policy which threatens to unloose revolt in the Islamic world.
>
> For such a policy money is needed and speed to send agita-

---

[*] On February 21, Under-Secretary of War, José Asensio was dismissed, and soon arrested together with Colonel Villalba, for the betrayal of Málaga. War Commissar Bolivar, a Stalinist who had joined Villalba in abandoning headquarters, was *not* arrested. Nor was a word breathed—until the National Committee of the CNT got really desperate—for the moment—at the Stalinists' assaults—that Antonio Guerra, Stalinist representative in the Military Command of Málaga, stayed behind and went over to the fascists (CNT Boletin. Valencia, August 26, 1937). The day Gijon fell—eight months later—the government announced it would try the Málaga traitors—Asensio, his chief of staff, Cabrera, and another general. Why try these, and not those guilty at Bilbao, Santander, etc. etc.? Because Málaga fell under Caballero, while the far more brazen betrayals in the north took place under Negrin. . . .

tors and organizers to all centers of Arab emigration, to all the frontier zones of French Morocco. (*Guerra di Classe*, October 24, 1936.)

But the Loyalist government, far from arousing French and English fears by inciting insurrection in Spanish Morocco, proceeded to offer them concessions in Morocco! On February 9, 1937, Foreign Minister Del Vayo delivered to France and England a note, the exact text of which was never revealed but was stated later, without denial by the cabinet, to include the following points:

> 1. Proposing to base its European policy on active collaboration with Great Britain and France, the Spanish government proposes the modification of the African situation.
> 2. Desiring a rapid end to the civil war, now susceptible of being prolonged by German and Italian aid, the government is disposed to make certain sacrifices in the Spanish zone of Morocco, if the British and French governments should take steps to prevent Italo-German intervention in Spanish affairs.

The first inkling of the existence of this shameful note came a month after its dispatch, in the French and English press on March 19, when Eden made a passing reference to it. The CNT ministers swore they had not been consulted in its dispatch. Berneri addressed them bitingly: "You are in a government which has offered France and England advantages in Morocco, while from July, 1936, it should have been obligatory on us to proclaim officially the political autonomy of Morocco . . . the hour has come to make known that you, Montseny, and the other anarchist ministers are not in agreement with the nature and purport of such proposals. . . . It goes without saying that one cannot guarantee English and French interests in Morocco and at the same time agitate for an insurrection there. . . . But this policy must change. And to change it, a clear and strong statement of our own intentions must be made—because at Valencia, some influences are at work to make peace with Franco."

(*Guerra di Classe,* April 14, 1937.) But the anarchist leaders remained silent, and Morocco remained undisturbed in Franco's power.[*]

## The Aragon offensive against Saragossa-Huesca

Thumb through the Spanish or the French or American press of August–November, 1936, and note the sharp contrast between the Loyalist defeats on the central and western fronts and the victories on the Aragon front. The CNT, FAI, and POUM troops predominated in Aragon. They obeyed the military orders of the bourgeois officers sent by the government but kept them under surveillance. By the end of October, having captured the surrounding heights of Monte Aragon and Estrecho Quinto, the Aragon militias were in position to take Huesca, the gateway to Saragossa.

The importance of taking Saragossa can be readily understood by a glance at the map. It lies athwart the road from Catalonia and Aragon to Navarre, the heart of the fascist movement. Saragossa taken, the rear of the fascist army facing the Basque province would be endangered, as well as the rear of the forces converging on Madrid from the north. An offensive on this front, therefore, would have enabled the initiative in the military struggle to pass to the Loyalists. Moreover, Saragossa had been one of the great strongholds of the CNT, and had only fallen to the fascists because of the outright treachery of the civil governor, a member of Azaña's party and his appointee.

As late as the end of September, a general strike of the workers was still going on in Saragossa, though its leaders were being killed by slow torture for refusing to call it off. A strong attack on Saragossa would have been accompanied by an uprising of the workers within, as the anarchists pledged.

---

[*] The only official CNT pamphlet dealing with Morocco that I have been able to find is: "What Spain could have done in Morocco and what it has done," a speech by Gonzalo de Reparaz on January 17, 1936, telling how he tried to get the monarchy and the republic to organize things efficiently in Morocco, and how they did not! Not a hint that the only advice a revolutionist can give on the colonial question is: get out of Morocco.

To take the strongly fortified cities of Huesca and Saragossa, however, required planes and heavy artillery.

But from September onward, there developed a systematic boycott, conducted by the government against the Aragon front. The artillery and planes which arrived from abroad, beginning in October, were sent only to the Stalinist-controlled centers. Even in the matter of rifles, machine-guns and ammunition, the boycott was imposed. The Catalonian munition plants, dependent on the central government for financing, were compelled to surrender their product to such destinations as the government chose. The CNT, FAI, and POUM press charged that the brazen discrimination against the Aragon front was dictated by the Stalinists, backed by the Soviet representatives. (Caballero's friends now admit this.) The government plans for liquidating the militias into a bourgeois army could not be carried out so long as the CNT militias had the prestige of a string of victories to their credit. Ergo, the Aragon front must be held back. This situation, among others, drove the CNT leaders into the central government. The two principal figures of Spanish anarchism, Garcia Oliver and Buenaventura Durruti, transferred their activities to Madrid, Durruti bringing the pick of the troops of the Aragon front. But the boycott of the Aragon front continued despite all anarchist concessions. For it was fundamental to the strategy of the bourgeois-Stalinist bloc to break down the prestige and power of the CNT, no matter what the cost. Six months of anarchist and POUM press complaints and demands for an offensive on the Aragon front, met with dead silence from the bourgeois-Stalinist press. Then the Stalinists proceeded to slander the CNT militiamen's inactivity on that front, and to adduce that fact as proof of the need for a bourgeois army. The CNT-POUM counter-proposal for a unified command and a disciplined army under workers' control was defeated.

For many months the Stalinists denied to the outside world their sabotage of the Aragon front. But when the fact became too well known, the Stalinist produced an alibi: there were arms aplenty sent to the Aragon front but the "Trotskyists" diverted them across no-man's land to the fascists. (*Daily Worker,* October 5, 1937.) Like all Stalinist frame-up stories, this one carried its inherent falsity on its face. The POUM—the alleged Trotskyists—had at most ten thousand men on this front. The dominant force here was the CNT. Were they—with their press clamoring for these arms—such dolts as not to see what the POUM was doing? Or is this story merely a preparation for the day when the Stalinists will accuse the CNT of having connived with the POUM in diverting arms to the fascists?

The pitiful armament on the Aragon front has been described by the English author, George Orwell, who fought there in the I.L.P. Battalion. The infantry "were far worse armed than an English public school Officers' Training Corps," with "worn-out Mauser rifles which usually jammed after five shots; approximately one machine-gun to fifty men; and one pistol or revolver to about thirty men. These weapons, so necessary in trench warfare, were not issued by the government and could be bought only illegally and with the greatest difficulty."

"A government which sends boys of fifteen to the front with rifles forty years old and keeps its biggest men and newest weapons in the rear," concluded Orwell, "is manifestly more afraid of the revolution than of the fascists. Hence the feeble war policy of the past six months, and hence the compromise with which the war will almost certainly end." (*Controversy,* August, 1937.)

Thus, the government surrendered the opportunity provided in Aragon to wrest the initiative and carry the war into fascist territory.

### The northern front

Bilbao, and the industrial towns and iron and coal mines surrounding it, constituted a concentrated industrial area second only to Catalonia. For war purposes, it was even superior to the Catalonian area, which had to build its metallurgical plants up out of nothing when the civil war began. Bilbao should have become the center of Spain's greatest munitions source. From this material base, the northern armies should have driven sharply south toward Burgos and east against Navarre, to effect a junction with the troops from the Aragon front. The strategy dictated was of the most elementary kind.

The Basque capitalists, however, were the masters in the Biscayan region. As an English sphere of influence for centuries, it had no enthusiasm for joining Franco and his Italo-German allies. Neither, however, had the Basque bourgeoisie any intention of fighting to the death against Franco. Thanks to the support of the socialist and communist parties, the Basque capitalists had not had their factories seized by the workers after July 19. But they had no guarantee that a Loyalist victory over Franco would not be followed by seizure of their factories also.

The property question determined the military conduct of the Basque regional government. This was seen as early as mid-September, 1936, when the fascists advanced on San Sebastian. Before the attack was well launched, San Sebastian surrendered. Before the Basque bourgeoisie retreated, they drove out of the city the CNT militiamen who wanted to destroy factory equipment and other useful materials, to prevent them from falling into the hands of the fascists. As a further precaution, fifty armed Basque guards were left behind to protect the buildings. Thus, the city was delivered intact to Franco. The bourgeoisie reasoned: destroyed property is gone forever; but if we eventually make peace with Franco, he may give us back our property . . .

When this happened, I wrote, on September 22, 1936: "The northern front has been betrayed." The anarchist ministers have since revealed that this was the opinion in the Caballero cabinet. What delayed the completion of outright betrayal for six months, however, was the stupidity of Franco's officers who took over San Sebastian. The fifty guards left behind to protect the buildings were shot; bourgeois proprietors who had remained behind to make their peace with Franco were imprisoned, some of them executed. The inhabitants were terrorized. The Basque front stiffened—for a little while.

By December, however, the Basque government was again feel-

ing its way to an armistice. At a time when Madrid was still reject-
ing all negotiations, for exchange of prisoners, the Basques negoti-
ated such an agreement:

> The fact that the Basque group was negotiating in San Sebastian
> became known only yesterday. The writer learned, however, that
> the delegation had left Bilbao more than a week ago . . . proceeded
> to Barcelona but its mission there ended unsatisfactorily. The
> Basque delegates expressed their disappointment with the state
> of affairs in the Catalan capital . . . and it is thought that they
> also took offense at the attitude of the Catalans toward the church.
>
> In any case the result has been that they decided to sound out
> the San Sebastian leaders in the hope of arranging some sort of
> compromise and perhaps ultimately a truce.
>
> It is known that during the last month or two the northern
> front has been quiet, with much fraternizing between those in
> the opposing front lines. (Hendaye frontier dispatch, New York
> *Times*, December 17, 1937.)

Any doubt as to the substance of this report was dispelled the
same day by "Augur," the "unofficial" voice of the British Foreign
Office. "The British have been working to promote local armistices
between the rebels and loyalists. The offer of the Basque regional
government at Bilboa to conclude a Christmas truce was directly
due to discreet intervention by British agents who hope this may
lead to a complete suspension of hostilities." The French, added
"Augur," "are exercising similar influence in Barcelona where their
success is less marked because the desires of President Companys
to end the bloodshed have been overawed by the communists and
anarchists." (New York *Times*, December 17, 1936.)

Nothing of this, of course, appeared in the Loyalist press, where
the censorship now in full blast. Such circumstantial accounts,
particularly one bearing the name of "Augur," appearing in papers of the stature of the New York *Times* and the *Times* of London, required, at the least, a formal denial, if denial could be made.

Neither the government nor the Stalinist press, however, dared deny the facts: for they were true.

The Basque bourgeoisie simply had no basic stake in fighting fascism. If the struggle involved serious sacrifice, they were ready to withdraw. One of the factors which gave them pause, however, was the growing CNT movement in the Basque regions. Here the Stalinists and right-wing socialists, sitting in the regional government with the bourgeoisie (the CNT had been dropped when the Defense Junta gave way to the government), facilitated the betrayal. On the flimsiest pretext imaginable—the Basque government invited the CNT militiamen to join in celebrating Easter Week and the CNT Regional Committee and press indignantly denounced the religious ceremonial—the whole regional committee and the editorial staff of *CNT del Norte* were imprisoned March 26, and the printing presses turned over to the Stalinists! Systematic persecution of the CNT thereafter paved the way for going over to Franco.

The Loyalist government was aware of the danger, aware of Bilbao's failure to transform her plants for munitions purposes, aware of the criminal inactivity of the Basque front which enabled Mola to shift his troops southward to join the encirclement of Madrid. Why did the government do nothing about it? Of course, the cabinet sent numerous emissaries to Bilbao, flattered the Basques, went out of the way to please them, sent generals to collaborate with the Basque leaders—Llano de Encomienda, just freed by a court martial in Barcelona from charges of complicity in the uprising became commander-in-chief of the North!—but these measures naturally proved fruitless. There was *only one way* to save the northern front: by confronting the Basque bourgeoisie with a powerful united front of the proletarian forces in the region, ready to take power if the bourgeoisie faltered, and to prepare for this by ideological criticism of the Basque capitalists. That way, however, was alien to this government which, above all, feared to arouse the masses to political initiative.

But there was one sector of the northern front which was active, Asturias. We have seen how, within forty-eight hours of news of the rising, five thousand Asturian miners had arrived in Madrid. Within a few weeks, they had cleared out the fascists, except in well-fortified Oviedo, which had been the seat of a strong pretorian garrison since the crushing of the Asturian Commune of October, 1934. Every miner in Asturias would have given his life to take Oviedo. Armed with little more than rifles and crude dynamite bombs, the miners besieged Oviedo, soon taking its suburbs. The fall of Oviedo would have freed them for an offensive against Old Castille. Spokesmen for the Asturians begged in Valencia for a few planes and the necessary artillery to batter down Oviedo's defenses. They were sent away empty-handed. What was their crime? The Asturian workers abolished private property in land, collectivized housing and industry. The strong CNT movement, hand in hand with the UGT—here revolutionary in tendency, as was demonstrated by its organ, *Avance*, under the editorship of Javier Bueno—exclusively controlled production and consumption. It was known that they intended, when Oviedo was theirs, to proclaim there again, as in 1934, the Commune of Asturias . . . The government invited them to shed their blood everywhere except for the commune. Tens of thousands of them, for want of any other course, joined the Loyalists on all the fronts. Their fighting prowess became legendary. But enough of them remained before Oviedo, penning in the garrison, until the very end . . .

### Why Madrid became the key front

With Morocco and its communications lines with the mainland undisturbed, with the northern front quiescent thanks to Basque passivity, and with governmental sabotage of the Aragon front, Franco was in a position to dictate the course of the war, to choose his points of offensive at will. He never once lost the initiative to the Loyalists, who had to accept battle when and as the enemy willed.

Thus, Franco was enabled to throw his main forces against Madrid. By October the encirclement of Madrid was well on the way. Franco wanted the nation's capital in order to provide his German and Italian allies with a plausible basis for recognizing his régime.

And, indeed, by all accounts, German and Italian recognition were extended on November 9, 1936 in the belief that Madrid was about to fall and that recognition would provide the added incentive to make its fall speedy. By all accounts, too, Franco made his major strategical blunder here, when he attempted, in his haste, to take Madrid by frontal attack instead of completing its encirclement by cutting the Valencia road. The fascists stubbornly clung to this strategy for months, giving the Loyalists the opportunity to fortify the area sufficiently to withstand the flank attacks when they came in February and March.

The significant fact to note in the defense of Madrid was *the use of revolutionary-political methods*. If Madrid fell, the jig was up for the Stalinists. In Spain, their prestige was bound up with the Fifth Regiment of Madrid—in reality an army of over a hundred thousand men—and the Defense Junta which from October 11 was responsible for Madrid's defense and which was Stalinist-controlled. Internationally, the prestige of the Comintern and the Soviet Union would have collapsed irrevocably with the fall of Madrid. The retreat to Valencia and Catalonia would have found a new relationship of forces, with the Stalinists taking a back seat. Out of that new phase might have come a resort to a revolutionary war against fascism, which would have put an end to all the schemes of Eden, Del bos and Stalin. Madrid absolutely had to be held. In dire necessity, the Stalinists abandoned purely bourgeois methods—but only for a time and only within the confines of Madrid.

Methods of defense which, in other cities, were proposed by the local POUM, FAI, and CNT organizations and denounced as adventuristic, as alienating the liberal bourgeoisie, were sanctioned here by the Stalinists themselves, on November 7, when the fascist drive reached the city's suburbs. A CNT leaflet of that week is worth quoting:

> Yesterday we warned the people of Madrid that the enemy was at the gates of the city, and we advised them to fill bottles with gasoline and attach fuses to them to be lighted and thrown

onto rebel tanks when they enter the city.

Today we suggest other precautions. Every house and apartment in the district known to be inhabited by fascist sympathizers should be thoroughly searched for arms. Parapets and barricades should be set up in all streets leading to the city's center.

Every house in Madrid in which anti-fascists live must constitute itself a fortress, and every obstacle should be offered as invaders try to pass through the capital's streets. Fire on them from the upper stories of buildings, against which the fire of their machine-guns will be ineffective.

*Above all we must purge Madrid of the fifth column of hidden fascists.*

One of Mola's boasts—that four columns were converging on Madrid, with a fifth secretly forming inside—had given the workers the splendid slogan: smash the fifth column. Gone now were the governmental—and Stalinist—strictures against "illegal searches," "unauthorized seizures and arrests," etc., etc. Over five hundred Assault Guards were arrested and imprisoned in those days as fascist suspects—the first and last time the Stalinists sanctioned such a purge of bourgeois elements. The Stalinists were on record for "all power to the government of the people's front," and, therefore, hostile to workers' committees in the factories and districts. For once, however, desperation caused them to abandon this. The Stalinist-controlled Fifth Regiment issued a manifesto which, among other things, called for the masses to elect street and house committees for vigilance against the fifth column within the city![*] Workers' committees went through the streets, impressing all able-bodied men into building barricades and trenches. The defense Junta organized separate councils for food, munitions, etc., each of which swelled daily into a mass organization. Women's committees orga-

---

[*] Ralph Bates mentions this fact (*New Republic,* October 27, 1937) as if to imply it was typical of Stalinist policy. I challenge him to find a *single* other instance subsequently in which the Stalinists made a similar proposal.

nized kitchens and laundries for the militiamen. Means were found in this non-industrial city to begin—this too on initiative from below—the manufacture of ammunition. The Stalinists did not forget to continue their persecution of the POUM, but even this slowed down and the POUM militants were given room to function in the defense of the city. Those were glorious months, though laden with death: November, December, January. What was this? "The people in arms."

The Stalinists were even so desperate as to welcome the triumphal entry into Madrid of the picked troops from the CNT Aragon front columns, whose heroic conduct destroyed the slanderous myth, already being propagated by the Stalinists, about the Aragon militias. Shortly after bringing these troops, however, the greatest military figure produced by the war, the anarchist Durruti, was killed and the spotlight was turned on Miaja.

But the political methods pursued on the southern, northern and Aragon fronts, remained the same. The incessant campaign of the CNT, the POUM, and sections of the UGT for an offensive on all fronts as the best way to help Madrid, and the only way to lift the siege of the city, was ignored.

Nor did the "people in arms" remain the defenders of Madrid. By January the immediate danger was over, and the Stalinist-bourgeois bloc reverted to "normal." The house-to-house searches for fascists and arms by the workers' committees were discouraged and then suppressed. Soldiers replaced workers at the street barricades. The work of the women's committees was taken over by the army. Mass initiative was no longer invited. The current ran now the other way, although the siege of Madrid had not been lifted. *POUM,* a weekly, was permanently suspended in January. In February, the Junta seized the POUM radio and the presses of *El Combatiente Rojo.* The Stalinist, José Cazorla, the Junta's police commissioner, organized the repression both legally and illegally. If his arrests of workers were not sanctioned by the Popular Tribunals, he took "said acquitted parties to secret jails or sent them into communist militia battalions in advanced positions to be used as 'fortifications.'" Simultaneously, the bars were let down on the right, and Cazorla released many fascists and reactionaries. These charges were made by Rodrigues, Special Commissioner of Prisons (*Solidaridad Obrera,* April 20, 1937), and the CNT demand for an investigation was refused. The dissolution of the Junta completed the move to bourgeois-bureaucratic methods of conducting the defense of Madrid.

The sole military victory of the Caballero cabinet was the Guadalajara defeat of the Italian divisions in March—an unexpected victory as was indicated by the lack of preparations of reserves and materials to complete the rout of the Italians. The failure to coordinate the Madrid fighting with offensives on the other fronts, for the political reasons we have outlined, thus by default made Madrid the key front and simultaneously made impossible lifting of the siege of Madrid.

# 16

# The military struggle
# under Negrin-Prieto

That the "government of victory" would inevitably continue the disastrous military policy of its predecessor was apparent the day it was constituted. Prieto would continue his inactive naval policy and his political discrimination in the assignment of aircraft to the fronts. He was now also head of the army, with all services in a single Ministry of Defense, but the Supreme War Council, established in December, had already then been dominated by the bourgeois-Stalinist bloc through their majority of the ministries. (The Stalinist "demand" that the council function normally, raised on May 16, was simply a prop for the myth to make Caballero the scapegoat for the conduct of the war.) The political course which had dictated the previous military strategy—hostility to lighting the flame of revolt in North Africa, support of the Basque bourgeoisie against the workers, persecution of Catalonia and Aragon—all this continued, intensified.

In addition, the Negrin cabinet added new obstacles to prosecution of the war.

On the national question—relations with minority peoples— the Negrin régime moved not only to the right of Caballero, but also to the right of the republic of 1931–33. The bureaucratic centralization for which the monarchists and fascists stood had been an important factor in alienating from them the peoples of Catalonia, Euzkadi (Basques) and Galicia. Once the civil war began, the limited autonomy of the Catalans and Basques had broadened de facto. A declaration of autonomy for Galicia would have immeasurably facilitated the guerilla warfare there. It was not forthcoming because it would have provided a precedent for Catalonia to seize on. The Negrín régime proceeded, as we have seen, to wipe out Catalan autonomy. Where the Bolsheviks had gained strength for the prosecution of the civil war from the intensified loyalty of the autonomous minority nations, the Loyalist government quenched the fires of national aspirations.

The pay of militiamen was reduced from ten pesetas a day to seven, while the ascending scale for officers was: 25 pesetas for second lieutenants, 39 for first lieutenants, 50 for captains, 100 for lieutenant colonels. Economic distinctions thus sharply reinforced military regulations. One need scarcely emphasize the deleterious effect on the soldiers' morale of this and their increasing subordination to the officers.

The whole northern front was soon to be betrayed by the Basque bourgeoisie and officers, and by the "Fifth Column" of fascist sympathizers in the Assault and Civil Guards and among the civilian population. The struggle against the "Fifth Column" was indissolubly part of the military struggle. But, as Camillo Berneri had written even before the intensification of repression under Negrín, "it is self evident that during the months when an attempt is being made to annihilate the [POUM-CNT] 'uncontrollables,' the problem of eliminating the Fifth Column cannot be solved. The suppression of the Fifth Column is primarily to be achieved by an investigatory and repressive activity which can only be accomplished by experienced revolutionists. An internal policy of collaboration between the classes and of consideration toward the middle classes, leads inevitably to tolerance toward elements that are politically doubtful. The Fifth Column is made up not only of fascist elements but also of all the malcontents who hope for a moderate republic."

While the northern front was left to the Basque bourgeoisie, the Aragon front was subjected to a frightful purge. General Pozas initiated what was ostensibly a general offensive in June. After several days of artillery and aerial conflict, orders to advance were given to the 29th (formerly the POUM's Lenin) division and other formations. But on the day for the advance, neither artillery nor aviation was provided to protect it. Pozas later claimed this was because the air forces were defending Bilbao—but the day of advance was three days after Franco had taken Bilbao. The POUM soldiers fully realized that they were being exposed deliberately. But not to go into fire would have given the bourgeois-Stalinist bloc a case against the Aragon front. They went into the line of fire. One flank was ostensibly assigned to an International Brigade (Stalinist)—but shortly after the advance began, it received orders to withdraw to the rear. The lieutenant-colonel in charge of a formation of Assault Guards on the other flank later congratulated the POUM troops: "At Sarinena I was warned against you on the ground that you might shoot us in the back. Not only did it not happen but thanks to your bravery and your discipline, we have avoided a catastrophe. I am prepared to go to Sarinena to protest against those who sow the seeds of demoralization, to effect the triumph of their partisan political aims."

During this offensive, Cahué and Adriano Nathan, POUM commanders, were killed in action. Police were at that moment coming for Cahué, to arrest him as a "Trotskyist-fascist."

When the attack was over, the 29th was sent to the rear. That, customarily, had meant to give up rifles—there were still not enough for front-line and reserves simultaneously on this front! But the suspicious POUM troops refused to yield their arms. They declared themselves ready to return to the front. A few days later two battalions of the division were ordered to march on Fiscal (on the Jaca front) to repulse a fascist attack. Not only did they crush the attack but they reconquered positions and material previously lost. Then they were retired to await new orders—but not sent back to their division. Why? To disarm them. Pozas ordered it. They were concentrated in the village of Rodeano and surrounded by a Stalinist brigade. They were relieved of all their valuables—watches, chains, even good underwear and new shoes. Their leaders were arrested, the rest permitted to go—on foot. Hiking home, many were arrested in the towns on the way. The only reason the same methods were not employed against the rest of the division was that the news leaked out quickly and Pozas feared the CNT divisions would come to its defense. But a few weeks later the 29th was officially dissolved, the remaining men being distributed far and wide in small groups.*

The Ascaso (CNT) division was also cut to pieces. *Acracia*, CNT organ of Lerida, wrote:

> Now we know exactly why Huesca was not taken. The last operation at Santa Quiteria furnishes a good proof of it. Huesca was surrounded on all sides and only the betrayal of the aviation forces (controlled by PSUC) was responsible for the disaster with which this operation ended. Our militiamen were not backed up by the aviation and were thus left defenseless in face of an intensive machine-gunning by the fascist aviation. This is only one of the numerous operations which ended in the same manner on account of the same betrayal by the aviation.

Soon after there was a plenary session of the PSUC Central Committee in Barcelona. Among those prominently participating were "comrades" General Pozas, chief of the Aragon front, Virgilio Llanos, political commissioner of the front, and Lieutenant-Colonel Gordon, chief of staff . . .

Acceptance of control by the central government had been dangled before the Aragon front troops as the end of all their

---

* This account is that of the front correspondent of *Avanti* émigré (Paris) organ of the Italian Maximalist-Socialists, scarcely a POUM or Trotskyist source.

worries. Instead, it was used to break them down still further. The front correspondent of the anarchist (Paris) *Libertaire* wrote on July 29:

> Ever since the central government took over control, the financial boycott became accentuated. Most of the militiamen have not received their pay for a long time. In Bujaraloz, where the general staff of the Durruti column is located, both—officers and soldiers—have not seen a cent for the last three months. They cannot wash their clothes for lack of soap. In many a place visited after several months of absence, I found comrades whom I knew well: now they looked pale, thin and visibly weakened. The physical state of the troops is such that they cannot keep up any prolonged exercises; they cannot march for more than fifteen kilometres a day. In the region of Farlete the troops live by hunting, without which they would starve to death.

Systematic persecution of the chief forces of the Aragon front scarcely laid the basis for military victories, although at Belchite and Quinto the 25th division (CNT) gave a good account of itself. But the alleged success of the July offensive on the Aragon front was so much newspaper talk. "Results?" wrote the illegal anarchist organ, *Libertad* (August 1): "Two villages lost in the Pirineo sector and three thousand men lost. This is what they call a success. Disastrous, calamitous, shameful success!"

After the fall of Santander (August 26), the persecution of the CNT troops abated somewhat. But now came a terrible lesson in the consequences of creating counter-revolutionary forces of repression, such as the Stalinist-controlled Karl Marx division. In the midst of an offensive in the Zuera sector, "fifty officers of that division and six hundred soldiers passed over to the fascists. As a result of these desertions a battalion was destroyed. Despite the mettle of the CNT forces, the operation could not be terminated well. The enemy had the necessary time to recover and it was impossible to continue the attack. After a summary court martial that was immediately convened, thirty officers of the Karl Marx Division have been shot. In addition, the political commissar of the division, Trueba, a PSUC member, has been dismissed." (*Amigo del Pueblo,* illegal organ of Friends of Durruti, September 21.) Needless to say, the CNT press was forbidden to publish the facts.

## The northern front

As a government pledged to class collaborations even more completely than Caballero's, the Negrin government did nothing to counter the more and more brazen sabotage of the Basque bourgeoisie. This front was almost inactive throughout the period from November, 1936, to May, 1937, when the fascists moved to wipe it out altogether. Nor had those six months been utilized in economic-military preparations. One must emphasize again that the Euzkadi (the Basque country) was second only to Catalonia as an industrial region and superior to it in being a region of heavy industry, with iron and steel plants in the midst of iron and coal mines. *Nothing* was done to develop out of this a great war industry. For this crime, the Stalinists bore equal responsibility, for two party representatives were ministers in the autonomous government. The coup against the CNT in March, when its regional committee had been imprisoned and its press confiscated, was now followed by systematic repression of the workers, with public meetings prohibited. Thus, the one force which might have prevented betrayal was crushed by the Stalinist-bourgeois bloc.

In the Caballero cabinet, as we have said, there were constant fears about the loyalty of the Basques. Irujo's constant threats of giving up altogether merely reflected the fact that the bourgeoisie had no serious stake in the struggle against fascism and would not fight under conditions destructive of their property. Consequently, when Franco began to move in the north, Caballero planned a large-scale offensive on the southern Madrid front to draw the fire of the fascist forces. According to his friends, 75,000 fully equipped troops were to have gone into action but two or three days before the offensive was to begin, his resignation was forced. Negrin's first act was to withdraw these troops. Be that as it may, the fact was that no offensive was launched to relieve Bilbao, either on the Madrid or Aragon front, until mid-June—too late.

But the decisive factor in the loss of Bilbao was open treachery. "Not even the insurgent heavy guns," wrote the New York *Times* correspondent, "could have destroyed some of these underground fortifications with their three armored concrete tiers and block-houses spaced about three miles apart all the way to the Biscay coast. The Insurgents themselves say that the 'iron ring' of fortifications would never have been taken had not the Basques been out-manoeu-vred." "Out-manoeuvred," however, was a fascist euphemism for betrayal. After the city fell, this fact was admitted by the Basque delegation in Paris which put the blame on an engineer in charge of building the fortifications, who fled to Franco with the plans. Analy-sis of the delegation's story revealed that the engineer in question had fled *months before*. Why was not the intervening period uti-lized to re-design the fortifications? But the alibi was a subter-fuge. For, as any tyro in military science knew, mere possession of the plans could not have solved the problem for the fascists of breaking through the fortifications. *They were let through the iron ring.*

Suppose we were to accept the Basque alibi. Why, then, was Bilbao not defended in a siege such as Madrid—less advantageously situ-ated—had withstood? It is an elementary axiom of military sci-ence that no large city can be captured until its massive build-ings—veritable fortifications—have been razed to the point they offer no further protection to beleaguered troops. The process of razing buildings by shelling and bombing required enormous equip-ment such as the fascists did not have—less than an eighth of Madrid had been so razed after a year's shelling and bombing.

But the bourgeoisie did not wait for the shelling of Bilbao at all! On June 19, they surrendered the city, as they had San Sebastian the previous September. The uniform Basque policy of giving up cities intact has no parallel in any modern war, not to speak of civil war!

The pro-Loyalist correspondent of the New York *Times* (June 21, 1937) wrote:

> Details learned today of the last hours of Basque rule at Bilbao show that some 1,200 militiamen, who had before the civil war been soldiers of the regular army, decided in the early hours of the morning, after the bridges had been blown up, that chaos had gone far enough, and took control of the city in the capacity of police. The Asturian and Santander militiamen were driven out of the city.
>
> Assisted by some regular police and Civil Guards, this battalion accepted the surrender of their fellow-militiamen in the city and took their arms away, and afterwards hoisted a white flag on the telephone building. During the night they went around houses assuring the people that there was no cause for panic, placed guards on public buildings, and in the evening formed a cordon in the main street which prevented the excited crowds from pressing too closely on the National troops when they marched into the city.

Leisola, Minister of Justice in the Basque government, remained behind to superintend the betrayal. With the exception of seventeen (of whom we shall soon hear again), all fascist hostages were released and sent toward the fascist lines as a good-will offering before the troops had reached the city. Simply put: the regular army of the Basques, directed by the bourgeois leaders, joined hands with the "republican police" in attacking the Asturians and militia from the rear, disarmed as many as they could, and dismantled the houses and street barricades which the workers had prepared for street fighting. Shortly after the occupation, the same police donned Carlist berets and became Franco's regular police.

CNT and UGT press attempts to sound the alarm after the fall of Bilbao were cut to ribbons by the censorship. The Basque general staff was permitted to remain in command of the retreating troops. When, within a few weeks, the fascists began a second offensive, the industrial town of Reinosa, key to Santander's defenses, collapsed, and once again the Basques made no attempt to defend the city itself.

Two days before the fall of Santander, the Basque general staff and remaining members of the government fled to France on a British warship. Under what terms, was revealed by the New York *Times* dispatch of August 25:

> At the time of the fall of Bilbao the Basques freed all their hostages except seventeen. Now these are considered to be in the gravest peril as the Basques admit that it is no longer possible to protect them from extremist elements in Santander.
>
> When the British Embassy agreed to take off the hostages, it arranged also to evacuate the Basques who have been guarding them as well as any remaining members of the Basque government. . . .
>
> It is hoped that the whole manoeuvre will be carried out before the more violent elements in Santander are aware of what is happening.

The next day (August 25), the British warship, *Keith,* with Basque and fascist representatives aboard, arrived at Santander and "rescued" the Basque officials and the seventeen fascists.

President Aguirre was not in Santander. He banqueted the way across Spain, saying nothing, then joined his colleagues at Bayonne, France, where they issued the following statement:

> The delegation of the Basque government, in refuge in Bayonne, take the responsibility of subscribing to the following: Franco's offensive against Reinosa ended in terrible consequences. In a terrain composed of great mountains and deep gorges, Franco's troops advanced with incomprehensible velocity. The military technicians were amazed at the rapidity of this advance, not only of the infantry, but of the heavy and mountain artillery, as well as the cumbersome services belonging to the

different regiments and arms.

This was an impossible or very difficult achievement and proves that the accidents of terrain were not utilized for resisting Franco's army.

In the face of this advance the troops of the Santander army offered no resistance to the enemy. Not only did they not come into contact with the enemy, but they did not lend themselves to retreating in a way that could be organized for defense.

The Santander army's organization was undone from the moment the offensive began. Neither communications, nor the sanitary services, nor means for avoiding surprise attacks, functioned. No line of resistance could be established, for the battalions which did not surrender at the first encounter were on the run through the countryside in the most complete disorder.

Neither the general staff of Santander nor that of the Army of the North controlled the offensive at any moment. Once past Reinosa they could find neither the positions nor the situation of their troops, nor any unity on which they could count.

Reinosa was surrendered to the enemy with no time for evacuating the population. The artillery factory fell into the hands of the rebels, with its shops for naval construction almost intact, and all the material in construction, including 38 batteries of artillery.

The only resistance that the enemy encountered in its advance is that which the Basque battalions offered, rushing to the front. The incomprehensible conduct [of the others] ended by making the corps of the Basque army realize that it had been the victim of treachery, and that the advance of the Franco troops was being facilitated in such a way that the whole Basque army should fall into his power.

The Basques, having resisted nearly ninety days against a brutal offensive [against Bilbao] incomparably more terrible than that of Reinosa, without having the means at its disposal that the Santander army had, cannot explain in any reasonable way the fact that in such a manner a terrain of eighty kilometers was lost in eight days. It is necessary to add to these data that the offensive against Euzkadi was a surprise while that of Reinosa had been announced and was anticipated.

When the real situation was confirmed to it, the high command of the Basque army preoccupied itself in saving its troops and in preventing its effectives from falling into the hands of the enemy. To this mission it has consecrated all its efforts with the aid of the Basque government, which in this grave and difficult moment continued to give proof of its capacity and serenity.[*]

Somebody committed treachery, but not us, was the sum and substance of this amazing document, apart from its slander of the Asturian and Santander militiamen, fifteen thousand of whom had been executed by machine-guns after being surrounded in Santander.

A Paris press dispatch of August 26 named some of the traitors, reporting that the commandant of the Assault Guards, Pedro Vega, the commandant of the Basque troops, Angel Botella, and Captain Luis Terez, presented themselves to the nearest outpost of the fascist troops and offered the surrender of Santander, but warned that a battalion of the FAI militia had decided to fight to death.

Who, knowing anything of the CNT and Asturian militiamen, would imagine that they had not stood at their posts ready to fight to the death? A thousand instances of their last-ditch heroism can be told. Why should they surrender or not fight, above all, the Asturian militiamen, who had learned in October, 1934, that agreements ruling out reprisals were not kept by the reactionaries? On the other hand the Basques could not name a battle in which they stood up to the last. The Aguirre document's alibi was threadbare. There was no striking contrast between what they did at Bilbao and the events at Santander. On the contrary, they merely followed the same pattern.

We repeat: the bourgeoisie had no serious stake in the struggle

---

[*] From the original Spanish text (*Boletin*, Valencia, CNT, Sept. 11).

against fascism. Surrender of their property intact to Franco, with a prospect of eventual reconciliation, was infinitely preferable to them than destruction of their property in a death struggle. That they had not gone over to Franco to begin with was primarily due to their British connections. But during the offensive against Bilbao, that problem was "solved": The British had come to an understanding with Franco concerning the Basque provinces. As revealed by the authoritative Frederick Birchall in the New York *Times*, British banks had extended to Franco, via Dutch connections, vast credits which were to be secured by products from the Bilbao region. Then came the gap in the "iron ring." But even without a final settlement with Britain, the fascists would have received Bilbao and Santander untouched, as San Sebastian bad been delivered to them the previous September.

That others were also treacherous, we are ready to concede to Aguirre. Once again, before the fascist troops entered Santander, yesterday's "loyal" Assault and Civil guards were patrolling the streets, disarming Asturian militiamen and preventing street fighting. These police were under the Ministry of the Interior (a Prieto man), and directly under a Stalinist director-general of police, who had dissolved the councils of anti-fascist guards for cleansing the police of dubious elements.

What of that Supreme War Council, the "real functioning" of which had been one of the Stalinist demands which was not satisfied by Caballero, which could only be satisfied by Negrin?

What of the two Stalinist ministers in the Basque government, who had fled from Bilbao—we may be sure they knew their colleagues better than we!—even before Aguirre? What eyewitness testimony could they offer? It is a fact that their having ever existed cannot be discovered from the Stalinist press!*

The Basques had shifted the blame from their own shoulders with vague accusations. That treachery had occurred, they had au-

---

* Except that, six months after the fall of Bilbao, one minister was expelled from the Communist Party—a crude move to provide a scapegoat for Stalin's crimes.

thoritatively testified to. It is a fact that the government instituted no investigation, no hearings, and made no statement on this question!

The UGT and CNT's comments on the loss of Santander were cut to ribbons by the censor, for they sought to draw some lessons. Nevertheless, a wave of bitterness shook the masses. Was it for this that they had fought? Verbal concessions, at least, had to be made. Even Prieto's organ, *El Socialista* (August 31) had declared: "Without revealing any secret we can make this affirmation: treachery was present in Malaga; it was present in Bilbao; it was present in Santander . . . The general staff abandoned Malaga without a fight; military leaders made their way to France when Bilbao was in danger; others were in agreement with the enemy to facilitate his entrance into Santander."

The Stalinists attempted to unload all blame onto the Basque bourgeoisie, in a statement of its Political Bureau in mid-September. Its critical paragraphs corroborate our analysis:

> The long inactivity of these [Bilbao and Santander fronts] was not made use of in order to organize the Army or seriously to fortify our positions. The cadres which were undermined by treachery were not purged; the promotion of new elements to commanding positions was not encouraged. . . .
>
> In the Basque provinces, in Santander, the policy which would have satisfied the desires of the workers and peasants was not carried out. The big landlords and the owners of big undertakings which maintained connections with the fascists retained their privileges, and this cooled the enthusiasm of the fighters.
>
> A rotten liberalism secured impunity for the Fifth Column . . . the prohibition of public meetings, isolated the government and even the People's Front from the active strata of the people and prevented the utilization of the courage and enthusiasm of the citizens for defending the towns.
>
> The questionable behavior and the dishonesty of means employed as well by certain elements (besides other causes which

cannot be examined now) helped to undermine the enthusiasm of the population, to weaken the strength of the soldiers . . . (reprinted, *Daily Worker,* October 25, 1937.)

Note that the statement did not—and could not—refer to previous agitation by the Communist party for curtailing the privileges of the bourgeoisie, for the very good reason that, precisely in the name of anti-fascist unity, the party led the struggle *against* interference with the big bourgeoisie. Let us recall the party leader, Diaz' declaration, at the previous plenary session of its Central Committee:

> If in the beginning the various premature attempts at "socialization" and "collectivization," which were the result of an unclear understanding of the character of the present struggle, might have been justified by the fact that the big landlords and manufacturers had deserted their estates and factories and that it was necessary at all costs to continue production, now on the contrary they cannot be justified at all. At the present time, when there is a government of the People's Front, in which all the forces engaged in the fight against fascism are represented, such things are not only not desirable, but absolutely impermissible. (*Communist International,* May, 1937.)

After this, what utter hypocrisy to complain that "the big landlords and the owners of big undertakings which maintained connections with the fascists retained their privileges."

Even more important, the Stalinist statement ended, not with criticism of the bourgeoisie, but with the usual denunciation of the Trotskyists and the attribution of the reverses in the north "to the lack of unity of firmness of the anti-fascist front." A pseudo-Marxist critique was thus put at the service of a program of intensified class collaboration!

At the October first session of the Cortes, the Basque delegation appeared, most of them coming from Paris and returning there afterward. La Pasionaria spoke for the Stalinists: not a word about the treachery of the Basque bourgeoisie. Instead: "We know that the salaries which the workers earn are not sufficient to take care of their homes . . . In this sense, we have the example of what can occur, when the workers are not satisfied; we have the example of Euzkadi, where the workers continued with the same salaries because the same capitalist establishments continued." How can one characterize these base words? No other conclusion could be drawn from them, except that the dissatisfied workers had lost the military struggle. The only blame of the bourgeoisie was that they hadn't given the workers better salaries! If the pseudo-radical reference to "the same capitalist establishments" were anything but demagogy, why did not Pasionaria go on to demand that the other capitalist establishments in remaining Loyalist Spain be given to the workers? On the contrary, the cabinet was systematically taking factories and land away from the workers and giving them back to the old proprietors, as we have seen.

### The fall of Asturias

The Asturian and Santander militiamen—largely CNT and left Socialist—bitterly contested every foot of the ground. The terrain here was even more favorable to the defense than the hilly Santander region. The Asturian dynamiters were still unshakably holding their grip on the suburbs of Oviedo, immobilizing the garrison there since July, 1936. The workers had a small arms and ammunition factory at Trubia in their hands and raw materials from the mining district, and this, with the considerable military stores brought from the Santander region, provided the material basis for holding the north indefinitely. All told nearly 140,000 armed troops were in the Loyalist area of the north. As long as the north held, Franco could launch no big offensive elsewhere. The striking contrast between the defense put up by the Asturians and the previous surrender of Bilbao and Santander was indicated by the fact that not a village was given up before the fascist artillery had razed it. And when encirclement did force retreat, nothing usable was left behind. "The retreating

Asturians seem determined to leave only smoking ruins and desolation behind them when they are finally forced to abandon a town or village . . . The insurgents found them all dynamited and usually burned to the ground." (New York *Times,* October 19, 1937.) Every foot of ground cost the fascists huge expenditures of materials and men—until the fall of Cangas de Onis.

Then something happened. Not in the Oviedo region, where the militia held firm. Not among the forces which, after retreating from Cangas de Onis, had established new lines. But in the coastal region east of Gijon, where the Basque troops were, and which was under the direct command of the general staff stationed in Gijon. The fascist Navarrese advanced along the coast from Ribadesella, pushing twenty-eight miles through towns and villages in three days . . . Even so the chief insurgent forces were fifteen miles east of Gijon when the city surrendered, on October 21.

Why was Gijon not defended? There were still sufficient military stores to conduct a struggle for a period. Again we must repeat: a city of buildings is a natural fortress which must be razed before being taken. The one alternative—to retreat elsewhere—was not present, for there was nowhere else the 140,000 soldiers or the civilians could go. There could be no illusions that Franco would not execute thousands upon thousands, especially of the Asturian militiamen. Yet the government left these men to the mercy of Franco. Already on the 16th, the Associated Press reported the arrival in France of the Governor of Asturias and other governmental officials, who, the customs officers reported, carried papers showing that the central government had authorized their flight. (The next day's dispatch reported that the Spanish crew of the vessel which had brought them had refused to feed them!) On the 20th, the United Press reported arrival at the Biarritz airdrome of "five Spanish Loyalist war planes and a French commercial plane, bringing *fugitive officers from Gijon.*" "The aviators declared they left Gijon on orders from the chief of their squadron when fighting broke out among the defenders in the streets, and they were cut off from communication with other military units . . . After questioning, the aviators were liberated and turned over to the Spanish consular authorities at Bayonne." From the same source, the same day: "The Spanish government renewed pressure today on the French and British to speed up the evacuation of civilians from Gijon *and insure the removal of officers* of the Loyalist army of 140,000 men forced to retreat to the sea." Belarmino Tomas, Governor of Gijon, fled to France on the 20th. Thus, the government saved its functionaries, leaving the armed masses to their fate.

Nor did these masses have the opportunity to die fighting, instead of before execution squads. As a concession to the workers, a Socialist, Tomas, had been made Governor of Gijon. But this was merely a left facade. No measures had been taken in the two months intervening to purge the officialdom of the Basque Army, or the Santander staffs, or the other officers, or to create worker-patrols to cleanse the city of the Fifth Column. The Civil and Assault Guards of Gijon were likewise not sifted. As a result, the masses found themselves in a death-trap.

> The coastal column [of the fascists] one of four leading the advance, was nearest to Gijon—fourteen miles away by road—when the city revolted. The Gijon radio opened at 10 A.M. with the sudden announcement: "We are waiting with great impa tience . . . Viva Franco!"
>
> Shortly before 3:30 P.M. the red-bereted troops entered the city. Meantime, the Gijon radio had explained that the night before, *when the government leaders left*, secret organizations of Insurgents had gone into the streets in armed groups and had taken over the city. (New York *Times,* October 22, 1937.)

Three days later, one discovered the rôle of the "loyal republican police." "The same police force that has always maintained public order and regulated traffic was on duty there today." Once again the pretorian forces of the government and its bourgeois allies had gone over to Franco. It was linguistically appropriate that the formal offer of surrender to Franco came from Colonel Franco, a "loyal republican." Nothing had been destroyed: the small ammunitions plant, the factories, etc., etc., fell intact to Franco. That fact illumined the relation of the governmental officers and functionaries who had fled. Either they had directly aided in the treachery, therefore, the city was intact or, more likely, they dared not inform the soldiers that the city was not to be defended, and, therefore, fled secretly, giving no warning to the armed masses to organize their own defense . . .

"El gobierno de la victoria," Pasionaria had christened it. Six months demonstrated the grotesque ludicrousness of that christening. The one conceivable "justification" for its repressions against the workers and peasants might have been its military victories. But precisely from its reactionary politics flowed its disastrous military policies. Whether Spain remained under this terrible yoke and went down to the depths, or freed herself from these organizers of defeat and went forward to victory—whatever happened, history had already stamped the government of Negrin-Stalin with its true title: "the government of defeat."

# 17

# Only two roads

Sixteen months of civil war have conclusively demonstrated that all the roads pointed out to the Spanish people reduce themselves to but two choices. One is the road we point: revolutionary war against fascism. All other paths lead into the road marked out by Anglo-French imperialism.

Anglo-French imperialism has demonstrated that it has no intention whatsoever of aiding the Loyalists to victory. Even the Stalinized *New Republic* (October 27, 1937) was at long last compelled to admit: "It is clear that by now the concern of France and England over a fascist victory in Spain has become—if it was not from the start—a completely secondary consideration."

The Spanish question is but one factor in the conflict of interests among the imperialist powers, and will be finally "settled"—if the imperialists of both camps have their way—only when they come to the point of a general settlement of all questions, i.e., the imperialist war.

Having most to lose, the Anglo-French bloc holds back from the war, although it must eventually fight to hold its own. Until that moment it avoids decisive showdowns, in Spain as elsewhere. It permitted a trickle of aid to the Loyalists from the Soviet Union because it did not want a victory for Franco while his Italo-German allies dominated his régime. British interests have employed the interim to arrange with Burgos for joint exploitation of the British-owned Bilbao region. The first week of November, Chamberlain announced establishment of formal relations with Franco (as small coin to anti-fascist sentiment, the diplomatic and consular officials were designated merely as "agents"), while Eden assured Parliament that a Franco victory would not mean a régime hostile to Britain. Thus, the masters of the Anglo-French bloc prepared themselves for a Franco victory.

Whatever fears the Anglo-French bloc may have had about a Franco victory, it never wanted a Loyalist victory. An early victory would have been followed by social revolution. Even now, after six months of repressions by the Negrin government, the Anglo-French rulers still doubt that a Loyalist victory would not be followed by social revolution. They are correct. For the millions of CNT and UGT workers, held in leash by the civil war, at its victorious completion would shatter the bourgeois limits of the People's Front. Moreover, an imminent Loyalist victory would be such a blow to Italo-German prestige that it would be countered by invasion of Spain on an imperialist scale of warfare and an attempt to bottle up the Mediterranean. The danger to the "life-line of empire" of the Anglo-French bloc would bring war on the immediate order of the day. Anglo-French desire to postpone the war, thus led directly to opposition to Loyalist victory.

The only reason the Anglo-French bloc did not openly court Franco was that it dared not abandon its chief advantage in the coming war: the myth of democratic war against fascism, by which the proletariat is being mobilized to support the imperialist war.

The main pre-occupation of Anglo-French imperialism from the first was: how postpone the war, maintain the democratic myth, and yet begin to edge Hitler and Mussolini out of Spain? The answer was also obvious: a compromise between the Loyalist and fascist camps. As early as December 17, 1936, Augur semi-officially stated that English agents were working for a local armistice in the North, while French agents were doing likewise in Catalonia. Even the social-patriot, Zyromski, stated in *Populaire* (March 3, 1937): "Moves can be seen that are aiming at concluding a peace which would signify not only the end of the Spanish revolution, but also the total loss of the social victories already achieved." The Caballero Socialist, Luis Araquistain, Ambassador to France, from September, 1936 to May, 1937, afterward declared: "We have counted too much, in illusion and hope, on the London committee, that is to say, on the aid of the European democracies. Now is the hour to realize that we can expect nothing decisive from them in our favor, and from one of them much against us, at the least." (*Adelante,* July 18, 1937.)

The Negrin government put itself entirely in the hands of the Anglo-French bloc; and Negrin's speeches, notably that to the Cortes on October 1, in dwelling on the need for preparing for peace, and his speech after the fall of Gijon, revealed that his government was ready to carry out the Anglo-French proposals for compromise.

The face of Negrin was turned not to the battle fronts but to London and Paris. The government's orientation was summed up succinctly by the pro-Loyalist Matthews, after the fall of Gijon: "On the whole, there is more discouragement here over the London discussion than what has happened in the north." Matthews continued:

> There was a passage in Premier Negrin's broadcast last night which so perfectly expressed the government's opinion that it deserves to be put on record: "Once more our foreign enemies are trying to take advantage of the *ingenuous candor of European democracies* by fine subtleties . . . I am now warning the free countries of the world, for our cause is their cause. *Spain will accept any means of reducing the anguish of this country,* but let the democracies not be seduced by the Machiavellianism of their worst enemies and let them not again be the victim of a base decision." (New York *Times,* October 24, 1937.)

Truly that passage perfectly expressed the government's opinion. Were not the consequences of this policy so tragic for the masses, one would roar with laughter at the picture of the "ingenuous candor" of perfidious Albion and the Quai d'Orsay. Fearing that he was to be abandoned altogether, Negrin was thus begging his imperialist mentors to remember that he "will accept any means of reducing the anguish of this country." Had he not already proved that by his repressions of the workers?[*]

That the Loyalist government had already agreed to support a compromise with the fascists is attested to, not only by authoritative revolutionary and bourgeois sources, but also by a Stalinist source:

> A Spanish government representative who attended King George VI's coronation outlined to Foreign Minister, Eden, Valencia's plan for ending the civil war. A truce was to be declared. All foreign troops and volunteers serving on both sides would then be immediately withdrawn from Spain. During the truce no battle lines would be shifted. Non-Spaniards having been eliminated, Great Britain, France, Germany, Italy and the Soviet Union were to devise a scheme, which the Spanish government *pledged itself in advance to accept,* whereby the will of the Spanish nation regarding its political and social future might be authoritatively ascertained. (Louis Fischer, *Nation,* September 4, 1937.)

At the best, such an arrangement would mean a plebiscite under the supervision of the European powers. With Franco in possession of territory including more than half of the Spanish people, and with the Italo-German and Anglo-French blocs competing for Franco's friendship, one can imagine the outcome of the plebiscite: unity of the bourgeois elements in both Spanish camps in a Bona-

---

[*] "Chautemps reflects the bourgeois and fascist dislike of Valencia. He, therefore, constantly urges Valencia to moderate its action and emphasize the democratic character of the régime." This testimony is Louis Fischer's! (*Nation,* October 16, 1937.)

partist régime, decked out at the beginning with formal democratic rights, but ruling the masses primarily through the armed might of Franco's armies.

Such was the end of the road pointed out by the Anglo-French imperialists and already accepted by the Negrin government. There were still objective difficulties in the way: Franco hoped to win everything and was encouraged to fight on by Italy and Germany. But this much was clear. If not a complete Franco victory, to which England and France were already reconciled, then the best that can come from Anglo-French "aid" was a joint régime with the fascists.

Stalin might find this a bitter pill to swallow. However a compromise with the fascists would be dressed up, it would, nevertheless, be a terrible blow to Stalinist prestige throughout the world. But rather than break with the main objective of Soviet policy— the winning of an alliance with Anglo-French imperialism—Stalin was ready to submit to a settlement dictated by them. He would "find a formula." The same arguments which were used to justify Soviet entry into the non-intervention committee, if accepted, would justify the final act of treachery against the Spanish people.

Let us recall those shabby arguments. "The Soviet Union emphatically was not in favor of the non-intervention agreement. With sufficient support from the socialist parties, the labor and anti-fascist movements of the world, besides the support of the communist parties, the Soviet Union would have been able to stop the non-intervention move in its track."[*] Need we remind anyone that Stalin never tried to rally the world labor movement before he endorsed the non-intervention scheme? If the Stalin régime was powerless to stop the bandits, did it have to join them? The Stalinists understood quite well the rôle of England: "The Baldwin cabinet gauged its international action to retain the good will of the prospective fascist dictators of Spain [and] . . . to prevent a victory by the People's Front . . . Sufficient has appeared . . . to make positive the assertion

---

[*] Harry Gannes: *How the Soviet Union Helps Spain.* November, 1936. This was the official Stalinist apology for supporting the London committee.

that Britain has come to its own agreement with General Franco."* But what mattered the fate of Spain, the future of the European revolution? All that weighed nothing in Stalin's scale as against the tenuous friendship of imperialist France: "The Soviet Union could not come to an open clash with Blum on the non-intervention pact because that would have played into the hands of Hitler and the pro-Nazi faction in the London Tory cabinet which was trying to provoke just such a state of affairs."† Therefore? Pretend that the non-intervention committee has its uses: "Rather than to allow collusion between the Nazis and the Tory ministers to confront Spain, the Soviet Union strove to do *all it could within the non-intervention* committee to stop fascist arms from being shipped to Spain!"‡ Likewise, we have no doubt, Stalin will strive to do all he can *within the committee of compromise* to get an equitable arrangement for the participation of the Loyalists in the joint régime with the fascists.

Precisely in these last months, when the Anglo-French scheme was taking final shape, Stalin found a new alibi to supplement those provided by the Franco-Soviet pact and "collective security," with which to push the Loyalists into still greater dependence on the Anglo-French bloc. Louis Fischer gave it crudely enough:

> The Spanish war has assumed such large dimensions and is lasting so long that Russia alone, especially if it must help China also, cannot bear the burden. Some other nation or nations must contribute . . . If England would save Spain from Franco, Russia would perhaps be ready and able to save China from Japan. (*Nation*, October 16, 1937.)

Thus, China becomes an alibi for not decisively aiding Spain, while Spain remains an alibi for not saving China! "If England

---

\* Harry Gannes: *How the Soviet Union Helps Spain.* November, 1936.

† Ibid

‡ Ibid

would save Spain from Franco . . ."

The Spanish people were also directed down the road of Anglo-French imperialism by the Communist International, of course, and by the Labor and Socialist International. Apart from pious gestures of organizing fund-raising, the two internationals have called only for the workers to get "their" democratic governments to come to Spain's aid. The "international proletariat" is called upon to "compel the fulfillment of its main demands on behalf of the Spanish people, which are the immediate withdrawal of the interventionist armed forces of Italy and Germany, the lifting of the blockade; the recognition of all the international rights of the lawful Spanish government; the application of the statutes of the League of Nations against the fascist aggressors." (*Daily Worker*, July 19, 1937.) All these "demands" are calls for *governmental actions*. Since the French Socialists and British Laborites knew that serious governmental action could only take place in the event of war, and since their capitalist masters made plain they were not yet ready for war, they objected to too precipitate nudges from the Comintern. Their accusation of war-mongering, Dimitrov could only answer by terming "unworthy speculation on the anti-war sentiments of the masses at large"! But the socialists and Laborites were at one with the Stalinists in putting the fate of the Spanish people in the hands of "their" governments. For both had already pledged to support their capitalists in the coming war.

✳

Whence would come the leadership to organize the Spanish masses in implacable struggle against the betrayal of Spain?

That leadership could scarcely come from the ruling group in the CNT, not the least of whose crimes was its failure to steel the workers against illusions about Anglo-French aid. The very manifesto of July 17, 1937, addressed to the world proletariat, declaring, "there is only one salvation: your aid," launched a slogan perfectly acceptable to the bourgeois-Stalinist bloc: "Put pressure on your governments to adopt decisions favorable to our struggle." Roosevelt's Chicago speech was acclaimed by the CNT press. According to *Solidaridad Obrera* (October 7), it proved that "democratic unity in Europe will be achieved only through energetic action against fascism."

The CNT leaders clung to their old course, merely asking the face-saving formula of "anti-fascist front" to be substituted for Popular Front, in their return to the government. Many of the local anarchist papers, close to the masses, reflected their outrage at the conduct of the leadership. One wrote:

> To read a great part of the CNT and anarchist press of Spain makes one indignant or give vent to tears of rage. Hundreds of our comrades were massacred in the streets of Barcelona during the May fighting, through the treason of our allies in the anti-fascist struggle; in Castille alone, almost a hundred comrades have been cowardly assassinated by the communists; other comrades have been assassinated by the same party in other regions; public and covert campaign of defamation and lies of all kinds are conducted against anarchism and the CNT, in order to poison and twist the spirit of the masses against our movement. And in the face of these crimes our press continues speaking of unity, of political decency; asking loyalty among all, calm, serenity, sincerity, spirit of sacrifice, and all those sentiments we are the only ones to believe and feel and which only serve for the other political sectors to cover their ambitions and treason . . . Not to tell the truth from now on would be to betray ourselves and the proletariat. (*Ideas,* Bajo Llobregat, September 30, 1937.)

But the conduct of the CNT leadership grew even more shameful. The rage of the masses after the fall of Santander forced the Stalinists to utter some mollifying words, calling for a cessation of the campaign against the CNT. Whereupon even the most left of the big CNT papers immediately hailed "the rectification that undoubtedly has begun to be produced in the politics of the Communist party." (*CNT* October 6.) The fall of Gijon, isolating the government still more from the masses, led to negotiations for CNT support. All complaints forgotten, the CNT leaders hastened to declare their readiness to enter the government!

Of the UGT leaders, even less need be said. They had uttered not a word in defense of the POUM. Caballero made not a single public speech for five months, while the Stalinists prepared to split the UGT. The pact for united action, signed by the CNT and UGT on July 9, which could have organized the defense of the elementary rights of the workers, remained stillborn. Though obviously representing a majority of the provincial federations of the socialist party, the Caballero group went no further than to protest against the actions of the unrepresentative Prieto National Committee. Rather than an ally, the UGT leaders simply further weakened the already impotent CNT leaders.

Of the POUM, one can no longer speak of it as an entity. It was riven irrevocably. All the blows of the leadership had been directed against the left wing, while the right wing had been courted and flattered. *El Communista* of Valencia had openly flouted the party decisions, holding to a flagrantly People's Front line, moving steadily toward Stalinism. Finally, a week before the outlawing of the party, the Central Committee was driven to publish a resolution (*Juventud Comunista,* June 10) declaring: "The enlarged Central Committee . . . has agreed to propose to the Congress the summary expulsion of the fractional group that in Valencia has worked against the revolutionary policy of our dear party."

The party congress was never held. Scheduled for June 19, it was preceded by the June 16 raids. The POUM was entirely unprepared for illegal work, as the sweeping success of the raids indicated. Had the congress been held, it would have found the chief centers of the party, Barcelona and Madrid, aligned to the left against the leadership. One left-wing group called for condemnation of the London Bureau and for the creation of a new, the Fourth International. The other declared: "It has become clear that there does not exist in our revolution a real Marxist party of the vanguard."

It was not, then, to the existing organizations as such that one could look for new leadership to prevent a compromise with the fascists. Fortunately, events had only passed the leaders by. Among the masses of the CNT and UGT arose new cadres seeking a way out.

Of special significance were the Friends of Durruti, for they represented a conscious break with the anti-statism of traditional anarchism. They explicitly declared the need for democratic organs of power, *juntas* or soviets, in the overthrow of capitalism, and the necessary state measures of repression against the counter-revolution. Outlawed on May 26, they had soon re-established their press. Despite the threefold illegality of government, Stalinists and CNT leadership, the *Amigo del Pueblo* voiced the aspirations of the masses. *Libertad,* also published illegally, was another dissident anarchist organ. Numerous local anarchist papers, as well as the voice of the Libertarian Youth and many local FAI groups, were raised against the capitulation of the CNT leaders. Some still took the hopeless road of "No More Governments." But the development of the Friends of Durruti was a harbinger of the future of all revolutionary workers in the CNT-FAI.

The masses of the UGT and left socialists had long indicated their impatience with the pusillanimity of their leadership. But the first overt sign of revolutionary crystallization came only in October, when over five hundred youth withdrew from the "United Youth" to rebuild a revolutionary socialist youth organization. Simultaneously, the split in the UGT, forced by the Stalinists, effectively awoke many left-wing workers to the problem of saving their unions from the Stalinist destroyers. In this struggle were inescapably posed all the fundamental problems of the Spanish revolution, the nature of class-struggle unionism, the rôle of the revolutionary party among the masses. From it would crystallize forces for the new party of the revolution.

Here, then, was the Herculean task of the Bolshevik-Leninists. These Fourth Internationalists, condemned to illegality by the POUM leadership even at the height of the revolution, organized by those expelled from the POUM only in the spring of 1937, seeking a way to the masses, must help to fuse the left wing of the POUM, the revolutionary socialist Youth and the politically awakened CNT and UGT workers, to create the cadres of the revolutionary party in Spain. Could that party, if based on revolutionary foundations, be any but a party standing on the platform of the Fourth International?

Where else, indeed, would it seek for international comradeship and collaboration? The Second and Third Internationals were the organs of the betrayers of the Spanish people. Nor was it an arbitrary act, when the left wing of the POUM called for repudiation of the London Bureau, the so-called "International Bureau for Revolutionary Socialist Unity." For this center to which the POUM had been affiliated, had sabotaged the struggle against Stalin's frame-up system to which the POUM had fallen victim.

While the POUM itself had from the first denounced the Moscow trials and propagated a "Trotskyist analysis," the London Bureau had worked in the opposite direction. It had refused to collaborate in a commission of inquiry into the Moscow trials. Why? Brockway— then launching a joint I.L.P.-C.P. "Unity campaign"—blurted out the reason: it would "cause prejudice in Soviet circles." Brockway therefore proposed . . . a commission to investigate Trotskyism! When taxed with this course, Brockway defended himself by impugning the character of the Commission of Inquiry headed by John Dewey.

Meanwhile the London Bureau was blowing up. The S.A.P. (Socialist Workers Party of Germany) had first attacked the Moscow trials, but soon abandoned criticism of Stalinism, signing a joint pact for a People's Front in Germany. *Juventud Comunista* (June 3) reported the split of the London Youth Bureau: "The S.A.P. Youth had placed itself in a Stalinist and reactionary position . . . The Youth of the S.A.P. had signed one of the most shameful documents which the history of the German workers' movement has known." On the very day the POUM leadership was arrested as Gestapo agents, *Julio*, PSUC youth organ (June 19) under the headline, "Trotskyism is synonymous with counter-revolution," had hailed the policies of the I.L.P. and S.A.P. youth groups and proudly pointed out that the Swedish affiliate of the London Bureau was steadily approaching a Stalinist People's Front policy.

Even fouler was the position of those other "allies" of the POUM, the Brandler-Lovestone groups. For a decade they had defended the Stalinist bureaucracy's every crime, on the basis of a false distinction between Stalin's policies in the Soviet Union and the erroneous policies of the Comintern elsewhere. When Zinoviev and Kamenev were done to death, these lawyers for Stalinism had hailed the dread deed as a vindication of Soviet justice. They had likewise defended the second Moscow trial in February, 1937. I was myself present at a public meeting in the Lovestone headquarters when Bertram Wolfe apologized because a POUM representative had just called the trials frame-ups! Only after the execution of the Red Generals had the Lovestone group—with no explanation—begun to reverse its course. In ten years they had done their utmost to aid Stalin in pinning the appellation counterrevolutionary on the Trotskyists, and even when they had been driven to accepting Trotsky's analysis of the Stalin purge, these foreheads of brass remained as ever the implacable enemies of the resurgence of the revolution in Russia as, indeed, elsewhere. As the S.A.P., the Swedish affiliate, etc., move out of one end of the London Bureau, they are being replaced by the Brandler-Lovestone movement. The change has scarcely brought improvement!

How did this International Bureau for Revolutionary Socialist Unity prepare for the defense of the POUM? Its meeting of June 6, 1937, adopted two resolutions. Resolution No. 1 said:

> The POUM alone has recognized and proclaimed the necessity of transforming the anti-fascist struggle into a fight against capitalism under the hegemony of the proletariat. This is the real reason for the ferocious attacks and calumnies of the *Communist party allied with the capitalist* forces in the Popular Front against the POUM.

Resolution No. 2 said:

> Every measure directed against the revolutionary working class of Spain is at the same time a measure in the interests of

French and British imperialism and a step towards compromise with the fascists.

In this hour of danger we appeal to all working class organizations of the whole world, and *particularly* to the Second *and Third International*... let us at last take up a unified stand against all these treacherous manoeuvres of the world bourgeoisie (my italics).

One resolution for the left, one for the semi-Stalinist right—that is the London Bureau.*

"But are not the principles you propose for the regroupment of the Spanish masses, are they not intellectual constructions to which the masses will feel alien? And is it not too late?"

No! We revolutionists are the only practical people in the world. For we merely articulate the fundamental aspirations of the masses, indeed, what they are already saying in their own way. We merely clarify the nature of the instrumentalities, above all, the nature of the revolutionary party and the workers' state, which the masses

---

* In the June 4 issue of the *New Leader*, the I.L.P. leader, Fenner Brockway, gave the POUM some advice at this critical juncture. Some revealing extracts: "It is important that POUM, together with other workers' forces, should concentrate on the fight against Franco... The Spanish Communist Party had justifiably criticized the absence of coordination at the front and the bad organization of the armed forces. POUM must be careful not to appear to resist proposals which will facilitate efficiency in the fight against Franco but that does not mean that it must accept without protest a return to the reactionary structure of the old army." This kind of advice a week before the POUM was outlawed! That *the* task of the POUM was relentless, implacable struggle against the government, placing no confidence whatsoever in the CNT and UGT leaders, to issue united front proposals for concrete, daily defense of elementary workers' rights, and to immediately combine legal with illegal work—this was naturally beyond Brockway. The same issue carries a letter from the I.L.P. representative in Spain, McNair, to the Stalinist leader, Dutt, beginning: "It is painful for me to be compelled to enter into controversy with a comrade of the C.P. in view of the desire I have to see unity among the working class parties... I still hold the point of view... 'the important thing to have in mind is that the Unity campaign in Britain should engender unity in Spain rather than allow Spanish disunity to break up the Unity Campaign in Britain...'"

need to achieve what they want. It is never too late for the masses to begin to hew their road to freedom. Pessimism and skepticism are luxuries for the few. The masses have no other choice except to fight for their lives and the future of their children.

If our analysis has not illuminated the inner forces of the Spanish revolution, let us recall a few words of Durruti on the battlefield of Aragon, when he was leading the ill-armed militias in the only substantial advance of the whole civil war. He was no theoretician, but an activist leader of masses. All the more significantly do his words express the revolutionary outlook of the class-conscious workers. The CNT leaders have buried these words deeper than they buried Durruti! But let us remember them:

> For us it is a question of crushing fascism once and for all. Yes, and in spite of the government.
>
> No government in the world fights fascism to the death. When the bourgeoisie sees power slipping from its grasp, it has recourse to fascism to maintain itself. The liberal government of Spain could have rendered the fascist elements powerless long ago. Instead it temporized and compromised and dallied. Even now at this moment, there are men in this government who want to go easy with the rebels. You never can tell, you know—he laughed— the present government might yet need these rebellious forces to crush the workers' movement . . .
>
> We know what we want. To us it means nothing that there is a Soviet Union somewhere in the world, for the sake of whose peace and tranquillity the workers of Germany and China were sacrificed to fascist barbarism by Stalin. We want the revolution here in Spain, right now, not maybe after the next European war. We are giving Hitler and Mussolini far more worry today with our revolution than the whole Red Army of Russia. We are setting an example to the German and Italian working class how to deal with fascism.
>
> I do not expect any help for a libertarian revolution from any government in the world. Maybe the conflicting interests in the

various imperialisms might have some influence on our struggle. That is quite possible. Franco is doing his best to drag Europe into the conflict. He will not hesitate to pitch Germany against us. But we expect no help, not even from our own government in the last analysis.

"You will be sitting on top of a pile of ruins if you are victorious," said Van Paasen.

Durruti answered:

We have always lived in slums and holes in the wall. We will know how to accommodate ourselves for a time. For, you must not forget, we can also build. It is we who built these palaces and cities, here in Spain and in America and everywhere. We, the workers, we can build others to take their place. And better ones. We are not in the least afraid of ruins. We are going to inherit the earth. There is not the slightest doubt about that. The bourgeoisie might blast and ruin its own world before it leaves the stage of history. We carry a new world, here, in our hearts. That world is growing this minute.[*]

*November 10, 1937*

---

[*] Interview of Durruti with Pierre Van Paasen, Toronto *Star,* September, 1936.

# POSTSCRIPT

The jailing of workers and peasants and the opening of the front lines by "republican" officers to the fascists: that is the story of Loyalist Spain from November, 1937 to May, 1938. There is time and space to add only a few words as this book goes belatedly to press.

General Sebastian Pozas adequately symbolizes the period: An officer under the monarchy; an officer under the republican-socialist coalition of 1931–1933; an officer under the Lerroux-Gil Robles *bienio negro* of 1933–1935. Minister of War before the fascist revolt broke out. He moved heaven and earth to get away from Madrid in the dark days of the siege in November, 1936. When Catalan autonomy was done away with and the CNT troops were at last subordinated entirely to the bourgeois régime, Pozas was appointed chief of all the armed forces of Catalonia and the Aragon front. He effectively purged the armies of CNT and POUM "uncontrollables," arranging for whole divisions to be wiped out when they were sent under fire without artillery or aviation protection. "Comrade" Pozas, who graced the plenum of the Central Committee of the PSUC, was "obviously" the man to hold the Aragon front against Franco. . . . Now he is in a Barcelona prison, charged—and the military story is only too clear—with betraying the Aragon front to Franco.

The consequences of the alliance with the "republican" bourgeoisie, of the People's Front program, are now apparent. The fascists have reached the Mediterranean. They have split the remaining anti-fascist forces in twain. For the time being the race between Franco and the regroupment of the proletariat has been won by Franco. The Stalinists, the Prieto and Caballero socialists, the anarchist leaders, have proven insurmountable obstacles on the road to regroupment, immeasurably facilitating Franco's victory.

These criminals will soon fall out among themselves. They will attempt to shift the blame on each other. In that attempt, much more will be revealed concerning the machinations whereby they bound the workers and peasants hand and foot, and made impossible a successful war against Franco. But already we know enough to say that no alibis will enable them to clear themselves. All—Stalinists, socialists and anarchists—are equally guilty of having betrayed their followers. All have betrayed the interests of the workers and peasants—the interests of humanity—to the bestial régime of fascism.

Many will escape from Franco, as did the Stalinist and social-democratic functionaries from Hitler. But the millions of workers and peasants cannot escape. For them, today, tomorrow, the next day, as long as life continues, the task of smashing fascism remains to be carried out. Fight or be crushed—they have no other alternative.

The Spanish proletariat—crushed, as Berneri said, between the Stalino-Prussians and the Franco-Versaillaise—may yet touch off a flame that will again light up the world. Passing beyond the Pyrenees, where the period of the People's Front, as in Spain, is closing, that flame can unite with the hopes of the French proletariat, now faced with a choice between naked bourgeois dictatorship and the road of revolution.

But if the revolutionary conflagration does not break out, or is smothered, what then?

The tragic lessons of Spain are, in any case, of profound concern to the American working class and have an immediate bearing upon "purely American" problems.

Here the issue will soon enough be posed as inexorably as in Spain or France. The simple truth is that American capitalism has arrived at such an impasse that it can no longer feed its slaves. An army of the unemployed as large as that of 1932 now receives at Roosevelt's hand a fraction of the inadequate hand-out offered in 1933. The production index drops at four and five and six times the rate of the 1929–1932 decline. The government prepares cold-bloodedly for imperialist war as a "way-out." Crisis, unemployment, war—these have become the "normal" characteristics of the declining capitalist order. Since 1929 America has been "Europeanized." We face here the problems which have been faced since the war by the European proletariat.

Pessimism, defeatism, these are the reactions of the few, who thereby deduce from the reformist betrayals in Europe a justification for abandoning the American masses to a like doom. But to the workers and the oppressed toiling masses of city and country, pessimism and defeatism are alien. They *must* fight or be smashed— they have no other alternative. The vast, inexhaustible vitality of the American working class is the richest capital of the international labor movement. It has yet to be used, yet to be thrown into the breach. In the last four years, the American proletariat has given such evidence of its resources and its power as many of us did not dream of in 1933. It has organized itself within the very citadel of American capitalism—steel, rubber, autos. It can overthrow that citadel—if it has the will to do so and a leadership capable of assimilating the lessons of these catastrophes.

The task of the book is to provide the class-conscious worker and his allies in America with materials for understanding why the Spanish proletariat has been defeated, and by whom betrayed.

The heroism of the Spanish workers and peasants must not be in vain. From their failing hands the banner of struggle to the death against capitalism can be taken up by the American workers. Let them grasp it with the aid of a vanguard which has assimilated all the terrible lessons of Russia, Spain and France, with a strength and assurance such as the world has not yet seen, and carry it through to victory, not only for themselves, but for the whole world of toiling humanity!

*Minneapolis, May 5, 1938*

# PUBLISHER'S EPILOGUE

By May 1938, when the postscript to *Revolution and Counter-Revolution in Spain* was finished, the fate of the Spanish Republic had been sealed; and the eleven months that remained before the cessation of active hostilities saw only increasingly futile resistance as Franco's forces conquered outpost after outpost of the Republic. On the Republican side, the final months of the military campaign were marked by betrayals by the general staff; withdrawal of armies without informing the population; deliberate physical destruction of revolutionary divisions—frequently by sending them into battle inadequately armed and without air or artillery cover; surrender of cities intact to the enemy; and desertion by members of the "government of victory."

In September 1938 the Munich pact set the stage for the beginning of World War II. A month later, the trial of the POUM leaders, who had been arrested in mid-1937, ended with their acquittal on charges of treason and espionage. They were, however, sentenced to prison for their rôle in the May 1937 upsurge. By November, the International Brigades were being withdrawn. The heavy bombardment of Barcelona that had begun in January 1938 ended a year later with the surrender of Barcelona to the fascists; Azaña fled to France, where he later resigned. On March 5, 1939, the Junta for National Defense, led by Colonel Casado, seized power from what was left of the CP-backed Negrín government, and concentrated on tracking down and shooting prominent Stalinists who had not had time to flee the country. The junta's other purpose was to hand the government over to Franco, which it accomplished at the end of the month. With this, the final illusions that the Allies might intervene at the last minute to prevent Franco's victory were shat-

329

tered. Only six months after the curtain fell on the military battle in Spain, it rose again on the Stalin-Hitler pact and the initial stages of the Second World War on the continent.

Readers interested in the Spanish revolution and Civil War will also want to read *The Spanish Revolution (1931–39),* by Leon Trotsky (Pathfinder Press, 1973). This book contains the Russian revolutionist's day-to-day political assessments of the Spanish events. Trotsky suggested one of its articles, "The Lessons of Spain—The Last Warning," as a preface to the first edition of *Revolution and Counter-Revolution in Spain.*

# GLOSSARY

*Adelante* – Socialist Party newspaper

**Azaña y Díaz, Manuel** (1880–1940) – head of the Republican Left; prime minister of the Republican government in 1931 and again in 1936; president from May 1936 until 1939

*La Batalla* – newspaper of the POUM

**CNT** – National Confederation of Labor, the Anarcho-Syndicalist trade union federation

**Communist Left** – the Trotskyists

**Communist Party** – the official (Stalinist) section of the Comintern

**Companys y Jover, Luis** (1883–1940) – head of the Catalan Esquerra; governor of Catalonia from 1934

**Durruti, Buenaventura** (1896–1936) – leader of the left-wing Anarchists; killed in the defense of Madrid

**Esquerra** – Catalan party of the lower middle class

**FAI** – Iberian Anarchist Federation, controlled the CNT; divided into a left wing (led by Durruti) and a right wing (led by García Oliver)

**Franco y Bahamonde, Francisco** (1892– ) – military leader of Nationalist Spain

**Friends of Durruti** – dissident Anarchists who denounced the class collaborationism of their leaders

**García Oliver, José** (1901– ) – a right-wing Spanish Anarchist; minister of justice from 1936

**Giral, José** – minister of the navy; prime minister, July-September 1936

**Ibarruri, Dolores** ("La Pasionaria") (1895– ) – a leader of the Spanish CP

**Largo Caballero, Francisco** (1869–1946) – leader of the Left Socialists; prime minister, September 1936–May 1937

**Lerroux, Alejandro** (1864–1949) – leader of the Radical Party; premier during the "bienio negro" of 1933–36

*Mundo obrero* – Communist Party newspaper

**Negrín Lopez, Juan** (1889–1956) – final premier of the Republic, replacing Largo Caballero in 1937

**Nin, Andrés** (1892–1937) – leader of the Spanish Trotskyists until they broke with Trotsky in 1935 and formed the POUM; murdered by the Stalinist police

**People's Front** – a governmental coalition of Communist and Socialist parties with bourgeois parties on a program of liberal capitalism

**POUM** – Workers Party of Marxist Unification, formed in September 1935 by a fusion of Nin's Communist Left with Maurin's Workers and Peasants Bloc

**Prieto y Tuero, Indalecio** (1883–1962) – a leader of the right wing of the Socialist Party; minister of air and navy in Largo Caballero's cabinet and remained in Negrin's cabinet until 1938

**PSUC** – the unified socialist and Stalinist party of Catalonia (from 1936)

**Republicans** – a general term for those parties and individuals supporting the People's Front government over the National Front forces of Franco; several bourgeois parties had the word "Republican" in their name

**Trotsky, Leon** (1879–1940) – a leader of the Russian Revolution exiled by Stalin, who organized the Fourth International to maintain the revolutionary traditions of Marxism and Leninism

**UGT** – General Union of Workers, the second major trade union federation in Spain; led by the Socialist Party

# INDEX

# THE FIGHT AGAINST FASCISM AND WAR

## THE STRUGGLE AGAINST FASCISM IN GERMANY
Leon Trotsky
  Writing in the heat of struggle against the rising Nazi movement, a central leader of the Russian revolution examines the class roots of fascism and advances a revolutionary strategy to combat it. $28.95

The Struggle Against Fascism in Germany
by Leon Trotsky
Introduction by Ernest Mandel

## THE SOCIALIST WORKERS PARTY IN WORLD WAR II
WRITINGS AND SPEECHES, 1940–43
James P. Cannon
  Preparing the communist movement in the United States to stand against the patriotic wave inside the workers movement supporting the imperialist slaughter and to campaign against wartime censorship, repression, and antiunion assaults. $22.95

James P. Cannon
WRITINGS AND SPEECHES, 1940–43
The Socialist Workers Party in World War II

## THE SPANISH REVOLUTION (1931-39)
Leon Trotsky
  Analyzes the revolutionary upsurge on the land and in the factories leading to the Spanish civil war and how the Stalinists' course ensured a fascist victory. $30.95

## WHAT IS AMERICAN FASCISM?
James P. Cannon and Joseph Hansen
  Analyzing examples earlier in the 20th century—Father Charles Coughlin, Jersey City mayor Frank Hague, and Sen. Joseph McCarthy—this collection looks at the features distinguishing fascist movements and demagogues in the U.S. from the 1930s to today. $8.00

# New International

## A MAGAZINE OF MARXIST POLITICS AND THEORY

U.S. IMPERIALISM HAS LOST THE COLD WAR. That's what the Socialist Workers Party concluded at the opening of the 1990s, in the wake of the collapse of regimes and parties across Eastern Europe and in the USSR that claimed to be communist. Contrary to imperialism's hopes, the working class in those countries had not been crushed. It remains an intractable obstacle to reimposing and stabilizing capitalist relations, one that will have to be confronted by the exploiters in class battles—in a hot war.

Three issues of the Marxist magazine *New International* analyze the propertied rulers' failed expectations and chart a course for revolutionaries in response to rising worker and farmer resistance to the economic and social instability, spreading wars, and rightist currents bred by the world market system. They explain why the historic odds in favor of the working class have increased, not diminished, at the opening of the 21st century.

## U.S. Imperialism Has Lost the Cold War

JACK BARNES

"It is only from fighters, from revolutionists of action, that communists will be forged in the course of struggle. And it is only from within the working class that the mass political vanguard of these fighters can come. The lesson from over 150 years of political struggle by the modern workers movement is that, more and more, to become and remain a revolutionist means becoming a communist."
In *New International* no. 11. **$14.00**

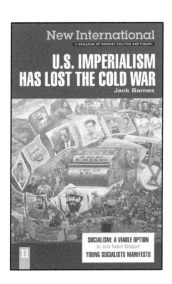

## Imperialism's March toward Fascism and War

JACK BARNES

"There will be new Hitlers, new Mussolinis. That is inevitable. What is not inevitable is that they will triumph. The working-class vanguard will organize our class to fight back against the devastating toll we are made to pay for the capitalist crisis. The future of humanity will be decided in the contest between these contending class forces."
In *New International* no. 10. **$14.00**

## Opening Guns of World War III

JACK BARNES

"Washington's Gulf war and its outcome did not open up a new world order of stability and UN-overseen harmony. Instead, it was the first war since the close of World War II that grew primarily out of the intensified competition and accelerating instability of the crises-ridden old imperialist world order." In *New International* no. 7. **$12.00**

# Also from Pathfinder

## Capitalism's World Disorder

Working-Class Politics at the Millennium

JACK BARNES

The social devastation and financial panic, the coarsening of politics and politics of resentment, the cop brutality and acts of imperialist aggression accelerating around us—all are the product not of something gone wrong but of the lawful workings of capitalism. Yet the future can be changed by the united struggle and selfless action of workers and farmers conscious of their power to transform the world. $23.95

## The Communist Manifesto

KARL MARX AND FREDERICK ENGELS

Founding document of the modern working-class movement, published in 1848. Explains why communism is derived not from preconceived principles but from facts and from proletarian movements springing from the actual class struggle. $3.95

## To Speak the Truth

Why Washington's 'Cold War' against Cuba Doesn't End

FIDEL CASTRO AND CHE GUEVARA

In historic speeches before the United Nations and UN bodies, Guevara and Castro address the workers of the world, explaining why the U.S. government so hates the example set by the socialist revolution in Cuba and why Washington's effort to destroy it will fail. $16.95

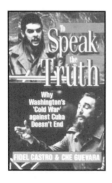

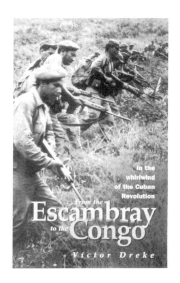

# From the Escambray to the Congo

In the Whirlwind of the Cuban Revolution

INTERVIEW WITH VÍCTOR DREKE

In this participant's account, Víctor Dreke describes how easy it became after the Cuban Revolution to "take down the rope" segregating blacks from whites at town dances, yet how enormous was the battle to transform social relations underlying all the "ropes" inherited from capitalism and Yankee domination. He recounts the determination, internationalism, and creative joy with which working people have defended their revolutionary course against U.S. imperialism—from Cuba's own Escambray mountains, to the Americas, Africa, and beyond. $17.00

# Thomas Sankara Speaks

The Burkina Faso Revolution, 1983–87

Peasants and workers in the West African country of Burkina Faso established a popular revolutionary government and began to combat the hunger, illiteracy, and economic backwardness imposed by imperialist domination. Thomas Sankara, who led that struggle, explains the example set for all of Africa. $19.95

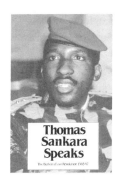

# Genocide against the Indians

GEORGE NOVACK

Why did the leaders of the Europeans who settled in North America try to exterminate the peoples already living there? How was the campaign of genocide against the Indians linked to the expansion of capitalism in the United States? Noted Marxist George Novack answers these questions. $4.00

## The Changing Face of U.S. Politics

Working-Class Politics and the Trade Unions

JACK BARNES

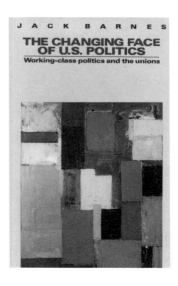

Building the kind of party the working class needs to prepare for coming class battles—battles through which they will revolutionize themselves, their unions, and all of society. It is a handbook for workers, farmers, and youth repelled by the social inequalities, economic instability, racism, women's oppression, cop violence, and wars endemic to capitalism...and who are determined to overturn that exploitative system and join in reconstructing the world on new, socialist foundations. $19.95

## Teamster Rebellion

FARRELL DOBBS

The 1934 strikes that built the industrial union movement in Minneapolis and helped pave the way for the CIO, recounted by a central leader of that battle. The first in a four-volume series on the class-struggle leadership of the strikes and organizing drives that transformed the Teamsters union in much of the Midwest into a fighting social movement and pointed the road toward independent labor political action. $16.95

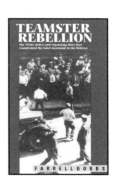

## By Any Means Necessary

MALCOLM X

Speeches tracing the evolution of Malcolm X's views on political alliances, women's rights, intermarriage, capitalism and socialism, and more. $15.95

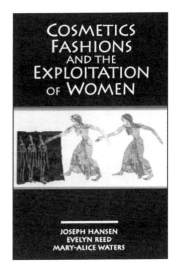

## Cosmetics, Fashions, and the Exploitation of Women

JOSEPH HANSEN, EVELYN REED, AND MARY-ALICE WATERS

How big business plays on women's second-class status and social insecurities to market cosmetics and rake in profits. The introduction by Waters explains how the entry of millions of women into the workforce during and after World War II irreversibly changed U.S. society and laid the basis for a renewed rise of struggles for women's emancipation. $14.95

## Making History

Interviews with Four Generals of Cuba's Revolutionary Armed Forces

Through the stories of four outstanding Cuban generals, each with close to half a century of revolutionary activity, we can see the class dynamics that have shaped our entire epoch. We can understand how the people of Cuba, as they struggle to build a new society, have for more than forty years held Washington at bay. Preface by Juan Almeida; introduction by Mary-Alice Waters. Also in Spanish. $15.95

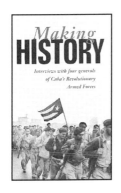

## The History of the Russian Revolution

LEON TROTSKY

The social, economic, and political dynamics of the first socialist revolution as told by one of its central leaders. "The history of a revolution is for us first of all a history of the forcible entrance of the masses into the realm of rulership over their own destiny," Trotsky writes. Unabridged edition, 3 vols. in one. $35.95

## The History of American Trotskyism

Report of a Participant, 1928-38

JAMES P. CANNON

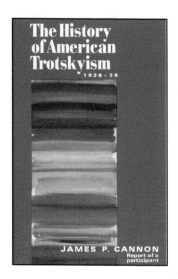

"Trotskyism is not a new movement, a new doctrine," Cannon says, "but the restoration, the revival of genuine Marxism as it was expounded and practiced in the Russian revolution and in the early days of the Communist International." In this series of twelve talks given in 1942, James P. Cannon recounts an important chapter in the efforts to build a proletarian party in the United States. $18.95

## Democracy and Revolution

GEORGE NOVACK

The limitations and advances of various forms of democracy in class society, from its roots in ancient Greece, through its rise and decline under capitalism. Discusses the emergence of Bonapartism, military dictatorship, and fascism, and how democracy will be advanced under a workers and farmers regime. $18.95

## Nelson Mandela Speaks

Forging a Democratic, Nonracial South Africa

Mandela's speeches from 1990 through 1993 recount the course of struggle that put an end to apartheid and opened the fight for a deep-going political, economic, and social transformation in South Africa. $18.95

## Imperialism: The Highest Stage of Capitalism

V.I. LENIN

"I trust that this pamphlet will help the reader to understand the fundamental economic question, that of the economic essence of imperialism," Lenin wrote in 1917. "For unless this is studied, it will be impossible to understand and appraise modern war and modern politics." $3.95